Advances in Artificial Intelligence
CIIAM 86

Proceedings of the 2nd International Conference on Artificial Intelligence

December 1-5, 1986
Marseille

Kogan
Page

Conference organized by

AGENCE DE
L'INFORMATIQUE

amédia

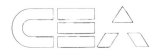

INSTITUT INTERNATIONAL
DE ROBOTIQUE ET
D'INTELLIGENCE
ARTIFICIELLE
DE MARSEILLE

IIRIAM

First published in 1986 by Hermes
51 rue Rennequin, 75017 Paris, France
Copyright © 1986 Hermes

English language edition first published in 1987
by Kogan Page Ltd, 120 Pentonville Road, London N1 9JN
Copyright © 1987 Hermes

British Library Cataloguing in Publication Data

International Conference on Artificial Intelligence
(2nd : 1986 : Marseilles)
Advances in artificial intelligence : proceedings of the 2nd International
Conference on Artificial Intelligence.
1. Artificial intelligence
I. Title
006.3   Q335

ISBN 1-85091-333-1

Printed and bound in France by Imprimerie Laballery.

Conference Chairman

Hubert CURIEN, Professor at Université Paris VI.

Organizing Committee

Chairman
Marc BERGMAN, IIRIAM, Marseille

J.-M. LE DIZES, AMEDIA / CETE / Aix les Milles
F. MORIER, CEA / Centre de Cadarache
J.-C. RAULT, ADI
S. ROBERT, IIRIAM

Program Committee

Chairman
Eugène CHOURAQUI, GRTC/CNRS, Marseille (France)

M. ADAM, IBM, Centre scientifique, Paris (France)
Y. ANZAI, Hokkaïdo Univ. (Japan)
M. ARRIDI, Univ. Stockolm (Sweden)
M. BENGIO, SCHLUMBERGER / Montrouge (France)
M. BERGMAN, IIRIAM / Marseille (France)
M. BIBEL, Univ. München (W. Germany)
A. BONNET, ENST / COGNITECH (France)
P.P. BONISSONE, GENERAL ELECTRIC / Schenect. (USA)
J. CAMPAGNE IBARCQ, COMPAGNIE BANCAIRE (France)
A. COLMERAUER, GIA / Univ. Marseille-Luminy (France)
N. COT, Univ. Paris VI (France)
L. DEMIANS D'ARCHIMBAULD, CIMSA (France)
R. DE MORI, Mc GILL Univ. Montréal (Canada)
H. FARRENY, Univ. Paul Sabatier, Toulouse (France)

Objectives

The object of this international conference is to encourage scientific exchange between academic reasearchers and industry concerning the development of knowledge based systems.

To assist this transfer of technology, the conference is organised along three main lines :

— Tutorials designed aid professionals to apply these new technologies.

— Presentation of the state of the art in scientific research and the methodologies used in developing applications.

— An exhibition of industrial products, prototypes involved in hardware and software.

Contents

Speech Recognition

Applications to Technical Domains: General Tools

Applications to Technical Domains: Process Control

Man-Machine Communication

Knowledge Acquisition and Representation

The Filtering Process: a Mechanism for Modelling Inheritance in Object Oriented Languages

P. Dugerdil

GRTC/CNRS, Marseille (France)

In this paper, we examine the inheritance process in object-oriented languages in the light of a general mechanism: the filtering process. This approach provides a basis for the analysis and comparison of inheritance processes. We begin with three hypotheses that constitute the axioms of our model and we introduce the notions of the filtering process and the transfer function of a filter. For these notions, we examine the inheritance process between objects. The paper ends with a description of the inheritance mechanisms incorporated in the object-oriented language developed at GRTC.

Introduction

In the object-oriented representation of knowledge, the concepts are represented by classes and relationships between classes. A class contains slots that represent the attributes of the concept described by class. An individual belonging to a concept is said to be an instance of the associated class. Usually a given class can share slots with other classes representing more general concepts. The former is said to be a subclass of the latter, its superclass, and can inherit slots from them through specific relations (Stefik and Bobrow 1986). Although the common case is simple inheritance, ie a class is a subclass of only one class, some artificial intelligence (AI) languages have introduced multiple inheritance (Fikes and Kehler 1985). The sharing of slots between classes is usually total, ie the subclass inherits all the slots of its superclasses. This process can be extended in fact to the case where classes share not all but only some of their slots (Chouraqui and Dugerdil 1986, Wright and Fox 1985). The mechanisms of sharing knowledge between objects can be seen as a filtering process. This view allows the inheritance mechanisms of existing object-oriented languages to be analysed.

The Inheritance Model

The first hypothesis states that a class is allowed to innerit slots from another class only if those slots contribute to the description of its associated concepts.

The second hypothesis states that the slots that describe a concept are those declared in the class representing the concept plus those inherited by this class, ie those belonging to the class.

The third hypothesis states that when an instance is created the slots to which one can assign values are those that belong to its class. One cannot add slots to an instance that is not declared or inherited by its class.

If this hypothesis was not satisfied, then, following the second hypothesis, the concept to which the instance belongs would be different from that of its class.

Many processes have been described to inherit slots in a graph of classes (Bobrow and Winograd 1977, Brachman and Schmolze 1985, Carbonell 1981, Etherington and Reiter, Ferber 1983, Wright and Fox 1985). Here we propose a paradigm to represent slot inheritance by objects: the filtering process. The specification of the inheritance properties for every object is made along two axes that fix the semantics of the corresponding inheritance relation:

1. selection of the objects from which to inherit information;
2. selection of the information inherited.

We model these selections with two filters located in the objects inheriting information:

1. an object filter (FO) whose input set is the set of all class names of the knowledge base;
2. a slot filter (FS) whose input set is the set of all the slots of the classes whose names are selected by FO.

Every inheritance relation can then be replaced by its equivalent FO and FS filters for the study of the inheritance process.

The Filtering Process

Intuitively a filtering process is a selection operation among the elements of a set. The output of this process is the new set of filtered elements. The filtering process is defined as the transfer function f of a filter F over an input set I is a Boolean function $f:I->\{0,1\}$. The result returned by this function is such that the output set of the filtering of I through F, denoted FI, is:

$$FI = \{ x \in I \mid f(x) = 1 \}.$$

Graphically, it can represented by:

Connecting filters in series

If filters are connected in such a way that the output set of one filter is the input set of the next filter, then those filters are said to be serially connected. Let F1 and F2 be two serially connected filters and f1 and f2 be their transfer functions, respectively. The global output set of this filtering process over an input set I, denoted F1F2I, is:

$$F1F2I = \{ x \in I \mid f1(x) \wedge f2(x) = 1\}$$

where $\wedge$ is the Boolean product. Graphically, it can represented by:

Connecting filters in parallel

If filters are connected in such a way that the input set is the same for every filter and that the output set is the union of the output sets of all the filters, then those filters are said to be connected in parallel. Let F1 and F2 be two filters connected in parallel and f1 and f2 be their transfer functions, respectively. The global output set of this filtering process over an input set I, denoted (F1+F2)I, is:

$$(F1+F2)I = \{ x \in I \mid f1(x) \vee f2(x) = 1\}$$

where $\vee$ is the Boolean sum. Graphically, it can be represented by:

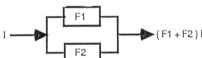

Properties

By the properties of the Boolean operators we obtain with regard to the global filtering characteristics:

1. the operation of connecting filters in series is commutative;
2. serial or parallel connections of filters are associative;
3. serial connection is distributive over parallel connection;
4. if the transfer function of a filter is independent of the input sets, then the filtering process is distributive over the union of input sets:

$$F(I \cup J) = FI \cup FJ.$$

The Inheritance Process

The set of slots belonging to a class is the set of slots declared in the class plus the set of slots inherited by the class (second hypothesis). Let the function Slot(c) be the

function returning the set of slots that belongs to a class of
name c. Let the functions Decl(c) and Inh(c) be the functions
returning the set of declared slots and the set of inherited
slots for a class of name c. Then we have:

$$\text{Slot } (c_j) = \text{Decl } (c_j) \cup \text{Inh } (c_j)$$

with Slot:C->P, Decl:C->P, Inh:C->P where C is the set of class
names of the knowledge base and P is the set of the parts of the
set of slots in the knowledge base.
Let c_i be a class. We note FO_{ci} the object filter of c_i so that
$FO\ C_{ci}$ is the set of the names of the classes from which c_i
inherits some slots. Since the slots inherited by c_i can depend
on the source of inheritance considered we note $FS_{ci,cj}$ the slot
filter of c_i that selects the slots inherited from c_j. c_j must be
a member of the set $FO\ C_{ci}$. From the definition of the FO and FS
filters we get the inherited slots of a class c_0 :

$$\text{Inh } (c_0) =_S \bigcup_{c_i \in FO_{c0} C} FS_{c0,ci} \left(\text{Decl } (c_j) \cup \text{Inh } (c_j) \right)$$

where the symbol $=_S$ means the smallest set satisfying this
expression (Deremer and Pennello 1982).
The inheritance of slots from a class c_j by a class c_0 is then
made through the serial connection of all the filters found along
the path from c_0 to c_j in the graph defined by the object filters
FO. If there is more than one path from c_0 to c_j, the resulting
filter is the parallel connection of the filters corresponding to
every single path.
An example of an inheritance graph (the arrows show the class
selected by the FO filters of every class) is:

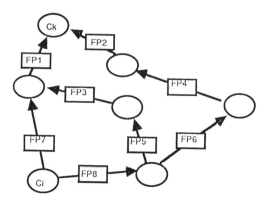

The set of slots inherited by the class c_i from the class c_k where FPi are slots filters is:

$$(FP7\ FP1 + FP8\ FP5\ FP3\ FP1 + FP8\ FP6\ FP4\ FP2)Slot(c_k)$$

Classifying Filters

Let X be the input set of a filter F having a transfer function f. If X is unordered, the set over which the transfer function returns 1 or 0 must be given explicitly.
Let $I = \{e_0, e_1, e_2, \ldots, e_n\} \subset X$ be such a set.
Then we note the following types of filter:

1. Null filter: $\forall x \in X : f(x) = 1$

2. Band-pass: $\forall x \in I : f(x) = 1 ; \forall x \in X \underline{and} x \notin I : f(x) = 0$

3. Band-cut: $\forall x \in I : f(x) = 0 ; \forall x \in X \underline{and} x \notin I : f(x) = 1$

Some important cases

An object filter is always of the band-pass type. Let FO_c be an object filter of a class c and C the set of class names of the knowledge base. If card(FO_c C)=1, then c inherits slots from only one class (single inheritance). If this is true for every class, then the knowledge base is made of trees of classes. If card(FO_c C)>1, then c inherits slots from several classes (multiple inheritance) and we have oriented graphs in the knowledge base.
If the slot filter $FS_{ci,cj}$ of a class ci is of the first type (null filter), then cj represents a concept of which the concept represented by ci is a specialization (vertical inheritance). An instance of ci can then have value for all the slots declared both in ci and cj. This kind of filter is represented through the inheritance relation ISA, AKO, etc.
From the first two hypotheses of our model if a class inherits only some of the slots of another class (slot filter.types 2 and 3), those classes represent different concepts and their instances will be distinct. Then, we can no longer speak of a hierarchy of concepts, and we have horizontal inheritance. The shared slots can be declared in any of the two classes and the other class will own the inheritance relation. It is the semantics of the inheritance relation associated with the cognitive interpretation of the classes that allows us to choose the class in which to declare the shared slots or the inheritance relation. The distinction between types 2 and 3 for horizontal inheritance may seem useless regarding our second hypothesis. But if it is generally admitted that with type 2 the two classes represent different concepts, it is a different story for type 3. In that case, a class inherits all but some of the slots of another class. Then the idea of vertical inheritance with

exceptions is sometimes used: the inheriting class represents a
subconcept for which some of the slots of the general concept are
not valid descriptions (Etherington and Reiter 1983, Froidevaux
1985)

More About Selective (Horizontal) Inheritance

In knowledge representation, a common case of selective
information sharing between two concepts is when those concepts
have a structural relationship (eg the part-of relationship).
There will then be selective inheritance between the classes
representing these concepts. Because of the structural nature of
the relation, it will be instantiated. Then the instances will
also share slots through the relation. Therefore, the inheritance
mechanism will now work at the level of instances, ie when a slot
is needed in an instance the process will look at classes to know
if the slot can be selectively inherited. If it can, the process
will travel along the instantiated structural relation towards
the other instance to get the slot.
  We can define object and slot filters at the instance level to
model the inheritance properties of the structural relations
between them. The object filter returns, for an instance, the set
of names of the instances from which it can inherit slots, and
the slot filter returns the set inherited slots from every
instance. Given that the same structural relation is modelled the
object and slot filters of a class have strong connections with
that of its instances. First, every instance selected by the
object filter of an instance must belong to one of the classes
selected by the object filter of that instance's class. Second,
the slot filter between two instances must be the same as the
slot filter between their class respectively.
  An important property of the inheritance between instances is
that it is bidirectional. If two classes share slots through a
structural relation then, following our three hypotheses, these
slots can be instantiated in any instance of those classes.
Therefore, it is not a priori known which one of the two
instances will have the shared slots instantiated. The direction
of the inheritance process is then from the instance that does
not contain the shared slot toward the instance that contains it.
But it is possible for this process to go one way to get a slot
and the other way to get another slot.
  For example:

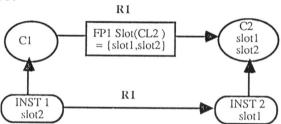

Cl and C2 are classes and INST1 and INST2 are instances. There is
a structural relation Rl between Cl and C2 with FP1 being the
slot filter for this relation. Cl can inherit the slots "slot1"
and "slot2" from C2 (or the slots "slot1" and "slot2" are shared
by the two classes). The structural relation Rl is instantiated.
As explained above, the two slots can be instantiated in any of
the two instances. Then, "slot2" has been instantiated in INST1
and "slot1" in INST2. So the inheritance process will go from

INST2 to INST1 for the slot "slot2" and from INST1 to INST2 for the slot "slot1".

Inheritance Mechanisms of the Object-Oriented Language under Development at GRTC

This language under development is built around Prolog and has multiple vertical inheritance and multiple selective inheritance mechanisms.

Vertical inheritance

It is given by the SORTE-DE (ISA) relation whose associated filters are FO: band-pass and FS: null filter. At the implementation level this relation is represented by a slot whose value is the list L of superclass names. "fo" is the transfer function of FO and C is the set of class names of the knowledge base:

$$L = \{ x \mid x \in C \text{ and } fo(x) = 1 \}, \, card(\, FO \, C) \geq 1.$$

Selective inheritance

It is given by the PARTIE-DE (PART-OF) structural relation whose associated filters are FO: band-pass and FS: band-pass. This relation is located in a class representing a part of a compound real object itself represented by another class. At the implementation level this relation is represented by a slot whose value is the list L1 of compound classes. We have when "fo" is the transfer function of FO and C is the set of class names of the knowledge base:

$$L1 = \{ x \mid x \in C \text{ and } fo(x) = 1 \}, \, card(\, FO_1 \, E) \geq 1$$

This slot possesses a distinguished facet named HERITAGE (INHERITANCE), whose value is the inheritance filter. This filter is the list L2 of 2-uples:

<name of the compound class, list of the names of the inherited slots from this class>. We have when C is the set of class names of the knowledge base:

$$L2 = \{ <x,y \, {}^{*}> \mid x \in FO \, C \text{ and } y = FS_x \, Slot(x) \text{ and } y \, {}^{*} = \bigcup_{p \in y} name(p) \}.$$

FS is then made of a set of band-pass filters (FSx) each one being associated with one class whose name is selected by FO. Although L1 is redundant with L2 by this syntax clearly we have separated the object and slot filters.

Conclusions

Here we have shown a model of inheritance between objects in the

form of a filtering process. This approach offers a common
conceptual model from which one can compare the inheritance
schemes of existing object-oriented languages. It has allowed us
to model interactions between multiple vertical inheritance and
multiple selective inheritance of slots in an object-oriented
knowledge representation language under development in our
laboratory (Chouraqui and Dugerdil 1986, Dugerdil 1985).
Moreover, this model is guiding us towards the implementation
step. The aim of our research is the development of an
intelligent computer-aided design (CAD) system for architecture
(Chouraqui et al. 1986).

References

Bobrow, D.G.; Winograd, T. (1977) An overview of KRL, a knowledge
representation language, "Cognitive Science" No. 1(1).

Borgida, B.T.; Greenspan, S. (1981) Data and activities:
exploiting hierarchies of classes, "Sigplan Notices" No. 16(1).

Borning, A.H. Multiple inheritance in Smalltalk-80, "Procedings
AAAI-82".

Brachman, R.J. (1985) "I lied about the trees" or default and
definition in knowledge representation, "The AI Magazine", fall,
pp. 80-93.

Brachman, R.J.; Schmolze, J.G. (1985) An overview of KL-ONE
knowledge representation system, "Cognitive Science" No. 9(2),
pp. 171-216.

Carbonell, J.C. (1981) Default reasoning and inheritance
mechanisms on type hierarchies, "Sigplan Notices" No. 16(1).

Chouraqui, E.; Dugerdil, P.H. (1986) Application des langages
orientés à la CAO de l´architecture, "Actes des journées AFCET
sur les langages orientés objet" No. 48, Janvier.

Chouraqui, E. et al. (1986) Le projet TECTON: un système expert
de CAO intégrant le savior architectural, "Actes des journées
internationales CAO et robotique en architecture et BTP",
Marseille, 25-27 Juin.

Deremer, F.; Pennello, T. (1982) Efficient computation of LALR(1)
look-ahead sets, "ACM Transactions on Programming Languages and
Systems" No 4(4).

Dugerdil, P.H. (1985) Une méthodologie orientée objet pour la
représentation des connaissances en CAO architecture, "Mémoire de
DEA en Informatique et Mathématiques´, Faculte de Luminy,
Université d´Aix-Marseille II.

Etherington, D.W.; Reiter, R. On inheritance hierarchies with
exceptions, "Proceedings AAAI-83".

Ferber, J. (1983) MERING: un langage d´acteur pour la représentation et la manipulation de connaissances, "Thèse de Docteur-Ingénieur, Université de Paris VI.

Fikes, R.; Kehler, T. (1985) The role of frame-based representation in reasoning, "CACM" No. 28(9).

Fox, M.S. (1979) On inheritance in knowledge representation, "Proceedings IJCAI-6".

Froidevaux, C.H. (1985) Exceptions dans les hiérarchies sorte-de, "Proceedings 5ème congrès AFCET: Reconnaissance des formes intelligence artificielle", Grenoble, November.

Roche, C. (1984) EAQUE-LRO Génération de systèmes experts. Application à des problèmes d´ordonnancement, "Thèse de Doctorat de 3ème cycle", Institut National Polytechnique de Grenoble.

Stefik, M. (1979) An examination of frame-structured representation systems, "Proceedings IJCAI-6".

Stefik, M.; Bobrow, D.G. (1986) Object-oriented programming: themes and variations, "The AI Magazine" No. 6(4).

Wright, J.M.; Fox, M.S. (1985) "SRL/1.5 User Manual", Intelligent Systems Laboratory, The Robotics Institute, Carnegie Mellon University, Pittsburg, 15 December.

A Framework for Object Functional Descriptions

M. Di Manzo, F. Ricci, A. Batistoni and C. Ferrari

University of Genoa (Italy)

RESUME

La reconnaissance est essentiellement un procédé de adaptation dans lequel des données visuelles sont comparees avec des classes de prototypes. Par conséquent, un point céntral, dans la vision artificielle, est le type de connaissance que l'on doit utiliser pour construire des prototypes et conduire le procédé de adaptation. Dans cet article nous proposons un paradigme pour décrire "à quoi un object sert" au lieu de "à quoi il resembles". Nous discutons une méthodologie pour construire des primitives fonctionnelles, et nous montrons, avec quelques éxamples, de quelle façon le procédé de reconnaissance peut être conduit par ce type de description.

Mot clés: Vision artificielle, Modelage cognitif, Description fonctionnelle.

ABSTRACT

Recognition is basically a matching process, where structured visual data are compared to class prototypes. Therefore, a central point, in artificial vision, is what type of knowledge do we use to build prototypes and drive the matching process. In this paper we suggest a paradigm to describe "what objects are for" instead of "what they look like". We discuss a methodology to build functional primitives, and show, with some examples, how the recognition process can be driven by this type of description.

Keywords: Artificial vision, Cognitive modeling, Functional description

1. INTRODUCTION

Recognition is basically a matching process, where structured visual data are compared to class prototypes. Therefore, a truly central point in machine vision is what type of knowledge do we use to build prototypes and drive the matching process. A very common strategy, in the past, has been to describe "prototypical shapes". In some cases, attempts have been made to capture the variability of shapes within each class by relaxing the matching constraints (see, for instance, the work done by Shapiro et al.[5]).

However, these experiences are pointing out that it is very hard to find a practical compromize between the needs for a high flexibility within each class and a high discrimination among different classes.

The poor performances of artificial systems, compared to the human skill, are probably due to the fact that humans beings think more in terms of "what objects are for" than in terms of "what they look like" [6]. So, we believe that the research in Artificial Vision should make a serious effort towards the definition of a paradigm for describing object functions.

In some previous papers [1,3] we claimed that the functional descriptions of a wide set of manufactured objects can be approached by decomposing them into networks of functional primitives. This is not surprising, since any major or minor detail of the shape of each object should result from the definition of a set of design goals, which account for the intended use, the constructive process, the stylistic choices, the economic constraints and so on.

Conversely, the design goals seem closely related to common sense object taxonomies, or even to technical ones in more specialized domains. For example, roughly speaking, we can say that an object belongs to the class of "chairs" if accomplishes the design goals of supporting a sitting human body, blocking its back—bending and ensuring stability in a proper position on a supporting plane surface (typically the floor); moreover, it belongs to the subclass of "rotating chairs " if, in addition to the previous ones, it accomplishes the goal of allowing a rotation of the part supporting the sitting body around a vertical axis, without moving its contact with the floor.

So, even if it cannot be proven, there is evidence for asserting that the recognition of an object, as a member of a given object class, is based on the identification of a subset of relevant design goals. If we are not concerned with stylistic goals (e.g. we do not create, in our taxonomy, the subclass of Luis XV chairs), the relevant design goals seem deal basically with the intended uses of objects. That is more interesting, in the analysis of many common objects classes a small number of design goals come out repeatedly as, for instance, supporting, containment, graspability, rotation, sliding, closure and so on.

Many object classes can be successfully characterized referring to this basic set of goals; objects are recognized as members of a specific class if and only if they accomplish a proper subset of goals. Since these goals describe expected object performances, we refer to them as "functional primitives", and use them as basic building blocks to define the overall functional characteristics which distinguish each object class.

One may ask what advantages do we expect from object functional description. It should be clear that functional decomposition is a task conceptually different from structural decomposition. Structural decomposition is based on the definition of geometric primitives and on the search for joints between them. Sometimes different functions are performed by different substructures, but this is not always the case: for instance, in a rotating chair, the same structural component (the legs) must accomplish both rotation and stability on the floor. So, we cannot hope to find simple geometric rules to match functional and structural decompositions. However, we are claiming that recognition is basically the process of inferring functions from shapes. This inference process is largely expectation—driven and relies on a deep knowledge of the constraints that functions impose on shapes.

The definition of a limited number of functional primitives as basic building blocks offers a practical approach to the binding of functions with shapes: the inner semantic of each primitive is defined by a set of rules which allow to verify whether a submitted shape is suitable to perform just that function.

We shall say more about primitives in the following; in the time being we assume to have an expert system, associated to each primitive, which can answer questions about the suitability of submitted structures. Now, let us look at what functional descriptions are, and how they can be used to drive the recognition process.

2. THE BASIC STRUCTURE OF A FUNCTIONAL DESCRIPTION

We told in the previous section that a structural decomposition may be a useless exercise. Nevertheless, each functional primitive describes a basic performance, and any performance involves a performer; in our case, it is typically a structural entity of the observed object. Thus the inference of function from the shape involves some type of structural decomposition, but this process must be driven much more by the knowledge hidden in the primitive experts than by the identification of geometric cues.

The need for a performer raises an interesting analogy with those systems which encode the meaning of natural language sentences by means of conceptual primitives (see, for istance [2]). Primitives are not isolated entities; they impose a structure to description, since they are the care of a network of "semantic cases", whose fillers must obey to the restrictions defined by a "conceptual grammar".

The basic, and mandatory, semantic case, is the ACTOR, which is filled by the primitive performer. The restriction which can be imposed to the ACTOR filler (and, generally, on all the case fillers) depend on the involved primitive, and are concerned with its dimensionality (i.e. it can be an edge, a surface or a volume).

All the other semantic cases are not mandatory. Usually a primitive is performed on some entity, which become the filler of the OBJECT case. Similarly to the other case fillers, the OBJECT filler may be either a structural entity of the described object, or an "external world entity" (typically another object). So in the description of a chair (Fig. 4) the primitive function SUPPORT is performed by the chair part "seat" on the external object "sitting_human_body".

The reason for the possible presence of external objects is that the role of the semantic cases is to define the current environment of the functional primitive; so, in a sense, they simply "communicate" to the primitive expert a set of constraints coming from the object itself or from its possible relation with other existing or virtual objects.

Further semantic cases are the DIRECTIVE, the QUANTITY and the INSTRUMENTAL cases. The DIRECTIVE case specifies the direction along which the function is performed: its filler is either one (or more) generic direction in the space or the orientation of a specific part of the object under exam (or of an external world object).

The QUANTITY case gives a qualitative measure of the involvement of the ACTOR filler in the function: its filler is a "quantity specification" expressed by means of adjectives as "large", "small" and so on. In this way we select different modalities in which the same basic function can be performed, allowing some factorization and parametrization of the related knowledge base.

The information about the tools that allow a particular primitive function to work properly, is expressed by the INSTRUMENTAL case.

The INSTRUMENTAL case is introduced when the primitive cannot be performed by the ACTOR filler, unless some other entity gives a specific support, whose nature depends on the semantics of the primitive itself. As shown in Fig. 1, we can say that a fluid (the ACTOR) flows out from a bottle by means a proper hole (the INSTRUMENT)in the body of the jug. If the hole is absent the fluid would not be allowed to flow out, and the function could not be performed. We note how the DIRECTIVE and the QUANTITY case work to express the fact "a small quantity of fluid flows through a hole, in any direction".

Other examples of the use of semantic cases are presented in Fig. 2 and Fig. 3.

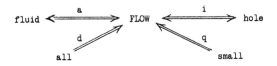

Fig. 1

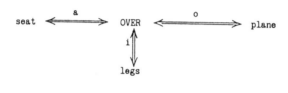

Fig. 2

hand ⟺ₐ GRASP ⟺ᵒ jug

Fig.3

3. TYPES OF KNOWLEDGE ENCODED IN THE PRIMITIVES

In our experimental prototype we are currently using about ten functional primitives, namely SUPPORT, GRASP, SLIDE, ROTATE, ENTER, CONTAIN, FLOW, PLUG, HANG, BLOCK_ROTATION and BLOCK_SLIDING. In Appendix we give a very brief explanation of their meanings; however they must be considered simply a working set to test the feasibility of our approach.

Most of the geometric knowledge, which allow to relate (naive) physics concepts to the observed shapes, is hidden in the primitive experts. Sometimes, however, a purely functional specification of some structural details would require an enormous amount of very sophisticated physical knowledge: on the other hand, the performed function may impose very restrictive constraints on the shape of the involved component. In this case, it is much easier and more efficient to maintain some geometrical relations explicitly at the description level. Thus, we have defined a further set of primitives, which are concerned with geometric restrictions and spatial relationships. The need for primitives even in this case, instead of, for instance, simple labelled arcs, derives from the nature of the spatial knowledge that they embody.

For example, when we say that a plane surface S must stay in a stable position OVER the floor with a defined orientation, we need something more than the capability of evaluating the relative positions of two surfaces; we need some knowledge to justify how that position can be maintained against the action of, say, the force of gravity, and to identify that part of the object structure which ensures this performance. Hence, more or less, even the assertion of a spatial relationship may involve some amount of sophisticated reasoning, and the situation that it describes may be constrained by the fillers of related semantic cases.

The geometric primitives currently used are OVER, UNDER, SIDE_S, LINKED, ON, OPPOSITE, PARALLEL, B_SURF, TOP (see Appendix).

4. MORE ABOUT EXPERTS: EXPERT COOPERATION

Hitherto we have assumed that experts answers yes/no questions about the suitability of submitted structural entities. However, in section 2 we noted that recognition presupposes a sort of knowledge–driven geometric decomposition. Indeed, what we ask to experts is often to extract relevant features from the submitted structures and/or identify substructures which may play a specific role in the accomplishment of the primitive function. The main reason for requesting this more sophisticated output can be found in the interaction between experts. A functional description is a network where the primitives share the fillers of their semantic cases. This means that the current environment of each primitive is typically defined by the results of the activity of its neighbours. Such a cooperation allows to avoid blind searching strategies, taking advantage of any partial discovery which may be used to focus the system reasoning on specific parts of the observed object. For example, when the SUPPORT expert of the chair definition (see Fig. 5) approves a submitted structure as a proper candidate seat, the search for a back, performed by the BLOCK_ROTATION expert, must be restricted to those substructures which are linked to the seat and properly placed in the space. This type of interaction may be controlled by constraining the position of external objects, as it happens in the seat–back example, or requesting expert to produce well–defined side effects. So, for instance, the CONTAIN expert, which looks for open containers, must output a directed axis that allows the cooperating experts to identify the relative positions of the opening and the bottom (see Fig. 6). Side effects are inherent to the semantics of each functional primitive; they are expressed by a specific relation, called RESULT, represented by arcs labelled by r. A second type of result arcs, labelled by R, are used in connection with variables, as explained in the following section. It is worth noting that the structural entities pointed by the r arcs are not necessarily related to the ACTOR filler, even if this is the most common case; the features or substructures, that they point out, are related to the filler of a semantic case whose choice depend on the definition of the primitive.

5. HOW TO USE FUNCTIONAL DESCRIPTIONS

Functional descriptions operate on a visual data base where we maintain an "analogic" description of the observed objects. This description can be considered as the result of an ideal bottom–up process which identifies surfaces and volumes, and makes inferences about local occlusions by means of perceptual rules [4]. Real systems have not yet this capability, unless they operate on very restricted domains, and it is even doubtful whether such a purely bottom–up system might ever exist. However, we are not concerned with these problems here; actually, for testing purposes the visual data base is filled with synthetic images.
To control the recognition process we need a further extension of the experts ability: they must check the appropriateness of a selected structural entity, when it has been isolated, or look for a possible proper candidate, when no specific suggestions are available. Isolated structural entities correspond to "labelled parts" in the visual data base; they describe possibly provisional results of the activity of some expert. The two expert operating modes must be distinguished at the description level; as we shall see in the following, this distinction is the basic tool for controlling the inherent concurrency of the expert activities. Therefore, in the functional descriptions, labelled parts are identified by names, and variables are introduced as case filler whenever the expert is requested to operate in searching mode. If the search is successful, the variable must be bound to a (new) labelled part; this binding is described by a "is–a" arc, which is the result (R arc) of the expert activity.
An example about the use of variables is shown in Fig. 4.
In Fig. 5 we show the complete graph corresponding to the functional description of a generic chair. In this graph you can recognize the basic elements that characterize the idea of "chairness": in fact a chair is presented as something having a part (the seat) devoted to support a sitting_human_body (refer to the SUPPORT expert), and another one (the back) able to block his backward rotation (see the BLOCK_ROTATION expert). Besides the seat surface has to stay at a proper height over a plane parallel to it by means the "legs" and finally the whole seat, back and legs must be stable on a plane (see the OVER and the ON expert).
Likewise the bottle is represented in Fig. 6, as something having a part (the body) devoted to contain fluids (see the CONTAIN expert). A hole in the body allows fluids to get in and out the

bottle (refer to the ENTER and the FLOW expert) and a neck, in the top of the body, can be plugged (see the TOP and PLUG expert). At last the bottle can be grasped by a hand and it stays on a plane (see the GRASP and the ON expert).

The whole recognition activity requires that the various experts are synchronized each other to avoid that they start to work without having all the information they need.

The basic idea is that the first running experts are those whose semantic case are filled with variables and external world entities: in fact they are the only experts with a definite context. As shown in Fig. 7 the CONTAIN and the GRASP experts are allowed to start working. When an expert finishes successfully it produces some results and define the context relative to other experts, that can now begin their activity.

In the above example, when the contain expert ends its activity successfully, it defines the "hole", the "body_axis" and the "body": consequently the FLOW, the ENTER, the ON and the SIDE_S become active while the PARALLEL expert is blocked until both the GRASP and the CONTAIN experts finish with a success. The last activated experts are the LINKED and the OPPOSITE experts that wait to have both the "handle", the "spout" and the "side_surface" defined: the recognition activity ends when all the experts are successful.

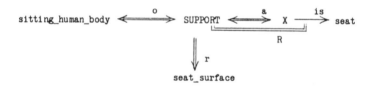

Fig. 4

6. CONCLUDING REMARKS

Many ideas discussed in this paper must be considered working hypotheses, since an experimental prototypes is still under development. Several important problems have not been addresses here. Firstly, a deeper investigation of the psychology and ergonomic foundations of the concept of functional primitive is necessary. Some advise may come from similar approaches in computational linguistics; however reasoning about objects is mostly related to our motor knowledge, while the semantics theories developed for language are much more concerned with abstract thinking. Secondly, the structure of experts, the type of knowledge that they embody (i.e. qualitative vs. quantitative), the relations between their organization and the activation rules of functional prototypes and several other related questions are still open research areas. Thirdly, strategies are needed to handle problems as large occlusions, which cannot be recovered with local algorithms. Finally, the problem of interfacing a functionally driven recognizer with a feature extractor in a real, noisy environment, is far from being assested. However, despite the primitive state of art of this approach to artificial vision, we feel that it is a very promising research line, which could give a substantial contribution to overcome the drawback of current systems.

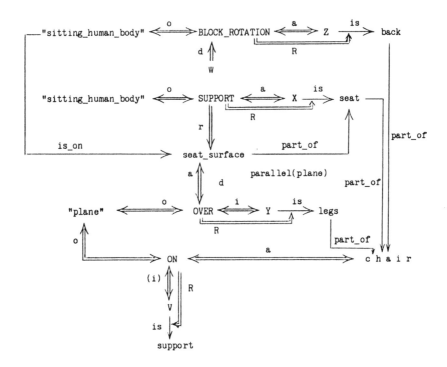

Fig. 5: THE CHAIR

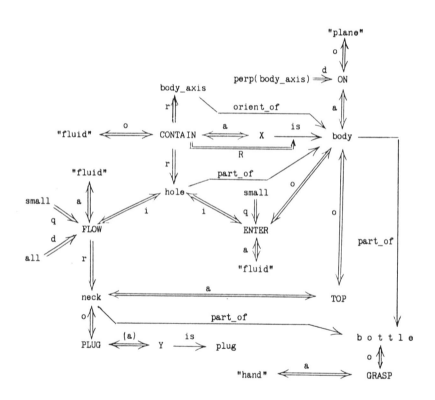

Fig. 6: THE BOTTLE

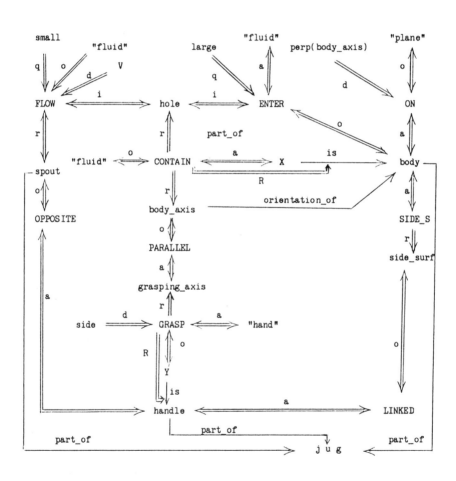

Fig. 7: THE JUG

APPENDIX

SUPPORT	:	the actor gives a support to the object.
GRASP	:	the actor grasps the object.
SLIDE	:	the actor slides on the object.
ROTATE	:	the actor rotates around the object.
ENTER	:	the actor enters in the object.
CONTAIN	:	the actor contains the object.
FLOW	:	the actor flows out the object.
PLUG	:	the actor plugs the object.
HANG	:	the actor hangs the object.
BLOCK_ROT	:	the actor prevents the rotation of the object.
BLOCK_SLID	:	the actor prevents the sliding of the object.
ON	:	the actor is on the object.
OVER	:	the actor is is over the object.
UNDER	:	the actor is under the object.
LINKED	:	the actor and the object are linked to each other.
OPPOSITE	:	the actor and the object are opposite.
PARALLEL	:	the actor and the object are parallel.
SIDE_S	:	it extract the side surface of a solid.
B_SURF	:	it extract the bottom surface of a solid.
TOP	:	it gives the top part of a given structure.

REFERENCES

[1] Giovanni Adorni, Mauro Di Manzo, Fausto Giunchiglia and Lina Massone "A conceptual approach to artificial vision", Proceeding ROVISEC 4, London (October 1984)

[2] R.C.Shank "Conceptual Information Processing", Noth Holland: Amsterdam 1985

[3] Giovanni Adorni, Mauro Di Manzo, Fausto Giunchiglia and Franca Ricci "Building Functional Descriptions", Proceeding ROVISEC 5, Amsterdam (October 1985)

[4] D.Waltz "Generating semantic descriptions for drawings of scene with shadows" in "The psychology of Computer Vision", P.H.Winston, Mc.Graw Hill, New York 1975

[5] Linda G.Shapiro, J.D.Moriarty, R.M.Haralick and Prasanna G.Mulgaonkar "Matching three−dimensional models", Proceeding IEEE Conf. on Pattern Recognition and Image Processing, Dallas 1981

[6] Patrick H.Winston, Thomas O.Binford, Boris Katz and Michael Lowry "Learning physical descriptions from functional definitions, examples and precedents", M.I.T. AI Memo 679, November 1982.

Knowledge Elicitation and Analysis for Approximate Reasoning Systems

R. Lopez de Mantaras, J. Agusti

Centre d'Estudis Avançats de Blancs (Espagne)

E. Plaza

Facultat d'Informatica, Barcelone (Espagne)

ABSTRACT

This paper describes a system and ancilliary methods based in Personal Construct Psychology for aiding knowledge engineers in the early stages of knowledge base design. System's semantics is based in fuzzy set theory in order to support the linguistic contrastive terms used by the human experts. Its basic approach is decoupling knowledge acquisition from implementation through the analysis and refining of knowledge in a stage prior to expert system implementation. Different analysis allow several perspectives of the knowledge base and its refining sticks to systematicity requiring concrete explanations.

Keywords: Knowledge acquisition, approximate reasoning, personal construct theory, knowledge base design, fuzzy set theory, contrastive sets.

1. INTRODUCTION

This paper describes a system and ancilliary methods based in Personal Construct Psychology for aiding knowledge engineers in the early stages of knowledge base design. This system has been developed in the framework of KESS project. Other topics being currently developed inside the Knowledge Engineering Support System project are consensual knowledge aggregation from different experts (Plaza et al.,1986) and the design of an environment to build prototypical knowledge sources for frame-based expert systems. Currently, expert system building tools focus on debugging already implemented knowledge bases. This approach requires an early definition of a subset of rules in order to be able to build a prototype system to pursue the knowledge acquisition process. Instead, we focus on the first

phase of knowledge acquisition (Figure 1) so that, before
deciding on the particular rule base implementation schema, the
following goals are achieved:

** Context acquisition: a   set   of   domain   objects   (e.g.
illnesses in a diagnostic system) that is representative of the
actual domain of expertise.

** Acquisition of the (almost complete) set of the   relevant
concepts used by the expert in the problem-solving process.

** Definition for each concept of its contrastive set, the
set of the linguistic values actually used by the expert.

These goals are   achieved   in   two   basic   stages: 1)   the
incremental   building   and   validation   of a conceptual base (the
relational base linking   concepts   and   objects   with   linguistic
values),   and   2)   the   generation   and   validation   of   a set of
inference   rules.   Although   this   paper   is   concerned   about
knowledge   acquisition   for knowledge-based systems (KBS) design,
this does not mean   that   after   this   phase   no   more   knowledge
acquisition   is   needed,   but   that this should be pursued by the
system building tool of the system architecture choosed.

2. REASONING WITH CONTRASTIVE SETS

Before dicussing theoretically the approach   used,   and   for
the   sake   of   clarity,   the   three   stages   of   the   knowledge
elicitation process are outlined in Figure 1:   Conceptualization,
Refinement   and   Inference   Validation.   The cycles depicted are
EAR* (Elicit-Analyse-Refine) iterations that   finally   produce   a
validated   rule-set   as   well   as a representative set of domain
objects and a set of relevant concepts for knowledge base design.

2.1 A Linguistic Approach

The issue of approximate reasoning is the issue of   dealing
with   imprecise   and   uncertain   information   in   an   inferential
system.   And the issue of vagueness and "exactness" is   an   issue
of   appositeness   to   a context: "Inexact" is really a reproach,
and "exact" is praise.   And that is to say that what   is   inexact
attains   its   goal   less   perfectly than what is more exact.   Thus
the point here is what we call "the goal"   (Wittgenstein,   1955).
Thus,   a   prime   desideratum of knowledge engineering for systems
using   approximate   reasoning   is   to   establish   the   apposite
precision   level   in   a problem solving domain in order to be able
to fulfill the expert   system   goal   (and   also   to   commmunicate
easily a KBS with experts and end-users).   Currently, most expert
systems (Hayes-Roth, 1983) and personal construct systems (Shaw &
Gaines,1980;   Boose,   1984)   use   numerical   estimates   of
"inexactness", but a problem arises: it is difficult   to   anyone
to   assert   consistently numerical   judgements in contexts where
they   are   not   employed.   An   experimental   research   developed
(Freksa & López   de Màntaras, 1984) showed that people asked to

give numerical estimations err almost every time and in a non-consistent way (overestimations and underestimations indistinctly) while judgements asserted using linguistic descriptions appear consistent in the same experimental situation. The reason for errors is the presupposition that a person (an expert) can make always a finer distinction over the objects of a context, but the fact is that forcing precisiation destroys the relevancy between the precision level used and the expert problem-solving knowledge.

The appropiateness of the linguistic approach to construct elicitation is founded on the claim that people discriminate, in a context, by means of a contrastive set. Contrastive set can be interpreted from a cognitive standpoint as a collection of "typical instances" of concepts used by the subject to discriminate in his reasoning and communication activity in order to achieve a goal. The study on colour categories (Kay, 1982) shows that people reach an agreement over the colour terms and at pointing out the 'typical examples', while there is no such agreement on colour boundaries. This "focal points" in the colour scale and other studies in psychology (see e. g. Johnson-Laird, 1983) suggest that many contrastive fields are mentally represented by prototypes or schemata of their typical member features, and that judgements about non-typical instances seem to depend on the 'distance' from the prototype schema.

The subject's working with the natural categories is plausibly the reason of consistency in linguistic (and context-dependent) judgements and inconsistency in non-linguistic (and context-independent) judgements shown in Freksa and Lopez de Mantaras (1984). By 'natural categories' we mean no more than a contrastive set apposite to the problem the subject is to solve. The linguistic approach simply states that in order to avoid unnacessary errors the 'metric' is not to be depended on external criteria, on the contrary, it is to be dependent on the contrastive fields used for each particular situation.

2.2 Contrastive Sets

In order to obtain an informational granularity apposite to the problem-solving goal we focus on the discriminating linguistic labels the expert effectively uses in discussing about and characterizing his expertise domain. The set of meaningful labels used to discriminate in a context is called in semantic analysis contrastive set. The Figure 2 shows some features of contrastive sets (Miller & Johnson-Laird, 1976). The semantic representation of the contrastive labels by possibility distributions allows to model most of the features of contrastive sets (López de Màntaras & Plaza, 1985). The contrastive set semantic denotation is contextually learned by means of an interacting adaptation of possibility distributions (Freksa & López de Màntaras, 1984), the only prerequisite being that a partial order may be defined over the objects of the universe of discourse. Furthermore, if there is an underlying metric scale consistency is assured (Figure 3), while if there is none consistency is dependent upon the expert experienceness.

Specifically, a contrastive set $K_i = \{k_1, \ldots k_m\}$ of m terms associated with concept C_i is admissible if:
i) the possibility distributions of K_i form a fuzzy coverage of the universe of discourse of C_i.
ii) for all terms k_r of K_i there exist an antonymic possibility distribution $k_s = k_r^-$ in K_i.
iii) there exists one possibility distribution k_r of K_i so that it is its own antonym : $k_s = k_r^-$ (undecided predicate).
Condition (i) is the <u>complete relevancy requirement</u> of the contrastive set (López de Màntaras & Plaza, 1985). In fact, this is a completeness condition imposed to the collection in order to be a contrastive set, exacting that the whole universe of discourse is covered completely with the possibility distribution collection. The second requirement states that the antonymy relationships hold in the contrastive set and express the particular constraint posed by construct polarity in the elicitation process (López de Màntaras & Plaza, 1985). The expert assertions are then fuzzy predicates of the kind "O_j is k_r C_i" where O_j is an object, C_i a concept and k_r a term of K_i. A fuzzy predicate induces in the representation structure of the system a fuzzy set k_r linking an oject and a concept
$$P_i(O_j) = k_r \quad \Longleftrightarrow \quad \text{"}O_j \text{ is } k_r C_i\text{"}.$$
For example,. being O_j a patient or an illness, C_i being "High blood pressure" (and C_i^- "Low blood pressure") a fuzzy predicate may be "O_j is dangerously C_i" if "dangerously" is a legal term of K_i.

If objects cannot be even partially ordered, the contrastive set is not represented as a whole and the linguistic terms are considered independent concepts, although the existence of the contrastive set is recognized in the logical analysis stage. The specific collection K_i used, determines the informational granularity of the contrastive set and other features of contrastive sets like the specificity and the extremism of predicates (Yager, 1983). Figure 3 shows an example of two contrastive sets representations.

As informational granularity is contingent upon the number of contrastive fields in a contrastive set (and, in a lesser degree, contingent upon the size of these fields represented by elastic constraints), so it is predicate extremism. Increasing contrastive field number increases the extremism (separation) of the predicates closer to the poles of the construct scale, but it is also dependent on the relative size of the predicates. As for different predicate specificity degrees, they can be modelled by relative size relationship between kernel and support set in possibility distributions.

2.3 Approximate Reasoning

Two main goals in knowledge elicitation for systems using approximate reasoning were considered to be achieved by the linguistic contrastive set approach: in the firts place, avoid inconsistencies in expert statements in order to minimize errors in the acquisition of knowledge. In the second place, distinguishing between imprecision of values and uncertainty in rules, it seems clear that not permitting the expert to state imprecise statements assertions (because of the inadequacy of the representation formulism) forces him to conceive of more uncertain rules. For this reason the second goal is to minimize inference rule uncertainty admitting imprecise statements about facts semantically represented by possibity distributions.

The knowledge elicitation process is the incremental building of the contrastive space (formed by the domain objects, the relevant concepts and its contrastive sets, and the fuzzy predicates):
$$\{C_i\,,\ K_i\,,\ O_j\,,\ P_i\,(O_j\,)=k_r\}\ \text{where}\ i=1..n,\ j=1..m,\ k_r\,eK_i\,,$$
and approximate reasoning is an elucidation process in the contrastive space. Specifically, KBS design is the formulation of a set of inference rules holding in that contrastive space satisfying the problem-solving goals. The system representation of an expert contrastive space is called <u>conceptual base</u>. Briefly, the contrastive set approach to approximate reasoning can be summarized with its requirements, assumptions, and limitations.
<u>Requirements</u>. Relevancy of concepts, appositeness of contrastive set informational granularity to the context, and representativeness of the elicited domain objects.
<u>Assumptions</u>. Approximate reasoning can be modelled as an elucidation process in the contrastive space.
<u>Limitations</u>. Those proper to KBS due either to data incompleteness (failure to achieve one of the requirements) or to the inappropiateness of the formulism employed to capture the relevant features of the problem-solving task.

3. BUILDING THE CONTRASTIVE SPACE

First section introduces notions of Personal Construct Theory, the second section describes the elicitation process, and the last one the analysis and validation of inference rules.

3.1 Personal Construct Psychology

Personal Construct Theory (Kelly, 1955) is a constructivist psychological theory with the basic tenet that a person, in oder to control and predict its environment, must construct a representation out of the flow of events. The features abstracted from reality (the distinctions made by a person) and subjectively deemed relevant are <u>constructs</u>: bipolar scales with two opposite (negation or antonimic) concepts as extreme poles. The construct system provides a basis for characterizing and predicting the environment which, in turn, in the light of experience may lead to the revision of the constructs used and, eventually, of whole construct systems (constructive alternativism: the revisions allow the problem to be viewed from a new standpoint). Kelly's work provided the <u>repertory grid</u> technique for eliciting the constructs relevant to a context which have been extensively applicated in interactive computer programs (Shaw & Gaines, 1980; Easterby-Smith, 1980). Viewing construct systems as the underlying knowledge structures in human

decision making (Shaw & Gaines, 1984) it can be shown they are
based in a "calculus of distinctions" underlying fuzzy and
probability uncertainty logics (Gaines, 1984). The system of
distinctions or constructs is the lowest level of the structure
of expertise knowledge (problem-solving decision-making) and
hence is the most general and primarial stage in knowledge
acquisition after the formulation of the problem. Personal
construct elicitation techniques have been recently used in the
knowledge engineering tasks (Gaines & Shaw, 1983; Boose, 1984)

3.2 Conceptual Base Construction and Refinement

This section deals with the man-machine dialogue situation
viewed by the linguistic approach. The EINA (Interactive
Elicitation and Analysis) program conducts a dialogue with the
expert that elicits the personal constructs (applying to a
domain) and the domain objects using fuzzy predicates. The set
of domain objects or elements elicited in a given domain is
called domain context.

3.2.1 Concept elicitation and analysis

From a knowledge acquisition perpective the elicitation
process based in the repertory grid techniques is the incremental
building of a conceptual base and corresponds to a
conceptualization process, i. e. the second stage of knowledge
engineering task (Hayes-Roth et al., 1983). The first stage,
identification of problem characteristics, is a previous informal
task (which may include same trial-and-error use of the
elicitation system) bound to establish the task goals and the
type of domain objects involved for the next stage of
conceptualization. The elicitation mode permits, starting from
an initial domain context, to build up a basic conceptual base
with the most clearcut constructs and domain objects. The
refining mode works out an analysis/disagreement/concrete
explanation cycle in function of two desiderata: that of domain
context representativeness and that of apposite characterization
of objects and constructs (apposite to the goal we are aiming at
in the current problem-solving situation).

At the beginning EINA enters the elicitation mode. The
experimental subject defines an initial domain context with a
minimum of three objects. Successively, domain context objects
are grouped combinatorially in triads. The subject is asked to
distinguish them by means of a similarity attribute between (a
common attribute of) two triad objects and a dissimilarity
attribute proper to the third object. This distinction is stated
by the similarity and dissimilarity attributes and represented in
the repertory grid by the opposite poles of a new construct. The
new construct is then applied to the domain context: the user
especifies linguistically (i.e. using the contrastive sets) the
degree to which the construct applies to each object (Figure 4).
To proceed in the elicitation mode the user supplies a new object
to the domain context and new tradic combinations are prompted
until this mode is quitted. This mode is necessary in the case
that an initial subset of relevant concepts is not clearly

defined; if there is one subset already defined the process starts directly in the refining mode.

Subsequently, EINA allows to enter the <u>refining mode</u> in which two interactive ressemblance analysis on both domain objects and elicited constructs, are performed. Construct ressemblance analysis displays the most similar constructs. The experimental subject is asked to point out the similarities he disagrees with, and to supply a <u>concrete explanation</u> to justify his disagreements. Similarly, domain context analysis displays the most similar objects and the user is asked to point out his disagreements and justify them, also by means of concrete explanations. A concrete explanation in construct analysis is an object used as a <u>counterexample</u>, i. e. an object such that, for the two similar constructs involved, the object applies to the pole of one construct <u>and</u> to the other construct <u>opposite</u> pole. The new object is then evaluated using fuzzy predicates over the set of the elicited constructs. A concrete explanation in domain context analysis is a <u>disambiguating construct</u> such that the two involved objects apply one to a construct pole and the other to the opposite pole. The new construct is also applied to all context objects. The refining mode also allows unconditioned addition to the repertory grid of new objects (thereafter evaluated by all the elicited constructs) and new constructs (subsequently applied to the domain context).

The two ressemblance analysis provides two different perspectives to explore the relationships of the conceptual base Expert disagreement with construct analysis makes apparent the poor characterization of (distinguishability between) constructs and it may be solved by a counterexample, i. e. the inclusion of a new object not so far envisaged. In this way, the lack of representativeness of the domain context with respect to the real domain is lessened. Besides, disagreed similarity between objects shows clearly the lack of <u>sufficient</u> object characterization (distinguishability). The supply of concrete explanations, new constructs, that distinguish more the objects, improves the characterization of context objects. Briefly, the incremental building of the conceptual base implements the trends toward the two goals mentioned at the Introduction: improvement of context representativeness of the domain and improvement of the discrimination and characterization power of the elicited concepts.

The <u>requirement</u> of using concrete explanations as justifications for expert disagreements resolution in expert knowledge acquisition has the advantage of <u>systematicity</u> in regards to conceptual base building: modifications brought about by disagreement resolution are focused by the expert/user on a given single point but the novelty's repercussion involves the whole conceptual base. This approach is used to develope the whole knowledge acquisition system including the inference validation and refining environment (López de Màntaras et al, 1985; Plaza & López de Màntaras, 1985).

3.2.2 Indistinguishability analysis

Construct analysis measures the indistinguishability degree
of personal construct use in a conceptual base. Domain context
analysis measures the indistinguishability degree of domain
object characterization for a given system of personal
constructs. Several indistinguishability relations have been
proposed to estimate ressemblence in classification problems; for
example Menger's probabilistic relation, Zadeh's similarity
relation, and Ruspini's likeness relation. The three of them are
F-indistinguishability relations, that is to say, they are
reflexive, symmetrical, and F-transitive binary fuzzy relations,
being F a triangular norm (t-norm):

F1. $R(x,x)=1$,
F2. $R(x,y)=R(y,x)$, and
F3. $F(R(x,y),(y,z))\leqslant R(x,z)$.

Since our interest, besides the interactive analisys, is to
produce a final analysis and a clustering of constucts and of
domain objects, it is apparent that the results obtained are
dependent upon the metrics associated with the
indistinguishability operator used for the analysis. The three
indistinguishability relations previously mentioned have been
studied (Lopez de Mantaras & Valverde) in regards to the validity
of the clusterings obtained. The validity criterion used is not
ad hoc but based on data themselves: an indistinguishability
relation based on membership degrees of each datum to the
different clusters is constructed and the validity criterion
states that the lesser the difference between the membership
degrees and the indistinguishability degrees, the better is the
clustering. The results obtained show that in most cases the
best t-norm is that of Łukasiewicz Aleph-1 corresponding to
Ruspini's likeness relation and using the usual negation relation
$\mathfrak{h}(x)=1-x$, the metric associated is the euclidean distance
restricted to [0,1]. For this reason it was decided to use this
option in the indistinguishability analysis on objects and
constructs in order to compute the two corresponding
indistinguishability matrices.

From the knowledge acquisition stance the hierarchical
analysis are useful as a summarization of the ressemblance
relations, presented individually in the interactive analysis,
holding in the repertory grid and allowing a global appreciation
of them, and eventually leading to an acceptance or refusal of
the conceptual base elicited structure in part or in whole.

3.3 Subjective inference analysis

The conceptual base builded already specifies a fuzzy
production rule system. The set of task goals is the set of
objects: Context = { O_j | j=1..m} and being the objects
characterized by the predicates applied to them
$$O_j = \{ P_i(O_j)=k_r \mid k_r \text{ of } K_i, \ i=1..n \}.$$
The resolution rule R_j having as conclusion object O_j is a fuzzy
rule with premises {C_i | i=1..n} whose values are fuzzy

restrictions of the corresponding contrastive sets:
$$\{P_i(O_j)=k_r \mid k_r \text{ of } K_i, \ i=1..n\} \implies O_j.$$
And the fuzzy production system rule base is the set of resolution rules
$$\{ R_j \mid j=1..m\}.$$

Although there are implemented systems using only resolution rules, it is more useful to use also inference rules (rules linking the concepts themselves) and next section presents an analysis detecting the implicational relationships holding in the conceptual base. However, independently of its implementation, the logical analysis of the concepts provides the expert with a new perspective of the conceptual base and thus with a new standpoint for validating and refining the elicited knowledge (section 3.4).

3.3.1 Logical analysis

The repertory grid logical analysis views the experimental subject predicates as truth valued assignments, i. e. as logical predicates (Gaines & Shaw, 1980). A logical predicate, as was introduced in construct analysis systems by Gaines and Shaw, induces the assignment of an object to a construct pole (in bivalued logic)· or induces a compatibility degree assignment of an object to a construct pole (typically, "John is 0.8 intelligent").

Repertory grid logical analysis (Gaines & Shaw, 1980) defines implicational relationships between construct poles in the usual way for fuzzy subsets over the universe of discourse of the elicited objets. Allowing fuzzy predicates in the system (typically "John is highly intelligent), the fuzzy subsets over the domain context are 2nd-type fuzzy sets. A 2nd-type fuzzy set A is a fuzzy set such that to each object x of the universe of discourse U, the membership function assigns a fuzzy subset of [0,1] called fuzzy degree or fuzzy level, i. e.
$$\mu_A(x) \subseteq [0,1].$$

We will denote 2nd-type fuzzy sets as following
$$A= (x \mid f_A(x))) \ , \text{ where } f_A(x)= (f \mid \lambda(f \mid x))$$

We will define an entailment relationship between construct poles represented by 2nd-type fuzzy sets as a natural extension of the semantic entailment in fuzzy sets. The semantic entailment between two fuzzy predicates p, q inducing two fuzzy sets P, Q (Zadeh, 1978) is defined as:
$$p \longrightarrow q \text{ iff } P \subset Q$$
where
$$P \subset Q \text{ iff } \mu_P(x) \leqslant \mu_Q(x), \text{ for all } x \in U.$$

A 2nd-type inclusion can be defined (Kauffmann, 1983) using a max-composition or 2nd-type union. The max-compositions of two 2nd-type fuzzy sets A, B is defined by:

$$A \underset{2}{\cup} B = \bigcap_{A \cup B}(w \mid x) = \\
=(\underset{\substack{u \in [0,w] \\ v=w}}{MAX} (\lambda_A(u \mid x) \wedge \lambda_B(v \mid x)) \vee (\underset{\substack{u=w \\ v \in [0,w]}}{MAX} (\lambda_A(u \mid x) \wedge \lambda_B(v \mid x))).$$

Now, a 2nd-type fuzzy inclusion can be defined:
$$A \subseteq_z B \text{ iff } A \cup_z B = B,$$
and therefore the 2nd-type entailment will be defined as follows
$$a \rightarrow b \text{ iff } A \subseteq_z B.$$

This implication relates construct poles the way we are interested in: it holds when the fuzzy levels of B are never lesser than those of A for each object of the domain context. Due to the antonymic relationships holding in the contrastive set it is apparent that whenever two construct poles satisfy a --> b then also their antonymic poles satisfy the dual entailment b̄ --> ā.

The logical analysis is implemented by the program ALIS (Subjective Inference Logical Analysis) that produces an inference network, a digraph where nodes stand for construct poles and weighted arcs stand for entailment strength. The entailment strength is given by the rate between the number of domain context objects satisfying the entailment and the domain context cardinality.

3.4 Inference Validation and Refining

The techniques for inference validation and refinement form the second EAR* iterative cycle of reformulation of the conceptual base prior to the prototype system implementation. The rules generated by ALIS are prompted to the expert and EVRI (Inference Validation and Refinement Environment) focuses the expert attention over the rules to which he disagrees. EVRI handles disagreements, as before, demanding a concrete explanations, but also taking into account that disagreements about the inference network may arise for different reasons like ambiguous or polysemic concepts, insufficient object characterization or domain context incompleteness, and must be handled in different ways. EVRI implements several different techniques for disagreement resolution.

A) Counterexample Proposal. Expert disagreement about a rule may be justified stating a counterexample that will be included in the conceptual base as a new concrete explanation. Inference rules are prompted ranked according to their uncertainty value so that the expert may compare them. Disagreement about an inference rule (or about its implicational strength) may be solved giving the system a new object as a counterexample (i.e. one or more objects in which the implication do not hold). This disagreement is then caused by a lack of representativeness of the context. Also, disagreement about resolution rules may be solved by one or more new concepts, for these disagreements stem from an insufficient characterization of objects. In both cases, the requirement of concrete explanation assures that the modification caused by a local conflict has a global repercussion for new objects and concepts also modify other rules.

B) <u>Revision of assigned values</u>. In view of the results the expert or the knowledge engineer may decide that it is necessary to revise and modify the assigned fuzzy linguistic values linking concepts and objects and an editing facility is then used. The reasons for revision may be that a contrastive set is problematical and must be redifined or relearned, or may be that different criteria of assignement had been used in the elicitation process and a consistent one is seeked.

C) <u>Laddering techniques</u>. Disagreements may arise due to ambiguous or polysemic constructs present in a rule. In this situations EVRI support the laddering techniques developed in Personal Construct Theory (Kelly, 1955). Briefly, laddering techniques consist in splitting a construct in one or more new constructs using simple WHY-questions and HOW-questions. The answers to these questions are new constructs that are applied to the context objects and the inference network recomputed in order to see if tehe disagreement is solved.

i) <u>WHY-questions</u>. They are questions like "Why is important concept C?". The answer creates a new construct (or several if the new ones are recursively subjects of Why-questions). Constructs generated are usually superordinate (more abstract or more general) than the original construct (Figure 5).

ii) <u>HOW-questions</u>. They are questions like "How can you explain concept C?" or "What means concept C?". How-questions generates constructs that are commonly subordinate (more specific or concrete) concepts (Figure 5).

D) <u>Stepback</u>. This EVRI option allows to return to the interactive ressemblance analysis of the refining mode (section 3.2.1).
More informal knowledge engineering is needed in case of unsuccesful disagreement resolution by the above techniques. A disagreement list is filed describing the characteristics of the unsolved disagreement loci and may be used as a script for a later human interviewing of the expert. Also, in case that the expert points out the inexistence of an intuitive rule in the inference network the knowledge engineer is needed, although he can handle it using the options supported by EVRI.

4. Conclusion

Once the inference network has been validated the knowledge base design phase is finished. Subsequently, an architecture to implement the knowledge based system is to be choosed and the analysis of the performenace of the implemented prototype system is the basis for a new process of knowledge acquisition. The election of the system architecture is postponed until a stage in which a large amount of structured knowledge is already obtained due to the decoupling of the knowledge acquisition and refining process from the knowledge base implementation. The structured knowledge consist of a representative set of domain objects, a set of relevant concepts with a high power of characterization and discrimination, and the terms of the contrastive sets effectively used by the expert. The knowledge elicitation supports conceptual base systematicity requiring concrete explanations of disagreements. Concrete explanations are required in concept analysis for validating context representativeness, in context analysis to enrich object characterization, and in rule validation (laddering techniques and counterexample proposal).

The system has been used in the context of the design of a knowledge based system for document retrieval (Cortès & Plaza, 1985). In this experience we remarked the insight provided by the different perspectives on the elicited data, the easiness in eliciting the conceptual repertoire and generating a tentative inference network, and, outstandingly, the incremental building of a representative context was most significant for it was possible to design a knowledge base from a limited but representative set of documents instead of being necessary to use the whole amount of documents of the library.

Future research focuses on two areas. The first one is the elicitation and integration of knowledge from multiple experts using personal construct methodology. Knowledge is elicited, shared and negotiated in a structured way by several experts in a conversational process which aim is to detect disagreements and achieve consensus. The knowledge engineer drives the process using analysis of the experts sociological patterns and techniques for synthesizing judgements (Plaza et al., 1986). The second research area is the development of new analysis methods like conceptual clustering for fuzzy values and the development of dialogue protocols for eliciting new types of knowledge like justification and explanation of reasoning.

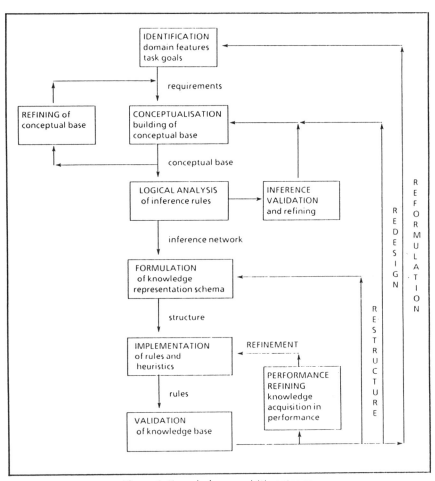

Figure 1. Knowledge acquisition stages

```
                   CONTRASTIVE SETS

   SIZE {male|female} ------- {integers}

   GENERIC / SPECIFIC

   {solid | liquid | gas} -------- taxonomies

   DIMENSIONALITY

   1-D (age) || 3 or 4 D (colours) || 6   or   more
   (kinterms) || unknown D (shape)

   GRADED / NON-GRADED

   Graded ------ {hot | cold}
   Discrete ------- {married | single}
   Debatable Gradability ----- {true | false}

   CRISP / FUZZY BOUNDARIES OF TERMS

   days of week -------- colou terms

   ANCHORAGE

   Absolutely anchored terms (measurement units)
   Deictically anchored terms (personal pronouns)
   Not Anchored at all terms (fast, slow, etc.)

   EXPRESSED

   by Affixes ----- (singular / plural)
   by Affixes & Words ---- (English tenses)
   by Words

   MEMBERSHIP

   precisely known (compass points names)
   vaguely open-ended (furniture articles names)

   ORDERED / UNORDERED

   COMPATIBILITY

   strictly exclusive ------ (taxonomies)
   may be fuzzy -------- (names of emotions)
```

FIGURE 2. Several features of contrastive sets.

```
                    CONTRAŞTIVE  SET  BUILDING
         Consider MICHAEL.
         Is MICHAEL VERY-SHORT ? no
         Is MICHAEL SHORT ? no
         Is MICHAEL RATHER-SHORT ? no
         Is MICHAEL MEDIUM ? no
         Is MICHAEL RATHER-TALL ? no
         Is MICHAEL TALL ? yes
         Is MICHAEL VERY-TALL ? undecided

         >>> CONFLICT <<< - RETURN to continue>show

         >>> CONFLICT #1 of type (NO RIGHT IN YES)
         >>> for RATHER-TALL.
         >>> Do you want to redifine label set ? no

         > > > > HANS (186) RATHER-TALL YES
         > > > > MICHAEL (185) RATHER-TALL NO

         Reconsider HANS
         Is HANS VERY-SHORT ? no
         Is HANS SHORT ? no
         Is HANS RATHER-SHORT ? no
         Is HANS MEDIUM ? no
         Is HANS RATHER-TALL ? no
         Is HANS TALL ? yes
         Is HANS VERY-TALL ? no

         Reconsider MICHAEL
```
                                                            (a)

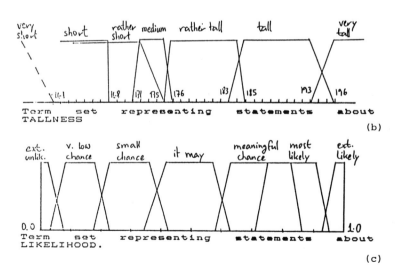

Term set representing statements about
TALLNESS
                                                            (b)

Term set representing statements about
LIKELIHOOD.
                                                            (c)

FIGURE 3. A contrastive set (b) and the adaptive building process (a).
The contrastive set (c) was obtained by Meyth-Marom using semantic
analysis methods.

Elicitation Mode

Elements are grouped in triads. User   supplies
similarities and dissimilarities.

Which two of A, B and C are more similar?
*** A and C
In which trait A and C are similar?
*** BROAD EXPERIENCE FIELDS
In which trait B is not like A and C?
*** NARROW EXPERIENCE FIELDS
In which degree A is BROAD EXPERIENCE FIELDS?
*** EXTREMELY
In which degree B is BROAD EXPERIENCE FIELDS?
*** VERY LOW

FIGURE 4.   A sample dialogue in elicitation mode.

Laddering Techniques

WHY Questions

Why is important ACCIDENT RISK?
*** (it is a feature of) WORKING ENVIRONMENT
Give me two antonyms for WORKING ENVIRONMENT
*** ADVERSE
*** GOOD

HOW questions

How can you explain EFFORT?
*** PHYSICAL EFFORT
*** INTELLECTUAL EFFORT
***
Give me to antonyms for PHYSICAL EFFORT
*** PHYSICAL EFFORT
*** NOT PHYSICAL EFFORT
Give me two antonyms for INTELLECTUAL EFFORT

ETC...

FIGURE 5.   Sample dialogues using Why-questions and How-questions.

REFERENCES

Boose, J H (1984), Personal construct theory and the transfer of human expertise, in F O'Shea (Ed.) Advances in Artificial Intelligence, ECAI-84. Elsevier North-Holland: Amsterdam.

Cortès, U & Plaza, E (1985), Descriptors' relevance in classification processes and prototype construction. Proceedings of the International Fuzzy Systems Association Congress 85: Palma de Mallorca.

Easterby-Smith, M. (1980), The design, analysis and interpretation of repertory grids. Int. J. Man-Machine Studies,13, 3-24.

Freksa, C & Lopez de Mantaras, R (1984), A learning system for linguistic categorization of "soft" observations. Colloque Association Recherche Cognitive, p. 331-345. Orsay (France).

Gaines, B R (1984),Fundamentals of decision: probabilistic, possibilistic and other forms of uncertainty in decision analysis, in L A Zadeh and B R Gaines (Eds), Fuzzy Sets and Decision Analysis. TIMS Studies in Management Sciences 20. Elsevier Publ.:New York.

Gaines, B R & Shaw, M L G (1983), Foundations of expert systems, in J Kacprzyk & R Yager (Ed.) Management decision support systems using fuzzy sets and possibility theory. TUV Verlag: Köln.

Hayes-Roth F, Waterman D A & Lenat D B Eds. (1983) Building Expert Systems. Addison-Wesley: Reading, Massachussets.

Johnson-Laird, P N(1983), Mental Models. Cambridge Univ. Press: Cambridge.

Kauffmann, A (1983), Complements sur les Conceptes Flous. Recherces et Applications. Tomme II. Mimeo. no publicat.

Kay, J(1982), Color perception and the meaning of color words. Mimeo: University of California.

Kelly, G A (1955), A Theory of Personality. The Psicology of Personal Constructs. W W Norton & Co.: New York.

López de Màntaras R, Cortes U, Plaza E, Sierra C & Villar A(1985), MILORD: An expert systems building tool with approximate reasoning, in C V Negoita & H Prade (Eds) Fuzzy Logics in Knowledge Engineering. TUV Verlag.

López de Màntaras, R & Plaza, E (1985), A linguistic approach to conceptual knowledge elicitation and analysis. Research Report CEAB: Blanes.

López de Màntaras, R & Valverde L (1984). New results in fuzzy clustering based on the concept of indistinguishability relation. 7th Int. Conference Pattern Recognition. IEEE Press: Montreal.

Miller, G A & Johnson-Laird, P N(1976), Language and Perception. Cambridge University Press: Cambridge.

Plaza E, Alsina C, López de Màntaras R, Agustí J & Aguilar J (1986), Consensus and knowledge acquisition. International Conference on Information Processing and Management of uncertainty in Knowledge Based Systems: Paris.

Plaza E & López de Màntaras R(1985), Knowledge acquisition and refinement using a fuzzy conceptual base. Proceedings NAFIPS Workshop on Fuzzy Expert Systems and Decision Support, October 24-25, Georgia St Univ: Atlanta.

Shaw M & Gaines B R (1980), New directions in the analysis and interactive elicitation of personal construct systems. Int. J. Man-Machine Studies, 13, 81-116.

Shaw M & Gaines B R (1984), Deriving constructs underlying decision, in H J Zimmerman, L A Zadeh & B R Gaines (Eds.) TIMS Studies in Management Sciences, 20, 47-65. Elsevier Pb.: New York.

Wittgenstein, L(1955), Investigacions Filosofiques. Ed. Laia(1983): Barcelona

Yager, R (1983), Opposites and measures of extremism in concepts and constructs. Int. J. Man-Machine St., 18, 249-291.

Zadeh, L(1978b), PRUF - A meaning representation language for natural language. Int. J. Man-Machine St., 10, 395-460.

Natural Language

Translating Natural Language Geometry Statements into a Many-Sorted Logic

J. Veronis

Groupe Représentation et traitement des connaissances,
CNRS, Marseille (France)

Abstract

We describe some difficulties that arise in using first-order logic to represent theorems and problems in a CAI system for geometry and/or as a background for syntactic and semantic analysis. We propose a many-sorted logic with restricted quantification based on a Boolean lattice of sorts and ad hoc overloading polymorphism, which is more appropriate from both the mathematical and linguistic point of view. In particular, this logic enables us to solve elegantly problems such as discourse consistency verification, polysemy and many cases of syntactic ambiguity and anaphora resolution.

Introduction

This work was carried out within the context of the realization of an interface for translating geometry theorems and problems from natural language to logic which is to be integrated into a CAI system for plane geometry. We show here that, although the part of geometry used is within the scope of first-order logic (FOL), FOL does not provide a well-suited framework, neither for representing theorems and problems nor for natural language processing. We propose a many-sorted (first-order) logic with restricted quantification based on a Boolean lattice of sorts and including ad hoc overloading polymorphism, which is more appropriate from both the mathematical and linguistic point of view. In particular, this logic enables us to solve elegantly problems such as discourse consistency verification, polysemy and many cases of syntactic ambiguity and anaphora resolution.

Restricted Quantification

Theorems and problems have very similar statement forms. In fact, any theorem can be transformed into a problem and any problem into a theorem by adding or suppressing a clause such as "Prove that ...". Both will then receive the same kind of logical representation and very similar syntactic and semantic processing.

Some difficulties arise in using FOL as a target language and/or as a background for syntactic and semantic analysis. Let us take the following theorem as an example:

Given D the perpendicular bisector of segment [AB], PA the

open semi-plane of edge D, M a point, if M belongs to P ,
                                                          A

then MA<MB.

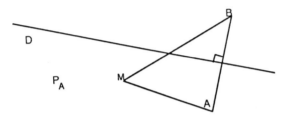

Expressed in standard FOL it corresponds to the following formula (put in an easily understandable form):

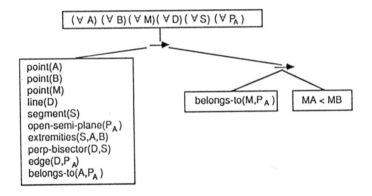

Clearly, this is not a good representation of the previous statement. It shows two embedded implications, whereas the statement was expressed with one conditional only. This would be of minor importance per se if it did not lead to more serious problems. The statement corresponding to the reciprocal of this theorem can be easily obtained by inverting the phrases following "if" and "then", respectively (this reciprocal happens to be true). Nevertheless, if we take the logical reciprocal of the previous formula, assuming that the reciprocal of:

$$(\forall x)\ (P(x) \rightarrow Q(x))$$

is:

$$(\forall x)\ (Q(x) \rightarrow P(x)),$$

we do not obtain a formula corresponding to the reciprocal statement. In fact, we obtain an odd formula, asserting that if {belongs(M,P)->MA<MB} is true, then A, B and M are points, etc.
          A

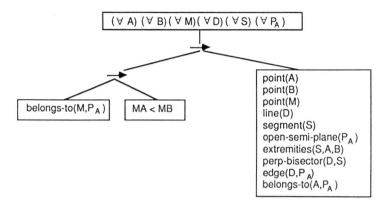

Moreover, this formula is false, whereas the reciprocal statement was true. The expected reciprocal is:

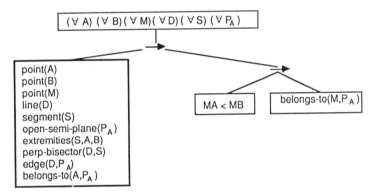

where the box outlined in bold remains unchanged. This does not correspond to the usual definition of the reciprocal operation. Theorems and problems are better expressed by restricted quantifications. Each quantified variable is then constrained to range across a given domain (Bourbaki 1970). The sentence "every dog barks", which corresponds to the FOL formula:

$$(\forall x)\,(\text{dog}(x) \rightarrow \text{barks}(x))$$

can be translated into:

$$(\forall x : \text{dog}(x))\,\text{barks}(x)$$

where there is no longer an implication sign and where "dog(x)" gives the range of objects for which we consider the property "barks". In general, we denote:

$$(\forall x : D)\,P \equiv (\forall x)\,(D \rightarrow P)$$
$$(\exists x : D)\,P \equiv (\exists x)\,(D \wedge P)$$

Restricted quantification presents more uniform notations than non-restricted quantification. We see, for example, that the

substitution of -> by ∧ when the existential quantifier is used
instead of the universal quantifier disappears in restricted
quantification. We have in restricted quantification tautologies
exactly analogous to those of non-restricted quantification but
generally expressed in a clearer way. Let us take, for example,
the negation. We have simply:

$$\sim(\forall x : D)\ P \leftrightarrow (\exists x : D)\ \sim P$$
$$\sim(\exists x : D)\ P \leftrightarrow (\forall x : D)\ \sim P$$

instead of:

$$\sim(\forall x)\ (D \rightarrow P) \leftrightarrow (\exists x)\ (D \wedge \sim P)$$
$$\sim(\exists x)\ (D \wedge P) \leftrightarrow (\forall x)\ (D \rightarrow \sim P)$$

As long as only truth values are considered restricted
quantification can be seen simply as a notation variant of
standard FOL. Nevertheless, one can also consider restricted
quantification as a theory in itself, and this enables in
particular a correct representation of reciprocals, which is not
possible in FOL. The reciprocal of:

$$(\forall x : D)\ (P \rightarrow Q)$$

is then naturally:

$$(\forall x : D)\ (Q \rightarrow P).$$

We also use multiple variable (restricted) quantifiers which
enable us to clarify:

$$(\forall x_1 : D_1)\ (\forall x_2 : D_2)\ ...\ (\forall x_n : D_n)\ P$$

which can be replaced by:

$$(\forall x_1, x_2, ... , x_n : D_1 \wedge D_2 \wedge ... \wedge D_n)\ P$$

Put in restricted quantification form our theorem will be (all
domains are placed into the rectangular box associated with the
quantifier):

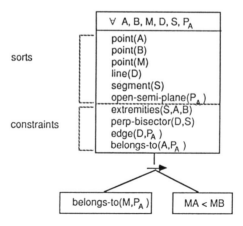

We now have a structure rather close to the natural language statement, which is expressed in two parts: a declaration part ("given ...") and a conditional part ("if ... then ..."). Moreover, the reciprocal of conditionals in natural language now corresponds exactly to the inversion of the implication branches in the new formula. In general, restricted quantification is well-suited to natural language. For example, quantified NP always give a domain "every dog", "a man", etc. Better still, there is no natural way to express non-restricted quantification in ordinary language. We must use variable names as in "whatever x, if x is a dog, x barks" (McCawley 1981).

Let us now examine the constitution of the domain. It includes two parts. First, each object must be attributed a category (point, line, etc), which we call a "sort". It is necessary to assign sorts in the domain since relations between objects are only defined for arguments of given sorts. We discuss this point in detail below. Second, objects may be related by additional constraints such as perp-bisector(D,S). These constraints can be put in the domain or not without changing the truth value as shown in:

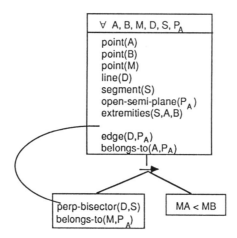

Nevertheless, the reciprocal of this new formula is not the same as previously (in addition, it is now false). Hence, the choice of the expert is constrained by the reciprocal he wants to give to the formulae. We summarize this situation in the following diagram, showing that formulae can be logically equivalent but not their reciprocals:

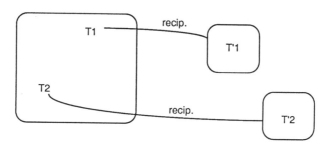

Many-Sorted Logic

In most expert systems, the universe is divided into categories
and inter-object relations are defined only between given
categories. For example, mid-point is only defined for ordered
pairs of a point and a segment. In standard FOL, this is handled
by giving the truth value "false" to mid-point(x,y) whenever x
and y are not a point and a line. A better solution is a three-
valued logic in which, in addition to the usual truth values,
"true" and "false", a third value exists which can be interpreted
as "undefined" (Lukasiewicz 1920, Kleene 1938, Van Frassen 1969,
Rescher 1969). Various systems can be found depending upon the
value given to a compound formula in which a component has the
value "undefined" but each of these systems presents serious
drawbacks (Seuren 1984). Herein, we use another approach in which
ill-sorted formulae do not belong to the logic language. Hence,
the problem of their truth value does not even arise, no more so
than if they were syntactically ill-formed.
A logic based on a sort system is generally called a many-sorted
logic. The interest of many-sorted logic in computer science in
general has not been overstressed, since it often makes automatic
deduction easier by cutting down the search space (Walther 1983,
Cohn 1985). In addition, it is also an efficient knowledge
representation tool (Hayes 1971). Various many-sorted logic have
been proposed (Wang 1952, Gilmore 1958, Hayes 1971, Henschen
1972, McSkimmin and Minker 1977, Reiter 1981, Cohn 1983) but all
have in common the following fundamental features. The universe
is divided into categories called sorts and individuals are
related to these sorts by an "is-a" relation. Sorts are not
always disjoint and a given object may belong to several sorts
(eg an object can be both an isosceles triangle and a right-
angled triangle). Sorts are related by a partial order relation
"a-sort-of" denoted $\leq$ (eg iso-tri$\leq$right-tri). In addition, for
each predicate p of a many-sorted logic there exists a
corresponding coherence relation (denoted p) that imposes precise
sorts on the arguments. For example, the predicate orthocentre
will be associated with the coherence relation
orthocentre(point,triangle). An automatic formula $p(t_1, t_2, ..., t_n)$ is generally said to be coherent or well-sorted if, given the
sorts $s_1, s_2, ..., s_n$ of terms $t_1, t_2, ..., t_n$, there exists $s'_1, s'_2, ..., s'_n$ such as $s_i \leq s'_i$ and $p(s'_1, s'_2, ..., s'_n)$.
For example, if T is an isosceles triangle and A is a point, the
formula orthocentre(A,T) is well-sorted since iso-tri$\leq$triangle
and orthocentre(point, triangle). This enables us to verify (to
some extent) discourse consistency.
We use a particular many-sorted logic which has some
similarities to that proposed by Cohn (1983) but also some
differences (unfortunately, we have no room here to go into
technical detail). In the logic proposed, the set T of sorts
constitutes a Boolean lattice for the relation $\leq$. We show that
this hypothesis is not at all a restrictive one, since the set of
subsets 2^U of the universe U of interpretation is really a
Boolean lattice for set inclusion and since there exists a rather
natural Boolean monomorphism φ which maps the sort lattice into

U
2 . This morphism can be understood in the following way: given a
sort s, φ(s) is the subset of individuals "which are" of sort s.
Therefore, the relation x "is-an" s can be translated by xεφ(s).
Hence, the Boolean sort lattice is a perfect mirror of the
organization of the universe and it is just as easy for an user
to give it as to give a common partial order.

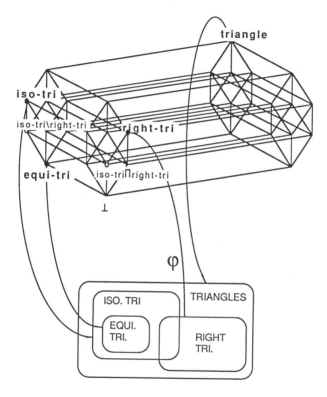

There is no need, of course, to describe in extenso the sort
lattice by giving a name to each sort. We have eponymous and
anonymous sorts. Eponymous sorts are those which are actually
named, and correspond to sort predicates (eg triangle, iso-tri,
right-tri, equi-tri). Anonymous sorts can be automatically
expressed (only when the inference engine uses them) in terms of
the eponymous sorts by means of the lattice operators |‾|, |_|
and \ (eg iso-tri |‾| right-tri will be associated with triangles
which are both isosceles and right-angled, iso-tri\equi-tri with
those which are isosceles but not equilateral, etc).
In addition, we use (ad hoc overloading) polymorphic predicates
and functions (Strachey 1967) which increase the expressiveness
of many-sorted logic. Thus belongs-to(x,y) is well-sorted in
several cases where (x,y) is an ordered pair (point,line),
point,circle), (line,direction), etc. We thus allow non-
functional coherence relations. This enables us to handle
"misuses" of terms which are frequent in statements and are a
particular form of polysemy. Thus, sides or heights of a triangle

are seen sometimes as lines, sometimes as segments; one can speak
of perpendicular lines as well as perpendicular segments, and
even about a line perpendicular to a segment. Purists may
consider that one should use distinct predicates since one has
actually different mathematical relations. Nevertheless, this is
an unnecessary imposition on the user and generally leads to
larger axiomatizations due to duplication of information. Using
polymorphic predicates and functions enable one to simplify
considerably the system and to maintain a one-to-one
correspondence between words and predicates. Appropriate
treatment precludes contradictions and this is a better
modellization both from the cognitive and linguistic viewpoint.

Sort Computation

The goal of natural language analysis is to obtain a closed
formula of this logic in which (as shown above) each variable is
associated with a domain and with a single sort. The sort of each
object appearing in a statement may or may not be expressed.
Phrases such as "circle C" or "A is a point" explicitly assign
sorts to objects since the words "circle" or "point" correspond
to sort predicates. In this case, the rest of the statement must
be checked in order to verify consistency with these sorts. Quite
often, however, the sort of objects is not expressed. For
example, "A and A´ belong to D and D´, respectively and are
distinct from O". Entire statements can be given in this fashion.
In this case, the analysis system (and the human reader) must be
able to reconstruct the sort of each object in a single way.
 Due to polymorphism this sort computation is not a purely
trivial one. From a sentence such as "S is the base of T" we
cannot directly infer unique sorts for objects S and T. Following
the analysis of each sentence (or part of a sentence)
corresponding to an atomic formula, we create a sort array in
which we keep track of the well-sorted domain of this formula,
that is to say the greatest sorts which can be given to each
variable with respect to coherence. Sentence combination is the
mirror of logical operations on formulae: conjunction,
disjunction, negation, implication. We assume that a compound
formula makes sense only if each of its constituents does and
this leads us to define a meet operation between sort arrays.
Basically, well-sorted domains corresponding to constituent
formulae are intersected to give the well-sorted domain of the
compound formula as shown below:

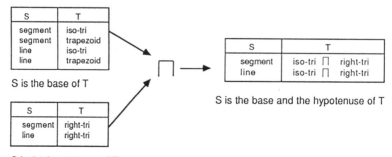

S	T
segment	iso-tri
segment	trapezoid
line	iso-tri
line	trapezoid

S is the base of T

S	T
segment	right-tri
line	right-tri

S is the hypotenuse of T

S	T	
segment	iso-tri ⊓	right-tri
line	iso-tri ⊓	right-tri

S is the base and the hypotenuse of T

If the resulting array is empty, no sort can be attributed to variables in order to render the formula coherent. The formula is therefore ill-sorted and discourse inconsistency is detected.
Various cases of inconsistency can be distinguished and this enables us to give an intelligent diagnosis instead of a standard laconic message such as "sentence rejected" which could hardly help the user to repair the mistake.
When the analysis of the statement is complete, if consistency is not detected, two cases can occur:

1. The final array enables one to attribute one and only one sort to each variable. If sorts are expressed in the statement for some objects, they must correspond exactly to this result. Domains can then be assigned to every variable in quantified formulae assuming that when anonymous sorts appear such as iso-tri | ̄|right-tri they can be translated by conjunctions of sort predicates [eg iso-tri(x)∧right-tri(x)].
2. The array contains several possibilities. If sorts are not expressed, the discourse is then ambiguous and this situation must be reported to the user.

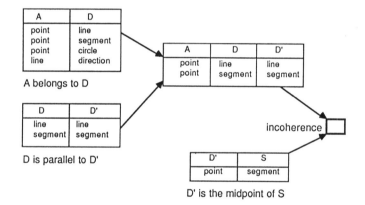

The sort computation also enables us to remove most syntactic ambiguities. Let us take for example the ambiguous sentence "[AB] is a chord of circle C of which D is the perpendicular bisector". Two syntactic parsings can be performed depending on whether the relative clause is attached to a chord or to a circle. The sort computation automatically gives the second analysis as inconsistent. Finally, this technique also facilitates the resolution of anaphora by cutting down the space of candidate objects.

Conclusions

A many-sorted logic based on a Boolean lattice of sorts and using polymorphic functions and predicates seems better suited to geometry statement understanding than standard first-order logic. Many problems such as the representation of conditionals and reciprocals, discourse consistency verification, polysemy, syntactic ambiguity and anaphora resolution are directly handled by the logic system. In addition, from a mathematical point of view this logic seems also better suited than standard first-order logic since it provides a good representation of the internal structure of theorems and problems and of inter-formulae relations such as reciprocal which are outside the field of truth theory. We believe that our approach is not dependent on the particular domain of geometry but on the contrary can be extended to various fields in which the universe of interpretation can be considered as a set theoretical universe.

References

Bourbaki, N. (1970) "Théorie des ensembles", CCLS, Paris.

Cohn, A.G. (1983) "Mechanizing a Particularly Expressive Many-Sorted Logic", PhD Thesis, University of Essex.

Cohn, A.G. (1985) On the solution of Schubert´s Steamroller in many-sorted logic, "IJCAI", 1169-1174.

Gilmore, P.C. (1958) An addition to Logic of many-sorted theories, "Compositio Mathematica" No. 13.

Hayes, P.J. (1971) A logic of actions, "Machine Intelligence" No. 6, Metamathematical Unit, University of Edinburgh, pp. 495-520.

Henschen, L.J. (1972) N-sorted logic for automatic theorem proving in higher order logic, "Proceedings ACM Conference", Boston, pp. 71-81.

Kleene (1938) On a notation for ordinary numbers, "Journal of Symbolic Logic" No. 3, pp. 150-155.

Lukasiewicz, J. (1920) O logice trojwartosciowej (On three-valued logic), "Ruch Filozoficzny V".

McCawley, J.D. (1981) "Everything That Linguists Have Always Wanted to Know", University of Chicago Press, Chicago.

McSkimmin, J.R.; Minker, J. (1977) The use of a semantic-network in a deductive question-answering system, "ICAJI" No. 5, Cambridge, pp. 50-58.

Reiter, R. (1981) On the integrity of first order data bases, "Advances in Data Base Theory, Vol. 1" (H. Gallaire, J. Minker and J.-M. Nicolas, eds), Plenum Press, New York, pp. 137-157.

Rescher, N. (1969) "Many-Valued Logic", McGraw-Hill, New York.

Seuren, P.A.M. (1984) Logic and truth values in language, "Varieties of Formal Semantics" (F. Landmand and F. Veltman, eds), Dordrecht, Foris.

Strachey, C. (1967) Fundamental concepts in programming languages, "Lecture Notes for International Summer School in Computer Programming", Copenhagen.

Van Frassen (1969) Presupposition, superevaluations and free logic, "The Logical Way of Doing Things" (K. Lambert, ed.), Yale University Press, New Haven.

Walther, C. (1983) A many-sorted calculus based on resolution and paramodulation, "IJCAI" No. 8, Karlsruhe, pp. 882-891.

Wang, H. (1952) Logic of many-sorted theories, "Journal of Symbolic Logic" No. 17.

Winograd, T. (1972) "Understanding Natural Language", Academic Press, New York.

Introduction of Grammar Rules

G. Francopoulo

LIMSI - CNRS, Orsay (France)

résumé:

Notre but est de construire un programme de "compréhension" de langage naturel, qui intègre les traitements syntaxiques et sémantiques. Le présent article traite de l'analyse syntaxique.

Parmi les différents algorithmes proposés, nous préférons le principe de l'analyse déterministe. Afin de reconnaître les diverses formes du français, les règles de traitement sont nécessairement complexes.

Nous présentons deux programmes basés sur les techniques d'induction symbolique (synthèse à partir d'exemples), qui permettent de créer et de modifier automatiquement les règles de grammaire. Ces règles sont ensuite incorporées dans notre analyseur syntaxique qui est pleinement fonctionnel. Afin de situer notre travail dans le courant actuel de la recherche, nous donnons une brève comparaison de notre système avec celui de Berwick.

mots clés: LANGAGE NATUREL
           APPRENTISSAGE ET ACQUISITION DE CONNAISSANCES

abstract:

Our goal is to construct a natural language "understanding" program, which integrates the syntactic/semantic processing. The present article is about syntactic parsing.

Of the various algorithms proposed, we prefer the deterministic analysis principle. In order to recognize the diverse grammatical templates of the French language, the processing rules are necessarily complex.

We present two programs based on symbolic induction techniques (knowledge synthesis from examples), that enable us to create and modify automatically the syntactic rules. These rules are then incorporated in our operational syntactic parser which is fully functional, no longer in the prototype stage. In order to situate our work in the current research stream, we give a brief comparison of our system with that of Berwick.

keywords: NATURAL LANGUAGE
           LEARNING AND KNOWLEDGE ACQUISITION

I INTRODUCTION.

Our goal is to construct a natural language "understanding" program, which integrates the syntactic/semantic processing. The present
article is about syntactic parsing.
   Of the various algorithms proposed [Winograd], we prefer the deterministic analysis principle (see [Rady] for the justification). In
order to recognize the diverse grammatical templates of the French
language, the processing rules are necessarily complex.
   We present two programs based on symbolic induction techniques
(knowledge synthesis from examples), that enable us to create and
modify the syntactic rules that:
             1) resolve lexical ambiguities.
             2) identify acceptable grammatical structures.
   These rules are then incorporated in our operational parser.

II PROBLEM STATEMENT.

II-A) REMINDERS ABOUT DETERMINISTIC GRAMMATICAL PARSING.

   Before getting into the details of our realization, we briefly
present the context in which the induced knowledge will be used. We
refer the interested reader to the reports of [Rady],[Sabah],
[Marcus],[Sampson], and the criticisms of [Briscoe]. It should be
noted that our work is an extension of that of Rady.
   The grammatical parsing is preceded by morphological processing
[Pitrat]. Each word produces a list (or several in cases of
ambiguity) of features composed of:
   * an entry name (a lexeme) in the dictionary.
     (the dictionary contains 10,300 entries).
   * categorization and sub-categorization features
     (e.g. PRONOUN PERSONAL)
   * depending on the former: the number, gender, person ...
     (e.g. PRETERIT 3_PERSON SINGULAR).
   * for a verb, some technical information about transformations.
     For instance, control of the embedded infinitive complement that
     will be used during the infinitive/completive transformation:
             I order you to eat.   -> I order you that [YOU] eat.
             I promise you to eat. -> I promise you that [I] eat.
   The purpose of the grammatical parsing is then to translate a
chain of words into a syntactic tree:
   * the root will be marked PRINCIPAL PROPOSITION.
   * the sub-trees will be marked NOMINAL-GROUP or VERBAL-GROUP ...
   * the words will be attached as leaves of the trees.
Our parser is composed of three modules:
   a) a four-cell buffer (S0, S1, S2, S3), each cell being either a
      word, or a tree under construction.
   b) a set of production rules.
      A rule is a pair: conjunction-of-conditions/sequence-of-actions.
      The conditions test the four-cell features: we call that the
      "Look ahead" process.
      Most of the time :
             . the tree we are in the way to build is in S0
             . the three other cells contain words
             . the actions manipulate just the first two cells (S0, S1).
      In contrast with the Marcus and Rady's models, our rules are
      unordered.
   c) an deterministic inference engine, that initialises the buffer
      with the beginning of the sentence and applies the rules until
      evaluation of the action "FINISH" in a right part of a rule. At
      every inference cycle, only one rule must applicable.

II-B) TWO CLASSES OF RULES.

An inference cycle proceeds in three phases:
1 application of the rules pruning the lexical ambiguities.
2 application of the grammatical rules.
3 buffer book-keeping, moving the unanalyzed words out of their stack into the buffer.

The first set of rules will try to prune the ambiguities at the word level, due to its knowledge of what is a legitimate sequence of words and what is an impossible sequence.
ex: the word "BLOCKS" is translated by the morphological analyser into: BLOCK = NAME PLURAL
                BLOCK = VERB PRESENT 3-PERSON SINGULAR
For instance, to parse the sentence: "THE BLOCKS IN THE BASKET ARE GREEN", we must remove the possibility containing the verb with a rule like:
```
IF      S1 HAS_THE_FEATURE NAME
    AND S1 HAS_THE_FEATURE VERB
    AND S2 HAS_THE_FEATURE PREPOSITION
    AND S2 HAS_THE_FEATURE ADVERB
    AND S2 HAS_THE_FEATURE ADJECTIVE
    AND S3 HAS_THE_FEATURE ARTICLE
    THEN  REMOVE_THE_SOLUTION_IN  S1  WHICH_HAS_THE_FEATURE  VERB
```
Thus, the first set of rules filters the structures, in order to ease the work of the second rules set.

The second set is composed of:
a) base rules that create syntactic groups (e.g. nominal-group).
b) transformation rules, whose function is to present a standard tree structure for the later semantic interpretation (e.g. passive/active transformation).
c) rules to remove some ambiguities that have not been processed by the first set. This is because, in certain circumstances, partial analyses is crucial in order to decide how to resolve ambiguities in the rest of the sentence.
As a matter of fact, this second set of rules is intrinsically more complex, there are two reasons for this additional complexity:
* the conditions test the word features but also the groups being constructed.
* the actions apply to rich structures (trees), they are thus relatively diverse and powerful.
We emphasize the fact that the two sets of rules are applied in the same cycle; the complete sentence parsing does not occur in two sequential phases. The absence of ambiguities is a necessary condition in order to build the tree, this is why we must begin by pruning the ambiguities.

II-C) LINGUISTIC VIEWPOINT.

In the context of deterministic parsing, there is no definitive description of a general parsing scheme for "current" French. Such a scheme would describe each rule in such a way that the conditions would be discriminating, because the parser must make the right choice without any backtracking or pseudo-parallellism.
Until recently, our parsers used hand-written rules. These rules were very interdependent; the conditions became so complex that it was impossible to improve the behavior of the parser without rewriting almost all the rules. The problem was in determining the conditions : on a precise sentence, we knew how to parse it, but we were not able to fix the compromise between a general condition and

a discriminating one. Thus, as G.Richie emphasized, [Richie], rule
set writing is the most delicate problem in deterministic parser
engineering.

III OUR SOLUTION.

III-A) PRINCIPLE

   Our objective is to define a general parsing scheme, taking two
points into account while respecting one property:
   point 1   . it is possible to present a set of sentences that are
                syntactically accepted by a french speaker.
   point 2   . for every sentence, it is possible to build a syntactic
                tree, except when the sentence is syntactically
                ambiguous (but that is rather rare).
   property   . in order to succeed in the long run, the building of
                the rule set must be incremental: adding a new rule
                must not modify the behavior of the existing model
                [Descles].
   Induction [Quinlan],[Dietterich],[Michalski], seems to be the best
method available to generalize a process which starts from point 1,
respects the property and ends in point 2.

   We start from the inductive hypothesis:
   "Given a wide range of examples with as few correlations as
possible; then the rules induced should be able to parse a significant sub-set of French".

   The system's behavior will be as follows:
   The input is a set of syntactically correct sentences. With each
sentence, we associate clues about the upcoming parsing; then considering the whole set of examples, the inductive program will generate
the processing rules.
   In other words, one needs to specify the understanding operators:
" HOW TO PARSE ", and the induction component will then build the
knowledge that states " WHEN TO PARSE AND HOW TO PARSE ".

III-B) INDUCTION OF RULES FOR PRUNING THE LEXICAL AMBIGUITIES.

   The induction proceeds in four phases:
            . manual preparation.
            . pruning the useless features and situations.
            . rule creation.
            . deletion of the superfluous rules.

1 MANUAL PREPARATION.

   We enter sentences in file F1, then we run the morphological
analyser, which produces a set of solutions for each word in the file
F2. For each solution in file F2, we specify (from the keyboard) the
correct solution.
   Thus, in the sentence: THE BLOCKS IN THE BASKET HAVE GREEN
POLKA-DOTS, we point out with an arrow, the correct solution:

THE	the	article	<---
BLOCKS	to block	verb	
	block	noun plural	<---
IN	in	preposition	<---
	in	adverb	
	in	adjective	
THE	the	article	<---

```
BASKET        basket      noun                <---
HAVE          to have     verb                <---
GREEN         green       adjective           <---
              green       noun
POLKA-DOTS    polka-dot   noun                <---
  .             .         final punctuation <---
```
In the same fashion, for THIS BOOK IS HER PROPERTY.
```
THIS          this        demonstrative adjective <--
BOOK          book        noun                <--
              to book     verb
IS            to be       verb                     <--
HER           her         possessive adjective <--
PROPERTY      property    noun                     <--
  .             .         final punctuation        <--
```
Note: in these examples, in order to simplify the understanding of the article, only the categorization and sub-categorization features are presented.

2 PRUNING THE USELESS FEATURES AND SITUATIONS.

The gender, number, person features are useless because:
. they don't indicate any syntactic grouping.
. the ambiguous gender, number, person features will be pruned after creation of the first syntactic groups because of the agreement constraints.
. if they are taken into account, they cause un explosion in the number of rules.

The necessary clues for induction are:
. syntactic categorization features (ex: pronoun).
. syntactic sub-categorization features (ex: personal).
. temporal features (ex: past-participle).

The entry names are ignored: thus, there is no specific rule for a given word.

The algorithm begins by forming the triplets:
SITUATION / GOOD SOLUTION / BAD SOLUTIONS, neglecting the similar triplets. The situation corresponds to the words "look ahead" of the parser.

Given the sentence THE BLOCKS IN THE BASKET HAVE GREEN POLKA-DOTS, seven situations are possible:
```
              S1a   from   THE BLOCKS IN
              S1b          BLOCKS IN THE
              S1c          IN THE BASKET
              S1d          THE BASKET HAVE
              S1e          BASKET HAVE GREEN
              S1f          HAVE GREEN POLKA-DOTS
              S1g          GREEN POLKA-DOTS .
```
For the sentence THIS BOOK IS HER PROPERTY, four are possible:
```
              S2a   from   THIS BOOK IS
              S2b          BOOK IS HER
              S2c          IS HER PROPERTY
              S2d          HER PROPERTY .
```

3 RULE CREATION.

3_1 SIMPLE ALGORITHM.

The algorithm will compare the different triplets:
SITUATION / GOOD SOLUTION / BAD SOLUTIONS that we note (S/GS/BS).
If BS is empty, this means that the triplet doesn't give us any new information. Each triplet (S/GS/BS) selected with a non-empty BS will

be compared with the others in order to detect the counter-examples.
We define a counter-example of (S/GS/BS) as the triplet (S'/GS'/BS')
with: . S being included in or equal to S'
                          . the intersection of BS and GS' being non-empty
   In other terms, a counter-example is a triplet such that the rule
we try to induce will improperly remove a good solution of the
morphological analysis. If we detect a counter-example, we don't
propose any rule; on the contrary, the suggested rule will be:
IF S THEN REMOVE BS.

3_2 FIRST EXAMPLE.

   In the processing of THE BLOCKS IN THE BASKET HAVE GREEN POLKA-DOTS
and THIS BLOCK IS HER PROPERTY, the triplets T1a, T1d, T1e, T1f, T2a,
T2c, T2d are neglected because their "BS" is empty.

The four selected triplets are:
   T1b = situation
                          (verb)(noun)
                          (preposition)(adverb)(adjective)
                          (article)
         good solution
                          (noun)
         bad solutions
                          (verb)
   T1c = situation
                          (preposition)(adverb)(adjective)
                          (article)
                          (noun)
         good solution
                          (preposition)
         bad solutions
                          (adverb)(adjective)
   T1g = situation
                          (adjective)(noun)
                          (noun)
                          (final punctuation)
         good solution
                          (adjective)
         bad solutions
                          (noun)
   T2b = situation
                          (noun)(verb)
                          (verb)
                          (possessive adjective)
         good solution
                          (noun)
         bad solutions
                          (verb)

   These four triplets are compared with the eleven others, there
is no counter-examples. Every triplet produces a rule:
   g00100 if S1 has_the_features VERB
              S1 has_the_features NOUN
              S2 has_the_features PREPOSITION
              S2 has_the_features ADVERB
              S2 has_the_features ADJECTIVE
              S3 has_the_features ARTICLE
          --> remove VERB   from S1
   g00101 if S1 has_the_features PREPOSITION
              S1 has_the_features ADVERB
              S1 has_the_features ADJECTIVE
              S2 has_the_features ARTICLE

```
               S3 has_the_features NOUN
         --> remove ADVERB     from S1
             remove ADJECTIVE from S
   g00102  if S1 has_the_features ADJECTIVE
             S1 has_the_features NOUN
             S2 has_the_features NOUN
             S3 has_the_features FINAL PUNCTUATION
         --> remove NOUN      from S1
   g00103  if S1 has_the_features NOUN
             S1 has_the_features VERB
             S2 has_the_features VERB
             S3 has_the_features POSSESSIVE ADJECTIVE
         --> remove VERB      from S1
```

3_3 SECOND EXAMPLE.

Let us add a third sentence: HE WALKS IN THE CITY, that will
produce four possible triplets:

```
    T3a    taken from  HE WALKS IN
    T3b                WALKS IN THE
    T3c                IN THE CITY
    T3d                THE CITY .
```

T3c is discarded because it is identical to T1c.
The set of example is thus composed of:

```
    T1a, T1b, T1c, T1d, T1e, T1e, T1f, T1g from the first sentence
    T2a, T2b, T2c, T2d                          second sentence
    T2a, T2b, T2d                               third sentence.
```

The triplets, selected such that BS is non-empty, are:
T1b, T1c, T1g, T2b, T3b.
T1b will be compared to the others, T3b appears as a counter-
example, no rule is created. T1c, T1g, T2b will induce three rules.
T3b will meet T1b as counter-example. Thus, from five triplets, the
algorithm will produce three rules.

3_4 IMPROVEMENT OF THE ALGOTRITHM.

3_4_1 PARTIAL INDUCTION.

In the simple algorithm, if the proposed triplet matches a counter-
example, no rule is created: . either we induce a rule
                              . or we consider that it is a failure.
This method is too cautious, the new algorithm is based on the fact
that a failure is not necessarily fatal. Instead, a failure will
weaken the actions: the rule resulting will be less powerful.
More precisely:
  . we begin the comparaison with the features list BS.
  . if we match a counter-example (S'/GS'/BS'),
    we do: BS <- BS - GS'
    if BS become empty, it is a fatal failure.
  . if there is no fatal failure during the comparison, the rule
    will be: IF S THEN REMOVE BS (BS being eventually weakened).

3_4_2 CREATION OF GENERAL RULES.

If no counter-example is encountered, the algorithm proposes a
rule with conditions testing two buffer cells instead of three. The
number of conditions is determined while searching for counter-
examples. This improvement has two advantages:
  a) the rules need less computing resources in their utilisation.
  b) it produces simpler rules that may be duplicated. The total
     number of rules is smaller, because duplicate rules will be
     deleted later.

3_4_3 AMBIGUITIES IN THE END OF THE SENTENCE.

A rule has a "look ahead" of three cells and removes one or several
ambiguities of S1. We do special processing in order to consider the
penultimate word of the sentence: the generated rule will test
S1,S2,S3 and remove the ambiguities on S2.

3_5 DELETION OF SUPERFLUOUS RULES.

   When the algorithm proposes a rule, it doesn't compare it with the
ones already built. Though we never construct duplicate triplets
(S/GS/BS), because of partial induction some rules are identical.
Another point is that there are general rules and specific rules
which have the same actions.
   Let's consider two rules:
     R1   if conjunction of conditions CC1
          then process the list of actions LA1
     R2   if conjunction of conditions CC2
          then process the list of actions LA2   such that LA1 = LA2
   If CC1 is included or equal to CC2, each time that R2 will be
applicable, R1 will be too; we can then remove the more specific rule
(R2). This simplification is made possible because the rules are
unordered. We simplify after a complete induction phase, rather than
progressively after each rule, in order to use the same program for
both sets of rules.

III-C) INDUCTION OF GRAMMAR RULES.

1 PRESENTATION.

   The principle is the same as for the first (lexical ambiguities)
set of rules, the difference being in the fact that the induced
information is more complex.
   For each sentence, we specify the actions needed to parse the
sentence. First we have to verify that processing the actions will
give us the desired tree; we use a small program which executes the
actions, progressively tracing the resulting structures.
   The actions being assumed correct, we run the inductive program
in order to generate the grammatical rules.

2 SOME LERTOL ACTIONS.

   The action's syntax, defined by [Rady], is called LERTOL (it looks
like PIDGIN in the Marcus's work).
   MARK <lf> <s>   add the new features <lf> to the existing
                      features of the structure <s>.
   INSERT <lf> <s>   create a syntactic group with the features <lf>
                      before the structure <s>.
                      The former element is pushed temporarily into a
                      stack.
   DETACH   pick up the structure that has been most recently
                      pushed.
   ATTACH <si> <sj>   join the structure <si> to the tree <sj>.
                      The place occupied by <si> in the buffer becomes
                      free and will be recovered at the end of the cycle.
   FINISH   signal the end of parsing.

3 RULE GROUPING.

The induction wil study the pairs: Situations/Actions. It is necessary to begin by determining the action part of the rules. The extreme choices consist of proposing: * a rule for every sentence
* a rule for every action.
The first proposition would mean that one rule would be sufficient to parse the whole sentence. However taking into account the three words in the beginning of the parse is not sufficient to determine the whole of the parse. Thus this proposition is not usable because the parsing scheme imposes that not more than one rule should be applicable at once.
The second proposition is possible; it has the drawback of provoking the generation of a great deal of rules.
It is possible to classify the actions according whether:
* they create or move structures (e.g. INSERT)
* they modify the contents of a structure (e.g. MARK).
In order to group the actions, we adopt the following heuristic compromise: THE ACTIONS IN THE RIGHT PART OF A RULE WILL PROVOKE
ONLY ONE CREATION OR MOVE OF A STRUCTURE.

4 ALGORITHM.

The parsings will be simulated in order to determine the pairs: situations/actions that will produce the rules.
We will do, until evaluation of the action FINISH:
* determine and memorize the situation.
* determine and memorize the actions.
* apply the lexical pruning rules.
* evaluate the actions
Then, the pairs situations/actions are compared with each other. The processing follows two seemingly contradictory principles:
1) the conditions must as simple as possible.
2) the conditions must be discriminating. The parser being deterministic, the rule must not be in conflict with another.
The first principle tends to make the rule more general, thus the rule must be general and specific at once.

A situation/action pair S/A, wil be said to be in conflict with S'/A' if: * S is included in or equal to S'
* A is different from A'

In order to satisfy the first principle, the comparison of successive situations will determine the pattern of the rule. We have decided on six levels of rules according to this increasing complexity:
level 1   test the root of S0.
level 2   test the root of S0 and S1.
level 3   test the root of S0, S1 and S2.
level 4   test the root of S0, S1, S2 and S3.
level 5   test the root of S0, S1, S2 S3
and the existence/absence of subtrees.
level 6   test the root of S0, S1, S2 S3
and the features of the subtrees.
The first four levels correspond with a "variable lookahead".

THE CHOICE OF THE COMPLEXITY LEVEL WILL BE DETERMINED AT THE END OF THE COMPARISON, SO THAT THE RULE SHOULD HAVE THE MINIMAL COMPLEXITY BEFORE CONFLICT.
Once the complexity level is fixed, the algorithm generates the rule. It is possible however, that the maximal complexity level were

not enough; the conflict is then brought to the user attention. The last process (as explained in chapter II-3-5) consists in deleting the superfluous rules.

It should be noted that the inductive algorithm is rather simple, for instance compared with the rule integration of [Steels]. This is because: being rich and complex, the handled structures produce enough clues to generate the conditions. In particular, it is not necessary (some testings have been made) to create negative conditions.

III-D) IMPLEMENTATION.

The programs are written in LE_LISP [Chailloux], then automatically translated in a portable sub-set of C_language [Francopoulo] and compiled. The LISP to C translater (which is called CROSSLISP) is used in order to be sure that the programs will run on most computers available on the market.

The rules in LERTOL are transformed into a discrimination tree so as to factor out the conditions that are common to several rules. The tree, which is a lisp program, is then compiled.

We use the examples quoted (between inverted commas) in a grammar book, in order to have a corpus of sentences as widely varied as possible. Let us note that the sentences entered are not syntactically ambiguous. Currently (April 86), our sentence set for the induction of the pruning rules is composed of the 580 sentences quoted in [Dubois]. For the second class of rules, we use the first hundred of these sentences. A sentence has an average of seven words.

The induction of the first class of rules takes four hours on an IBM-AT, the induction of the second set takes one hour.

For the first set of rules, when we increase the number of examples, we observe that the ratio "nb of rules / nb of examples" diminishes:

Thus, the   80 first examples produce   69 rules   (0.86)
           153   135 rules   (0.88)
           376   257 rules   (0.68)
           580   321 rules   (0.55)

We can't extrapolate these results in order to see the beginning of a stabilization because:

    a) various interdependent parameters come into play:
        .the first sentences in the grammar text are simpler than
         the following ones.
        .there are some similarities in sentences of a given
         chapter of the grammar book.
        .all the words combinations are not presented (e.g. there
         are a few adjectives in the chapter about passive trans-
         formations)
    b) there are not enough examples.

Induction of the second set of rules, from 100 examples produces 247 grammar rules.

When we apply the first set of rules to the sentences that are in the examples set, between 95% and 100% of the ambiguities are pruned. If we present arbitrary sentences, the rate varies between 80% and 85%; the remaining ambiguities being processed by the grammar rules.

In spite of the high number of rules, the parsing with the induced rules doesn't consume a lot of computer resources.

    * the deterministic parsing builds just one tree.
    * the condition complexity is optimal.

The whole syntactic parsing of a sentence takes (depending on its complexity) between half a second and a second.

IV COMPARISON WITH ANOTHER SYSTEM.

The closest system is that of Berwick [Berwick]. Indeed, R.Berwick who is developing Marcus's ideas at M.I.T, shares our two basic hypotheses which are determinism and induction.

Here is a brief overview of Berwick's system:
   a) Induction must provide rules for a deterministic parser.
   b) At the initial state, the system is composed of:
      . a lexicon.
      . a case grammar.
      . a deterministic parser modified in order to incorporate X-bar theory principles.
      . a learning algorithm that proposes an action in order to reduce the distance between the example pattern and the target structure [Head Complement Modifier] postulated by the X-bar theory.
   c) Induction processes according to the principle: "in a given situation, generate at most one rule". If a second rule becomes necessary, then the example parsing is considered as being beyond the parsers ability and the parsing is abandoned. Thus, the system progressively learns rules that are more and more complex, from examples that are more and more difficult.

It is possible to compare Berwick's system with ours, according to two criterions:
   1) The INDUCTION METHOD. Berwick's system proceeds more automatically than ours, because for each example, one doesn't need to provide the understanding operators (i.e. the rules actions). In return, more knowledge is incorporated definitely inside the parser: Berwick's parser is in bondage to the X-bar theory.
   2) The RESULT. Berwick's system generates 70% of the Marcus rules. Ours generates 100% of the rules.
To conclude, R.Berwick, motivated by a linguistic goal proposed an elegant and complex method; but as a development tool, it gives worse results than ours.

V CONCLUSION.

In our lab, the previous parsers used hand-written rules. The conditions became so complex that it was impossible to improve the behavior of the parser without rewriting almost all the rules.

Our solution makes easily feasable the progressive elaboration of a vast set of rules. Imagine that the parser is used as a man/machine interface: if an unknown sentence form is presented and the parser can't treat it, one needs only to add it to the set of examples and to rerun the induction to integrate the parsing mechanisms for the new sentence (and all similar sentences).
Induction has a second advantage. It is almost impossible for a linguist, to optimally fix the complexity of the rules conditions. The induction program takes into account the "variable lookahead" and the tests depth in the trees; it then generates optimal complexity rules that don't require a lot of computing resources.

However, there are still some unresolved points. In the induction of grammar rules, in certain situations, the maximal complexity in the conditions is not sufficient to determine the discriminating conditions. These conflicts are due to the lack of semantic

information (such as case grammar) attached to the verb.
    Our long term target being syntactic/semantic integration, we are
presently working on a semantic learning system which will integrate
(among other things) a case grammar.
    Furthermore, it would be interesting to make use of vast
inventories of word usage protocols such as that of Gross [Gross].

bibliography:

BERWICK R.   The acquisition of syntactic knowledge.
                 MIT Press 85. Cambridge, Massachusetts.
BRISCOE E.   Determinism and its implementation in Parsifal.
                 in JONES & WILKS: Automatic language parsing.
                 Ellis Horwood 83. Chichester, United-Kingdom.
CHAILLOUX J.   Le_lisp: manuel de référence.
                 INRIA 84. domaine de Voluceau, 78 Rocquencourt,
                 France.
DESCLES J.P.   Enoncés et énonçables.
                 lingua e stile. Anno XIII 05/78.
                 Società Editrice di Mulino 78. Bologna, Italy.
DIETTERICH T.   & MICHALSKI R. A comparative review of selected
                 methods for learning from examples.
                 in MICHALSKI, CARBONELL & MITCHELL: Machine learning.
                 Tioga Press 83. Palo Alto, California.
DUBOIS J   & DUBOIS-CHARLIER F.
                 Eléments de linguistique française: syntaxe.
                 Larousse 70. Paris, France.
FRANCOPOULO G.   Crosslisp: traduire du lisp en C (manuel de référence).
                 ELSA-software 85. 4,place des planches ORSAY, France.
GROSS M.   Méthodes en syntaxe.
                 Hermann 75. Paris, France.
MICHALSKI R.   A Theory and methology of inductive learning.
                 in MICHALSKI, CARBONELL & MITCHELL: Machine learning.
                 Tioga Press 83. Palo Alto, California.
MARCUS M.   A theory of syntactic recognition for natural
                 language.
                 MIT Press 80. Cambridge, Massachusetts.
PITRAT J.   Réalisation d'un analyseur-générateur lexicographique
                 général. Rapport de recherche C.F.Picard 101-130 1979.
                 Univ. Paris VI. 5,place Jussieu Paris, France.
QUINLAN J.   Semi-autonomous acquisition of pattern-based
                 knowledge.
                 in HAYES J.,MICHIE D.& PAO Y. Machine intelligence 10.
                 Ellis Horwood 82. Chichester, United-Kingdom.
RADY M.   L'ambiguïté du langage naturel est-elle la source du
                 non-déterminisme des procédures de traitement ?
                 Thèse de doctorat d'état PARIS VI 1983.
                 Univ. PARIS VI 5,place Jussieu Paris,France.
RICHIE G.   The implementation of a PIDGIN interpreter.
                 in JONES & WILKS: Automatic language parsing.
                 Ellis Horwood 83. Chichester, United-Kingdom.
SABAH G.   & RADY M.
                 Deterministic syntactic-semantic parser.
                 proc.IJCAI 83. Karlsruhe, Germany.
SAMPSON G.   Deterministic parsing.
                 in KING: Parsing natural language.
                 Academic Press 83. London, United-Kingdom.
STEELS L.   & VAN DE VELDE W.
                 Learning in second generation expert systems.
                 proc. European Working Session on Learning 86.
                 LRI Orsay, France.
WINOGRAD T.   Language as a cognitive process.
                 Addison Wesley 83.Reading, Massachusetts.

Applications to Technical Domains: Diagnosis

A Methodology for Automating Expert Diagnosis in Expert Systems

A. Dionisi Vici, F. Malbocchia and L. Sisto

RESUME

La recherche courante sur la technologie des Systemes Experts diagnostiques aspire à fournir une methodologie qui incorpore les "Expert Strategies", comme la connaissance du control appliqué à des taches diagnostiques. Le but est de fournir un reseau pour l'Explication et l'Acquisition de la connaissance, deux importants aspects de la recherche et de l'industrialisation des Systemes Experts. Pour obtenir un reseau suffisamment general, il faut definir un processus diagnostique et un processus de decision.

Dans une recherche qui aspire à l'industrialisation du "mixed mode approach" au diagnostic, nous proposons une methodologie qui puisse reunir dans les Systems Experts la connaissance diagnostique et la connaissance de decision necessaires dans la detection des pannes. Cette methodologie comprend quatre phases: enonciation, generalisation, modelage, incorporation.

La description de cette methodologie se rapporte à un prototype experimental developpé dans notre recherche. Les resultats de cette recherche sont la definition et l'implementation des instruments qui supportent le transfer de la connaissance entre l'Expert humain et l'Expert automatique.

Mots clés: Systemes Experts, Acquisition de la connaissance, diagnostic

ABSTRACT

Current research in the technology of diagnostic Expert Systems aims to provide a methodology to embody expert strategies as control knowledge applied to diagnostic tasks. The goal is to provide a framework for explanation and knowledge acquisition, two major aspects of research and industrialization of Expert Systems. In order to achieve a sufficiently general framework, it is necessary to define a diagnostic process and a decision process.

In a research aiming at industrializing the mixed mode approach to diagnosis, we propose a methodology for embodying in expert systems the diagnostic and decision knowledge needed in fault finding. This building methodology consists of four steps: enunciation, generalization, modelling and embodying.

The methodology is described referring to an experimental prototype developed in our research. Achievements of this research are the definition and implementation of tools supporting the knowledge transfer between human and automated experts.

Keywords: Expert Systems, Knowledge acquisition, diagnosis

1. Introduction

Diagnosis and maintenance are a widely investigated application domain for Expert Systems (ESs). Main reasons for this choice are that it is a relevant industrial problem and at the same time it is a complex problem to stress the capabilities of expert systems [Dav 83].

Currently there are three approaches to expert systems for diagnosis: symptom based, model based and mixed.

The symptom based approach, which enumerates explicit associations among fault symptoms and fault causes (shallow knowledge) has been deeply investigated. Tools supporting the building of "shallow" diagnostic ESs tools range from empty shells to be filled in with specific knowledge, to intelligent knowledge acquisition systems [Dav 82]. In order to define a framework for the decision process and a taxonomy for diagnostic knowledge, abstract control knowledge has been proposed as a mean for explaining explicit strategies [Cla 83]. This framework has been discussed by the author in the context of a symptom based diagnostic system, but it can be applied to model based diagnostic systems achieving the mixed approach.

This approach has some severe shortcomings, since ESs built according to it are product dependent. That means that each new application requires a considerable effort for its development, and thus their industrialization possibility is limited. Furthermore, symptom based ESs typically represent the behaviour of field experts: i.e. experts that derive their expertise from practice. Sometimes they cannot express why their expertise is correct.

On the other hand, model based ESs reason starting from first diagnostic principles. Using the description of structure and function of the equipment under diagnosis, they generate hypotheses of structural faults and verify their consistency against actual misbehavior [Gen 82].

In the model based approach ESs carry out troubleshooting alternating test steps with diagnostic steps. Tests have to be generated in order to compare the behaviour of the faulty circuit with the correct (fault free) model. When differences are recognized, a diagnostic step can be made in order to infer all consequences from the discrepancy detected. These steps are repeated until fault has been found or when the diagnosis cannot go further (e.g. when we have a fault equivalence in the circuit).

Advantage of this kind of ESs is that they promise to be product independent. Their customization to a particular product is obtained by providing a descriptive model of the product (i.e. the equipment under test).

Besides, this descriptive model could also be obtained from a CAD database description of the product, thus making the model based approach promising if integrated to design.

In the case of model based Expert Systems, problems arise by the "generality" of the approach, which implies long run time computations.

This problem is faced with mixed mode Expert Systems which, similar to a model based Expert System, integrate heuristic strategies, dependent on complex problem solving situations, in order to reduce the cost of run time computations [Cha 83].

In this paper we describe a methodology for organizing the interaction between an expert in diagnosis with a knowledge engineer, following the mixed mode approach [Gio 85], [Dio 85]. The methodology consists in the following four steps:

1. start from a session where the expert describes in a examples knowledge relevant to a specific application;

This work was supported in part by the European Community, within the ESPRIT project 96: Expert System Builder.

2. devise the first principles involved, by generalizing concepts used in diagnosis and decision making;

3. build a model of the equipment able to represent the knowledge required in diagnosis;

4. embody the reasoning process in the ES.

This methodology comes from our knowledge engineering practice, applied in the implementation of different diagnostic tasks. The second step is carried on by merging the analysis of [Cla 83] and [Dav 83]. The third and fourth step are reflected by our ES architecture, described in the next section.

In section 2 the underlying concepts justifying the methodology adopted are presented. The same section contains also a schematical explanation of the four steps. Sections 3 to 6 contain the discussion step by step of a sample application of this methodology.

2. Justification of the methodology

The methodology presented in this paper is the result of a research on diagnostic ESs relying on a model of the equipment under test. This research is split in three phases. The first one devoted to devise a general architecture for diagnostic ESs [Gio 85]. The second phase to define a methodology for allowing the information transfer from the human expert to the ES. The third will be the implementation of tools in order to support this knowledge transfer.

The methology described in the following sections entails the organizaton of the building process of a model based ES.

At the beginning of our interview with the expert, we have that diagnostic knowledge is contained in his mind. Our goal is to capture the knowledge of the expert and organize it in an ES architecture. In the following we will briefly describe the kind of data and knowledge structure in which the human expert knowledge has to be translated. The aim is to identify a mapping between the conceptual and operational use of diagnostic knowledge.

The proposed architecture is composed of four levels, each containing omogeneous entities. Components of the architecture are:

The model: the fault free equipment is represented from two different points of view, structural and behavioural. Structural point of view is related to the circuit topology. Behavioral point of view represents the functionality of the components. Main characteristics of this level are: the model is single and then shared among all the other entities in the system; it is a declarative model, in which all information relevant during diagnostic process can be easily accessed. Model is the lowest level (fourth) and acts as a data base for the ES.

Model access tools: this level contains some well known CAD tools (e.g. simulator), together with other new ones that have been made possible due to the chance of having a declarative model. This (third) level acts conceptually like a DBMS for the ES.

Diagnostic tasks: at this level are present the diagnostic tasks given by the expert. Such diagnostic tasks make use of the model access tools in order to manipulate and inspect the model. This (second) level contains the base level problem solvers for the ES.

Control heuristics: at this level varius control information is represented, like stop conditions (e.g. fault equivalences), fault assumptions made by the diagnostic tasks (e.g. nonintermittency, single fault) and a description of the diagnostic stages in which each task can be succesfully applied. This (first) level acts as the system meta-level, specifying situations where strategies are applicable.

The four levels described before are meant to group together the omogeneous types of knowledge that can be contained in a diagnostic ES. This separation among levels makes it easier to build, understand and modify the ES. Besides, the four levels make more explicit the fact that each entity can use only entities contained in the next lower level in order to carry out its job. Thus control flows top-down.

As a final remark it is interesting to note that the same architecture without the third and fourth levels can be used for Symptom based ESs. In fact, it would actually allow to map the decision making model proposed by [Cla 83] for abstract control knowledge.

Having given an overview of the architecture in which diagnostic knowledge has to be mapped, the problem is now to give a methodology by which the knowledge of the human expert could flow into the ES.

The four steps of our methodology can be explained in this way:

Step 1: the diagnostic expert performs a sample diagnosis. This step is common to the first step given for the development process of Symptom based expert systems [Bar 81]. In our case we found that its relevance and justificatons remain unchanged. Here the expert exploits product dependent strategies for tackling diagnosis of a particular electronic device.

Step 2: the second step is the identification of the principles followed by the expert, the concepts adopted in diagnosis and the strategies applied in decison making. The devised principles are mapped onto the diagnostic tasks level of the ES. These tasks actually define a general diagnostic process. Heuristics applied in decision making are meant to reduce the complexity of diagnostic tasks and are mapped onto strategies (Control heuristics level of the ES). At this step fault assumptions have to be explicitly identifyied since they define the actual link between general diagnostic tasks and situations where strategies are applicable.

Step 3: After having devised the diagnostic tasks prescribed by the expert, we have now the problem of interfacing this task with the model of the circuit. In other terms we have to devise all the information required by the expert and make it available to the diagnostic task. If the ES is based on the functional and structural model of the electronic equipment we must provide tools which interpret the knowledge implicit in the model to provide the knowledge explicitly required by each diagnostic task. The most conventional of such tools/interpreters is the simulator. In the example reported in the next sections we present a less conventional one, capable of evaluating the functional dependencies of outputs on inputs. Aim of this step is to choose the correct model access tools and to provide the requirements of new ones to the knowledge engineer.

Step 4: Fourth step is the implementation of the devised entities, and their embodying into the ES. This phase is the one more promising to be automatically supported with the introduction of tools in the third phase of our research.

The four steps above are iterated until a knowledgeable behaviour is achieved. As can be noticed, the idea here is of starting from the expert knowledge, trying to classify it in four kinds of knowledge: knowledge about the model, about its manipulation, about the diagnostic strategies and about their management. The idea of classifying the expert knowledge depending on its type (or level) has been also considered in [Nec 85]. There the classification is different due to the fact that it is claimed to be generallly applicable. Here the classification is instead provided for the solution of HW troubleshooting problems, and therefore we can be more specific.

3. Example of expert diagnosis enunciation

The circuit chosen by the expert for performing the sample diagnosis is the AM2910 (Fig. 1) microprogram sequencer [ADM 83]. The rationale for this choice is that it is an integrated circuit containing most of the components appearing in real problems (registers, PLA's, stacks etc.) and which generally make diagnosis an expert task.

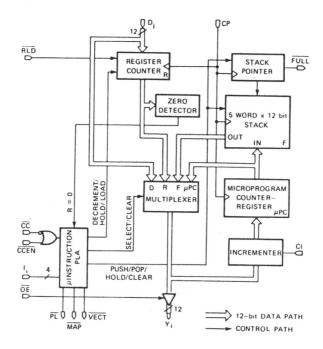

Fig. 1 - AM2910 microprogram sequencer.

In the example shown in figure 1, the expert, by comparing the expected output value [2] with the correct one 9, used at once this information, to conclude that the faulty output could only have been caused by the OE (output enable), the multiplexer, or two out of its five inputs: i.e. D and SELECT/CLEAR. The reasons for this early decision are due to the following facts:

a. OE could be wrong, and the outputs from the multiplexer may be ruined by a faulty value on this pin. This suspect was later discarded because it drives a three state output and if it were wrong we are unlikely to have observed a value like 9.

b. Multiplexer could be wrong. This conclusion was then rejected in a subsequent stage of diagnosis because of the fact that the multiplexer is implemented using a bit slice technology, and then the single fault assumption insures us that a 9 could not become a 2. Anyway we are interested in diagnostic principles, and then we will stop at this stage, still considering the multiplexer as a plausible fault module.

c. SELECT/CLEAR could carry a faulty value. Alternatively to the multiplexer, we can say that if SELECT/CLEAR is expected to select input D, it might have incorrectly selected the wrong input.

d. Input D to the multiplexer could be wrong, then SELECT/CLEAR selects correctly the input D. In this case the misbehaviour is caused from a faulty value on D. The remaining parts of the system are no longer supected.

4. Generalization of expert reasoning

At this point we have to answer the question "why the expert drew these conclusions ?" or better "what is the diagnostic principle applied by the expert in the previous example ?". Failing to find the general concept underlying the enunciation, would only allow to generate a heuristic valid for the multiplexer. In this case it could be expressed in this way:

> RULE : When applying test 000000000010 1 0 1 0010 0 0, to
> the AM2910 we found that the output is wrong
> =>
> Suspects are: multiplexer, and paths from
> input D and SELECT/CLEAR.

On the other hand we can generalize by stating that when the output of a module is proved to be wrong, responsible for this misbehaviour could be only the module itself and those inputs that could have affected the given wrong output in the given situation.

In other words we have have to discover in the situation above which inputs (in our example were F, PC and R) are not enabled to contribute to the observed faulty behavior.

The diagnostic concept generalized from the enunciation is: given one or more faulty outputs, under the single fault assumption suspect modules are only those a) structurally connected to the observed fault and b) functionally enabled to cause the observed fault.

In summary, the generalization step has identified:

- a diagnostic assumption (single fault);

- a causal principle (faults propagate along structural connections);

- a heuristic strategy (selection of functionally dependent inputs only).

5. Modelling

In step 2 the expert said that the information relevant in this case are: a) the expected behaviour of the system, b) the observed one and c) the ability, given a module, of answering to the question "which inputs affect the behaviour of the considered module in the known situation ?". This question can be answered when we avail of two information, the current context, i.e. the current snapshot of the correct model, while the second is the declarative representation of the system functionality. The current expected context is the model itself. It has been manipulated by the simulator, that has produced the expected behavior of the system. The second information needed is the behavioral model of the system.

EXAMPLE: the multiplexer contained in the AM2910 circuit is represented by the following function:

```
(deffunct multiplexer
  (cond ((= (in 1) 0) (out 1 (in 2)))
        ((= (in 1) 1) (out 1 (in 3)))
        ((= (in 1) 2) (out 1 (in 4)))
        ((= (in 1) 3) (out 1 (in 5))))))
```

A model access tool answering the question about functional dependency has been implemented: DEPENDENCY CHECKER.

It accepts the functionality of a module and its inputs and returns the list of inputs that may have affected the current output.

As a second step this tool has been expanded for dealing with sequential modules and now it is contained in our ES with the name of TEMPORAL DEPENDENCY CHECKER.

EXAMPLE: In our case the application of the TEMPORAL DEPENDENCY CHECKER to the multiplexer, gives the following result.

(t-d-c 'multiplexer 1 1)

((1 1) (2 1))

that means that at time 1 the inputs that may have affected the output one of the multiplexer are: input 1 (at time 1) and input 2 (at time 1).

The definition of this tool allowed to make available to the diagnostic task the information required.

This tool can be considered as an example of qualitative reasoning, as functions are searched for analytical properties, as opposed to quantitative numerical computations.

6. Embodying

As a final step, the knowledge devised during step 3 is inserted into the ES. The diagnostic task defined in this example is implemented using MRS rules [Gen 84]. The most important rules are shown below.

R-1

```
(if (and (incorrect $o)
         (primary-output $o)
         (connected $connection $o)
         (connection $connection))
;first we start from mismatches at primary outputs and
;trace the connected wires
         (assumed-faulty $connection))
```

R-2

```
(if (and (assumed-faulty $component-x)
         (connection $component-x)
         (connected ($component-y output $i) $component-x)
         (module $component-y))
;then we collect modules whose outputs are connected to
;suspect wires
         (assumed-faulty $component-y $i))
```

R-3
```
              (if (and (assumed-faulty $component $output)
                   (module $component)
                   (responsible-inputs $component $output $inputs))
              ;trace backward the module's inputs
                   (assumed-faulty $component $inputs))))
```

The model access tools (simulator and dependency checker) described here are, as all model access tools of the architecture, written in ZETA-LISP.

Dependency checker is applicable by the diagnostic task due to the heuristic strategy declared below specifying that temporal dependency checker has to be called when the question "which inputs did actually affect the observed output ?" arises.

(tofind (responsible-inputs x y z) TEMPORAL-DEPENDENCY-CHECK).

This heuristic strategy is applicable under the single fault assumption.

FINAL EXAMPLE: suppose that we asserted (instead of the discrepancy detection rule devoted to that)

        (incorrect   a m2910 4))   ; i.e. the output from the multiplexer.

the firing of the rules of the diagnostic task just seen, provides the following output answers:

```
              (ASSUMED-FAULTY CONNECTION-3-STATE-OUTPUT-4)
              (ASSUMED-FAULTY 3-STATE)
              (ASSUMED-FAULTY CONNECTION-OE-3-STATE)
              (ASSUMED-FAULTY MULTIPLEXER)
              (ASSUMED-FAULTY CONNECTION-SELECT-CLEAR)
              (ASSUMED-FAULTY PLA)
              (ASSUMED-FAULTY CONNECTION-D)
```

This is just what we can infer from the information given to the system (that are the same given by the expert during step 1). The described task now stops, because the diagnostic step just finished, and a test generation step has to be performed.

7. Concluding remarks

We have presented in this paper a four step methodology for implementing model based diagnostic ESs. The immediate relevance of this methodology is is that the roles of the diagnostic expert as well as of the knowledge engineer are extablished. Further relevance of this research has been the clear statement of the building process for a diagnostic ES.

These results are currently used for the definition and implementation of tools that will support the building process of a model based ES by the diagnostic expert only. Final goal of this research is to provide an environment in which a list of standard components of the ES will be available together with tools for building new components to be integrated with the existing ones.

The ES from which has been taken the example used for explaining our methodology has been now translated from MRS into ART, and has been succesfully experimented in the diagnosis of a multiplexing board, used in telephone exchange.

8. References

[ADM 83] Advanced Micro Device, Bipolar Microprocessor Logic and Interface, Am 2900 Family, 1983 Data Book.

[ART 85] "ART Automated Reasoning Tool Reference Manual" Inference Corporation Los Angeles.

[Bar 81] Barstow D.R., Buchanan B.G., "Maxims for knowledge engineering", Stanford Heuristics Programming Project, Report no. HPP-81-4, May 1981.

[Cla 83] Clancey W. J., "The advantages of Abstract Control Knowledge in Expert System Design" AAAI Proceedings 1983

[Cha 83] Chandrasekaran B., Mittal S., "Deep versus compiled knowledge approaches to diagnostic problem solving" in Int. J. Man-Machine Studies (1983) 19, 425-436.

[Dav 82] Davis R., "Applications of meta-level knowledge to the construction, maintenance and use of large knowledge bases" in "Knowledge-based systems in artificial intelligence. New York: Mc Grew Hill, 1982, 229-490.

[Dav 83] Davis R., "Reasoning from first principles in electronic troubleshooting", in Int. J. Man-Machine Studies (1983) 19, 403-423.

[Dio 85] Dionisi Vici A., Giovannini F., Malabocchia F., Sisto L., "Deep and shallow knowledge in an expert system for digital HW troubleshooting", CSELT TECHNICAL REPORTS, Vol.14, n.1, Feb. 86.

[Gen 84] Genesereth M.R., Greiner R., Grinberg M.R., Smith D.E., "The MRS dictionary", Stanford Heuristic Programming Project, Report no. HPP-80-24, January 1984.

[Gen 82] Genesereth, M.R. "Diagnosis using hierarchical design models", in Proc. AAAI 82, Pittsbourgh, Pennsylvania.

[Gio 85] Giovannini F., Malabocchia F., "A model based ES for HW troubleshooting driven by compiled knowledge", in Proc. Expert Systems '85, Warwick (U.K), Cambridge Univ. Press.

[Mit 85] Mittal S., Dym C.L., "Knowledge acquisition from multiple experts", in The AI Magazine, Summer. 1985.

[Nec 85] Neches, R., Swartout, W.R., Moore, J.D., "Enhanced maintenance and explanation of expert systems through explicit models of their development", IEEE trans. on Software Engineering, Vol. SE-11, N. 11, Nov 85.

Reasoning

Reasoning about Reasoning: an Example of Two Level Explanation with the Triangular Table Method

J.F. Picardat

Université Paul Sabatier, Toulouse (France)

ABSTRACT

One of the attractive aspects of rule-based reasoning programs is their ability to incorporate automated self-explanation procedures. The more used explanation method is based on the execution trace. It presents advantages as the consistency of the explanation with the program code. However, several problems can occur. It is proposed here a classification in three parts of this explanation approach. Then this paper focusses on the particular problem of making clear the relationships between the many inferences. In this way, it is shown how the triangular table of Fikes & al is a useful tool for explanation. An application is presented with two levels of triangular table.

Keywords : explanation, triangular table, rule-based program, reasoning modelling, planning

Introduction

Most of the Artificial Intelligence programs use reasoning for producing results (diagnosis, plan, ...), but few work has been realized to permit the automated analysis of this reasoning in order to explain or to correct it. Our attention has been focused for three years on the method of the triangular table [13][14], which seems interesting for several reasons: first this table records in a very useful and compact way the internal structure of a plan; second it permits to use this structure for analyzing each sequence of this plan. As far as we know, that technique has only been managed for error recovery in the robotics area. However, its advantages for analysing a sequence of acts lead us to study the use of this table for the reasoning explanation of a rule-based program. This is the object of this paper. In a first part, we study the different methods of reasoning explanation. Then, we successively make a description of the triangular table principle, and study how it can be useful for the explanation with an application at two levels in our rule-based plan-generator. We will try to discuss the interest of this approach.

1) Review of the explanation approaches

An explanation system is a system that attempts to answer questions pertaining to the system behavior. It is a particularity of rule-based programs to be able to explain their behavior in terms of conditions and consequences of each step. This is a positive point, among other ones, which makes them very interesting. Indeed, such a capability meets essentially three needs:

A- to help the debugging of expert systems, by tracing the execution of the program.
B- to facilitate the acceptance of results by users, who can follow the reasoning.
C- and to permit the transfer of knowledge from rule-based programs to students, who can test their beliefs by asking questions.

We make here a distinction between terms "explanation" and "question answering". Explanation is on a reasoning and its results (answer about the knowledge use), while the question answering systems [15][34][35] deals rather with static knowledge (as "what is the French capital ?").

Works on explanation have been developped correlatively with the studies on rule-based systems. Historically, one of the first study that pointed out the need of automated explanation, in these systems, was MYCIN [33]. It was in this way the descendant of previous question answering AI programs [34][15]. Shortliffe cited the importance of providing reasonable explanation, as well as good advice, for the rule-based programs to be acceptable to users. Thus MYCIN was designed so that it was able to give explanation of its decisions in terms of its rules and goals.

Since this one, several different approaches have been taken. Two major ones have been used: canned text and execution trace.

Canned text

The first one is the least sophisticated. The questions are anticipated during the rule-set writing, and the answers are stored in natural language. Only the text that has been recorded can be displayed, as for example error messages. Here, naturally, the explanation can be as elegant as desired. But, beyond this simplicity, three problems occur with canned explanation:

– first it is difficult to maintain the consistency between program code and canned text because they may be modified independently each other.

– second, all questions must be anticipated (which is of course impossible when the size of of the program increases).

– and then, the program does not "understand" what it is saying. So it can't detail or compute its response in order to take into account what the user expects.

Execution trace

This second approach is based on the execution of a rule-based program. Here the system keeps a record (the trace) of how it makes decisions during all its problem solving process. To answer a question, the system examines the trace in order to make the considered step (i.e. the rule) explicit. Thus for explaining why a fact has been settled, the system can print the premises of the rules which have been fired for this. Fig.1 shows an example of explanation made by MYCIN (which uses an execution trace).

user: Did you consider whether the patient was receiving steroids?
RULE543 could have used:
     whether J. Smith has received corticosteroids.
Clause 4 of RULE543 {the patient has received corticosteroids} was already known to be false.

user: How did you know that the patient had not received steroids?
RULE395 was used to conclude that J. Smith has received corticosteroids. The last question asked before the conclusion was made was 23.

user: What was question 23?
Question 23 was asked in order to find out whether J. Smith is a compromised host in an effort to execute RULE343.

<u>FIG.1 - A sample of MYCIN explanation capability (extracted from [5]).</u>

This method has several advantages compared to the precedent one:
    - explanation is issued from the program code so the problem of consistency disappears;
    - the system also answers "unanticipated" questions.
    - Moreover the facts used for both problem solving and response building have the same representation. So the program can use them in an other problem solving process of which the aim is to compute (or plan) the response to answer truthfully and informatively by taking account of what the user expects, and what the user knows [41][3][19][16].

However, three important disadvantages must be pointed out:
    - first, as the program code, most of the time, is not expressed in natural language (NL), this approach often <u>needs an NL generator</u> in order to translate the response into an understandable message by any user [38][21][22].
[i] - second, to print only activities trace is <u>quickly beyond the ability of a user</u> to assimilate the many inferences and their relationships, that is why some works propose to produce explanation from an abstract of the execution trace [26][37][7][17].
    - Third, the activity trace often keeps only the way that leads to the goal; which permits to answer positive questions (why) but <u>don't respond to negative ones</u> (why not). [31][40] try to treat these ones.
    - Fourth, a serious problem is that it may <u>possible that explanation is not in rules</u> because rules'author has written only the means of problem solving but not explicitly why this way is correct (as for example the order of premises). This is analysed in [5][39]. Swartout [39] proposes for this the use of a domain model to help the explanation system.

In spite of these disadvantages activity trace remains a popular means of explanation because both their are easily generated, and they provide more sophisticated explanation than canned text. this despite some work that tries to mix these two approaches [18].

With this quick presentation of the execution trace approach for explanation, we can decompose it into three different lines of research as shown in fig.2.

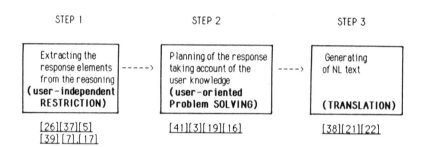

FIG. 2- A hierarchical model of the reasoning explanation

In conclusion, we can see that the field of research on explanatory capability is very large. In this paper we focus our attention on the first step: the extraction of response elements from the trace. So we will not consider the planning and the NL translation of the response.

We have seen (cf. **[1]**) that one of the problems which occur in this first step is how to structure the many inferences of the execution trace to make clear their relationships ?. We will try here to answer this question by showing the triangular table of Fikes & al [13][14] solve efficiently this problem.

2) The triangular table

Let us consider the action plan of a robot.
- Has the already executed sequence of plan given the expected results?
- Which sequence of plan can be executed in the present state of the world?

These are two of the questions about the plan execution control to which the triangular table method can answer [14] Indeed, this table stores with each action of the plan the preconditions for the execution of this action, so that it binds these preconditions to the effects of the previous actions. An example is given on fig. 4. The principle is to put on a row the conditions of the act of this row, and to put on a column the effects of the act which labelled this one.

a) Example of table

We are considering here the plan which achieves the following goal state:

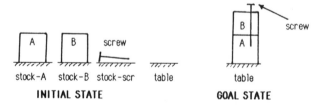

INITIAL STATE   GOAL STATE

FIG. 3- A classic problem

The triangular table of this plan is pointed out in fig. 4. The plan is printed on the diagonal line. The preconditions and the effects are stored as explained in lines and columns.

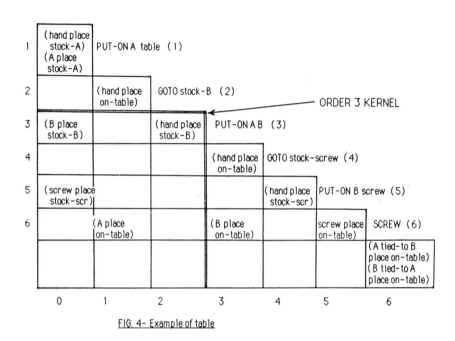

FIG. 4- Example of table

b) The research of kernel

kernel: a kernel is the set of conditions needed to execute a sequence. In the above scheme, we drew with a thicker line the 3d order kernel which corresponds to the terminal sequence:
PUT-ON A B/ GO-TO stock-screw/ PUT-ON B screw/ SCREW/ , that begins with the action n° 3. The Kernel Research (KR) during an attempt to recover a failing plan has been at the origin of the concept of triangular table [14]. The KR algorithm scans the table cell-by-cell from bottom to top, and from left to right. We refer the reader to Nilsson [24] for more details.

c) Precedent works on triangular table

In spite of these attractive aspects there wasn't any study, so far as we know, since [13][14], for developing this way of monitoring, though it has been mentionned in several A.I. synthesis books [4][24][30][32] and was recently shown [25] as a potential powerful tool for a robot programming language.

In our team, we have tried to develop this method by fitting it into our rule-based plan-generator: ARGOS-2 [8][10][27]. Except a study on sequence retrieval during planning [28], most of our works has considered the improvement of table building. For implementing these tables in ARGOS-2 program, a method has been designed [6] in order to automatically create the preconditions and effects lists of acts. It was based on a comparison of simulated world states before and after an act. Fade & al [9] show that the obtained lists in such a way are analogous to Delete (D) and Add (A) lists of STRIPS model, then points out the imperfection of Precondition (P) lists with this method. To improve this P-list, it proposes to collect all the rule trigger-parts through the reasoning chaining. In this way act conditions are inherited trigger-parts. So a correct (P, A, D) triplet can be build automatically to model acts of a rule-based plan-generator.

In other respects, any propositions have been made to use a hierarchy of triangular tables [25][29].

3) The use of the triangular table for explanation

Over all the previous uses of the Triangular Tables (TT), we can see that they have only been used for robotics plans. But this is not a limitation because in its principle the only restriction on an act is to be modeled by conditions and effects lists. Thus inference rules can be modeled as such acts. In order to experiment this, we have built the triangular table of a chaining of more sophisticated rules than STRIPS'ones (which were limited at one single primitive act), with ARGOS-2 (in which the acts are clearly distinct from rules).

a- Rule modelling

Let us remember that ARGOS-2 rules [8][10] are simultaneously driven by a goal and datas. The goal is decomposed into subproblem(s) and primitive action(s). The subproblem(s) replace the current goal in the problem stack, while the final actions are recorded in the building plan.

syntax: <u><rule>:</u> (<name> <trigger-part> < action-part>)

where, <u><trigger-part>:</u> (<problem-pattern> <fact-pattern>)

The principle used for building the rule table is here analogous to the one exposed in [9] for modelling final acts into a (P, A, D) triplet: two simulated world states are compared; those ones before and after the rule execution. However the difference between STRIPS or ARGOS-2 act model and the here-desired rule model is the considered world. In the case of a robotic act, only the environment facts set have been considered [14][6][9] because this final action modifies only the external world. Whereas ARGOS-2 rules modify a greater environment. Let us name the <rule environment> R.ENV. The whole R.ENV is:

R.ENV= (SEW, PS, MP)

where: SEW= Simulated External World model

PS = Problem Stack

PP = Plan in Progress

Indeed a rule modifies PS with subproblems, adds one (or more) act to the plan, and updates SEW according to the introduced act(s). So a first method to build the rule model -copied from the act one- is:

[c] < deletelist$_i$> = R.ENV$_{\text{before rule i}}$ − R.ENV$_{\text{after rule i}}$

< addlist$_i$> = R.ENV$_{\text{after rule i}}$ − R.ENV$_{\text{before rule i}}$

Nevertheless, this is not saving time because in the general case, the modifications are very few numerous compared to the memory (SEW, PS, or PP) dimension. **[c]** is admissible only for small lists. A more powerful method is to catch directly the modifications of R.ENV when they occur into current addlist and deletelist. We are now studying such a method as a development of ARGOS-2 inference engine; while **[c]** is implemented.

b- Application to a rule TT building

Once the rules are modelled under the form of a (P,A,D) triplet, we can build the TT of rules which are used in a "linear reasoning" (i.e: we don't consider here parallel processes, but it is not a limitation for the TT [13]). Let us now present an example of rule table with a simple robotic manipulation. Here the low level acts are the primitive LISP functions used to control a SCEMI robot in the NNS software environment [1][2]. The knowledge of the rule syntax is not necessary for understanding the following of the paper. Let us note only that the rules produce sub-problems (replacepb) and/or low level actions (record(plan...(update...))).

<u>Initial state:</u> SEW=((part on xp) (robot-hand on 0 state closed))
<u>goal:</u> PS=((take part))

<u>extract of a rules set:</u>
(**r1.go-to.1** ((go-to -pos))
        ((record (plan (*move_robot-hand* =pos))
                (update (modify ((robot-hand $*$)(on =pos)))))))

(**r5.calculate-fp.2** ((calculate-fp for -pos))

```
((record(plan  ( tmult =pos ( gentra '(00 100)) fp))
        (update (modify ((=fp *)))))))
(r7.take.1 ((take -obj) (robot-hand * state closed * on AFP *) NO(robot-hand * holds *))
    ((record(plan  ( open_robot-hand ))
            (update (modify ((robot-hand *)(state opened)))))
       (replacepb (take =obj))))
(r8.take.2 ((take -obj)  (robot-hand * state opened *)
                         (=obj * on -pos *)
                         (robot-hand * on AFP *))
       ((replacepb (go-to =pos) (take =obj))))

(r11.take.5 ((take -obj)  (=obj * on -pos *)
                          NO (robot-hand * on =pos *)
                          NO (robot-hand * on AFP *)
                          NO (robot-hand * holds *))
           ((replacepb (calculate.fp AFP for =pos)
                       (go-to AFP)
                       (take =obj))))
(r12.take.6  ((take obj)  (=obj * on  -pos * )
                          (robot-hand * on =pos * )
                          (robot-hand * state opened * ))
           ((record (plan ( close_robot-hand ))
                    (update (modify ((robot-hand * )(state closed) (holds  =obj)))))))
```

comments:

1- syntax: "*" replaces any segment (list -of symbolic expressions- without left/right brackets).

   "-⟨var⟩" is a variable which must catch a value.

   "=⟨var⟩" is an intantiated variable.

2- strategy: in a very simple way of obstacles avoiding, the robot-hand is moved (for the great displacements) hight over the assembly table to a fixed point AFP (Arrival Fixed Point) situated above the object to take; *tmult* and *gentra* are two low level actions, the first is the multiplication of two transformations, while the second generates the transformation of a translation from a vector.

Now, let us look at the result. The rule chaining (see Fig. 5-a) obtained for reaching the goal is:

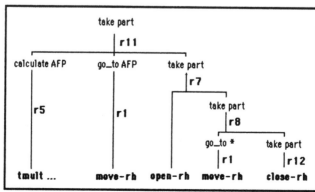

r11.take.5
r5.calculate-fp.2
r1.go-to.1
r7.take.1
r8.take.2
r1.go-to.1
r12.take.6

FIG 5-a) Backward chaining tree

while, the acts plan is: Tmult
                        move_robot-hand
                        open_robot-hand   (d)
                        move_robot-hand
                        close_robot-hand

and finally the rule table of the rule sequence is :

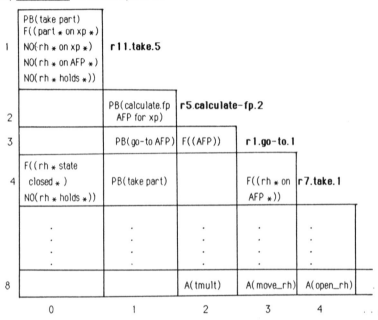

1	PB(take part) F((part * on xp *) NO(rh * on xp *) NO(rh * on AFP *) NO(rh * holds *))	**r11.take.5**			
2		PB(calculate.fp AFP for xp)	**r5.calculate-fp.2**		
3			PB(go-to AFP)	F((AFP))	**r1.go-to.1**	
4	F((rh * state closed *) NO(rh * holds *))	PB(take part)		F((rh * on AFP *))	**r7.take.1**
	. . . .	. . . .	. . . .	. . . .	. . . .
8			A(tmult)	A(move_rh)	A(open_rh)
	0	1	2	3	4

FIG 5-b: An ARGOS-2 rule triangular table
****

preliminary comments:
    0. rh= Robot-hand
    1. This table contains three groups of elements: Facts, Problems, and Acts which are marked with F, P or A
    2. The acts of the researched plan are written on the last row.
****

c- Use of the rule TTs for producing explanations

    This rule table (fig. 5-b) shows that the triangular table principle can be generalized in some way to all the rule-based expert-systems. But here what is the usefulness of such a table ?. One of its characteristics is to represent the internal structure of a plan (in its general definition: a sequence of steps) into a simple and clear form which presents several possibilities of tests and automatic manipulations.
    So, I have successfully used this table for writing a Reasoning Analysis Module (RAM) which is associated with ARGOS-2 (Fig. 6). RAM is now able to answer questions. We can ask essentially two kinds of questions about an element (problem, fact, act, or rule): where does it come from ?, and

what is its usefulness ?. Here is an example of dialogue, about produced acts plan –see (d)–, in the explanation option:

1– ? tmult ; (why has "tmult" act been introduced into the plan ?)
RAM --> **r5.calculate-fp.2**
　　　(comment: RAM has researched the column number in which "tmult" is, and has found **"r5.calculate-fp.2"** in top of this one.)

2– ? **r7.take.1** ; (why has been **r7.take.1** triggered ?.)
RAM -->　1– F((rh ∗ on AFP ∗))
　　　　　2– PB(take part)
　　　　　3– F((rh ∗state closed ∗) NO(rh ∗ holds ∗))

　　　(comment: RAM gives trigger-parts in the inverse order of their production in time; which facilitates the understanding of reasoning steps.)

3–? PB(take part) ; (why was the "take part" problem considered ?)
RAM --> **r11.take.5**
　　　When the response is a rule name, the user can require, as in MYCIN, RAM prints this one.

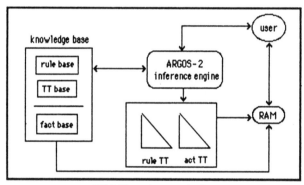

FIG 6: The system organization

4) Discussion of the explanation capability given by this table

　　　We have shown how a rule table is used, but of course we dispose of an other table: the act table, which is analogous to this one seen in fig.4. So we have two levels of triangular table. Each of these ones can be used for explanation producing. The rule table points out the motion of the three elements F, P, A: it is used for explaining the reasoning steps. While the second one, the action table, explicits the motion of facts between acts: it is used for explaining the result of the reasoning (the plan).

　　　Let us note that the rule triangular table is a structured record of the execution trace. And that we only consider here positive questions (i.e. no négative question as "Why not ..."; see [31][40] for this).

Advantages:

　　　One of the advantages of this method is to generalize the use of a tool: many procedures as table building and table treatment are common to the error retrieval and to the explanation production; which improves efficiency of the program.

But the first interest of this one for the explanation is to make clear the relationships between the inferences. Indeed, what the triangular table provides is a structured view of the motions of R.ENV along the time: the origin of each premise, the <u>aim of each consequence</u> , and the temporal order of use of both premises and consequences. So the explanation is beyond the rule-granularity of the execution trace. The explanation exceeds the step by step response.

Inconveniences:
One present limitation is that the explanations can only be produced after a program session because the table is build at the end of the inference chaining. We study now means to build it progressively during the plan generation in order to permit explanations in the course of a session. But this seems to us that it will not be too hard to implement.
A more serious disadvantage of this technique is actually the time used for finding in the table the key-word considered by the question. It is a pattern-matching procedure. So, this limitation is analogous to the well-known slowness of the pattern directed inference systems.

Conclusion

We have shown here how the triangular table of Fikes & al can be used for the reasoning explanation. With a two level application, our program, RAM (of which the implementation is in progress for improvement), can explain as well the reasoning as its result (a plan). This has two major advantages:
- to generalize the use of this representation to both explanation and monitoring capability,
- and to produce informative responses from a structured execution trace record by making clear the relationships between different inferences (beyond the step by step explanation).

Acknowledgements

The author would like to thank Bernard FADE and Henri FARRENY for their helpful comments on this work.

****

Bibliography

Explanation:
[3], [5], [7], [11], [12], [15], [16], [17], [18], [19], [20], [21], [22], [23], [26], [31], [33], [34], [35], [36], [37], [38], [39], [40], [41]

Triangular table:
[4], [6], [9], [13], [14], [24], [25], [28], [29], [30], [32]

References:

[1] ALAMI R.,"Un environnement pour l'intégration et la mise en oeuvre de systèmes complexes en robotique", Thèse, INP, Toulouse, nov. 1983.

[2] ALAMI R.,"Apocalisp 2.2", rapport interne LAAS n° 85098, Toulouse, mai 1985.

[3] APPELT D.E.,"Planning Natural Language utterances to satisfy multiple goals", Thesis, Standford University, 1981.- Abstracted in [36].

[4] BARR A.,FEIGENBAUM E.A. (Eds), "The handbook of Artificial Intelligence", Heuristic Press, vol 1, 1982

[5] CLANCEY W.J., "The Epistemology of a Rule-Based Expert System - a Framework for Explanation"; Artificial Intelligence 20 (1983) pp 215-251.

[6] CORNUEJOLS A., "Le contrôle d' exécution de plan pour système décisionnel de robotique". LSI, rapport interne n° 223, Toulouse, 1983.

[7] ERIKSSON A., JOHANSSON A., "Neat proof trees", Proc. of the 9th IJCAI, pp 379-381, 18-23 August 1985, Los Angeles.

[8] FADE B. ,"Contribution à la réalisation d'un résolveur automatique de problèmes", Thèse de 3° cycle, UPS, Toulouse, 1980.

[9] FADE B., PICARDAT J.F.,"About needed conditions for the execution of robotics planned programs",proc. of the 2nd int. conf. on Machine Intelligence, Londres, nov. 1985, pp.311-320

[10] FARRENY H., "Un système pour l'expression et la résolution de problèmes orienté vers le contrôle de robot", Thèse d'état, UPS, Toulouse, 1980.

[11] FERRAND P.,"SESAM: an explanatory Medical Aid System"; Proc. of the Europ. Conf. on Artif. Intellig.,pp 13-20, Pise, Italie, Sept. 1984, North-Holland.

[12] FIESCHI D.,"Contribution au système expert SPHINX: Application à l'enseignement médical". Thèse de 3° cycle, Université Paris 6, Mars 1984.

[13] FIKES R.E., HART P.E, NILSSON N.J., "Some new directions in robot problem solving", Machine Intelligence 7, Meltzer B. and Mitchie D. (eds.), Edinburgh University Press, Edinburgh, pp 405-430 (1972)

[14] FIKES R. E., HART P.E., NILSSON N.J., "Learning and executing generalized robot plans", Artificial Intelligence, vol. 3, n° 4,pp. 251-288, Winter 72

[15] FOX A.J.,"A survey of question-answering systems", in Medical Computing (M.E ABRAMS, ed.), American Elsevier Publishing Co. Inc., NY (1970).

[16] JOSHI A.,WEBBER B., WEISCHEDEL R.M.,"Living up to expectations: computing expert responses", Proceedings of AAAI-84, pp 260-263.

[17] KASSEL Gilles, "Expliquer, c'est raisonner sur le raisonnement: le système CQFE", proc. of the 6th Inter. Workshop on Expert Systems & their applications, pp. 973-990, Avignon, France, 28-29 avril 86.

[18] KASTNER J.K., WEISS S.M.,KULIKOWSKI C.A.,"Treatment selection and explanation in expert medical consultation, application to a model of ocular herpes simplex", Proceedings of MEDCOMP82 (1982), pp 420-427.

[19] LIPKIS T.,"Descriptive mapping for explanation production", Workshop on Automated Explanation Production, june 1982.- Abstracted in [36].

[20] LUCKAM D., NILSSON N.J.,"Extracting information from resolution proof trees", Artificial Intelligence 2, (1971), pp 27-54

[21] McDONALD D.D.,"Why to use a full-scale Natural Language generator", Workshop on Automated Explanation Production, june 1982.- Abstracted in [36].

[22] MANN W.C.,"Multiparagraph text generation", Workshop on Automated Explanation Production, june 1982.- Abstracted in [36].

[23] NECHES R., SWARTOUT W.R, MOORE J,"Explainable (and maintainable) expert systems", Proc. of the 9th IJCAI, pp 382-389, 18-23 August, 1985, Los Angeles.

[24] NILSSON N.J.,"Principles of Artificial Intelligence", Tioga publishing company, Palo Alto, Cal. 1980

[25] NILSSON N.J.,"Triangle tables: a proposal for a robot programming language", Technical note 347, Artificial Intelligence Center, Stanford Research Institute, february 1895.

[26] PAVLIN J., CORKILL D.D.,"Selective abstraction of AI system activity", Proceedings of AAAI-84, pp 264-268.

[27] PICARDAT J.F., "Manuel ARGOS II", Internal memo n°217, LSI lab., mai 1985

[28] PICARDAT J.F., "Reflexions sur le contrôle d'exécution de plan: la replanification retenue", Internal memo, LSI lab., sept. 1984

[29] PICARDAT J.F.; "Ebauche d'un modèle généralisé pour le contrôle de plan", LSI Lab., internal memo n° 216, nov. 1985.

[30] RICH E.,"Artificial Intelligence", McGraw-Hill Book company, New-York, 1983

[31] SAFAR B.,"Explication dans les systèmes experts", proc. of the 5th International Workshop on Expert Systems & their Applications, pp 585-599, 13-14 may, 1895, Avignon, France.

[32] SHIRAI Y., TSUJII J.,"Artificial Intelligence", John Wiley & Sons Ltd.,1984

[33] SHORTLIFFE E.H., "Computer-based medical consultations: MYCIN", American Elsevier, 1976

[34] SIMMONS R.F.,"Natural Language question-answering systems". Commun. ACM 13, pp15-30 (1970)

[35] SCHUBERT L.K., WATANABE L., "What's in an answer: a theoretical perspective on deductive question answering", Proc. of the 6th Canadian Conf. on AI, 21-23 may 86, pp 71-77

[36] SWARTOUT B., "Workshop on Automated Explanation Production". SIGART Newsletter (85) july 1983,pp 7-13.

[37] SWARTOUT B.,"The GIST behaviour explainer", Proceedings of AAAI-83, pp 402-407.

[38] SWARTOUT W.," GIST english generator", Proceedings of AAAI-82

[39] SWARTOUT W.R.,"XPLAIN: A system for creating and explaining expert consulting programs"; Artificial Intelligence 21 (1983) pp 285-325.

[40] WALKER A.,"Prolog/EX1, an inference engine which explains both yes and no answers", Proc. of the 8th IJCAI, pp 500-506, 8-12 August 1983, Karlsruhe

[41] WEINER J.L., "BLAH, a System which explains its reasoning", Artificial Intelligence 15 (1980), pp 19-48.

Support of Specification of Embedded Systems
A Practical Knowledge-Based Approach

R. Haataja, V. Seppänen

Technical Research Center of Finland, Electronics Laboratory,
Computer Technology Laboratory, Oulu (Finland)

This paper reports a knowledge-based system called PROduct
SPecification EXpert system (Prospex) supporting specification of
embedded computer systems, and of its first prototype PrOspex. It
has been designed as an intelligent workbench system to assist in
the specification and early design activities of embedded
computer systems. PrOspex supports the Structured Analysis for
Real-Time Systems (RT-SA) method. Using a commercial toolkit to
assist in the creation of graphics specifications and formatted
specification documents, the system is capable of analysing
specification on the basis of its knowledge base, consulting in
specification strategy and explaining its reasoning. Knowledge is
in the form of production rules, and the PrOspex system has been
implemented with Prolog. The Prospex prototype is inexpensive and
is a very promising implementation of a knowledge-based
specification support system in the field of microcomputers.

Introduction

Embedded systems where the computer is an essential part of a
larger technical and mechanical system (ANSI/IEEE 1983) are on
the increase (Mizuno 1983). At the same time, the software
engineering industry has encountered difficulties in producing
correct and consistent software products in a reliable way. Many
new ideas and research results have been reported, from
integrated software engineering environments (Huenke 1981) to
expert systems and other knowledge-based software production
assistants (Arango 1984, Kowalski 1984). Utilization of these
results generated by research is, however, a very slow tedious
process which must take into account technical, management and
psychological aspects related to the new concepts and ideas. The
interval between the research and putting the system into
practice can therefore be 10 years or more (Shaw 1985). Thus,
approaches based on innovative productive ideas and real
production environments are needed.
  System specification activities in the development of computer
systems are often considered one of the most difficult and error-
prone areas. This is particularly true for embedded systems where
computer hardware, software and electromechanical parts must be
specified consistently to meet the requirements of high quality
and efficiency.

One of the main difficulties in many existing specification
support systems is their impractical formal nature that reduces
their usability in a production environment: some specification
languages are thus likely to hinder production work. This on the
one hand, and the fact that less formal approaches often tend to
be based on vague ad hoc ideas, have left many companies in a
state of uncertainty. A simple, powerful well-formulated
specification method seems to be missing. Furthermore, any
tutorial material or organized courses on this method are not
available. If all these requirements are met, it is unlikely that
a computer system that supports the specification method can
result.

Knowledge-based systems, especially expert systems, that operate
successfully in many applications areas have been reported
(Hayes-Roth 1984). Practical software engineering and production
expert systems are, however, remarkably few in number or if not
they are kept confidential by the organizations that have
developed them. The entire software engineering field has also
been classified as too difficult a domain for efficient
knowledge-based support systems.

The Structure of Prospex

The PROduct SPecification EXpert system (Prospex) has been
designed to be an intelligent tool that can assist in the
difficult specification activities of embedded computer systems.
The objectives of the development of Prospex are:

1. to acquire and organize a knowledge base composed of
   perceptual, conceptual and strategic specification
   knowledge; to select a specification method to be supported
   on the basis of the production level requirements; to
   combine knowledge related to that method to knowledge
   realted to a set of products and companies in the domain of
   the embedded systems;
2. to use a commercial inexpensive graphics user interface for
   the creation of specifications and specification documents
   in order to enhance usability; to be able to concentrate on
   the knowledge-based functions of the system and to keep
   costs low;
3. to use knowledge in checking the quality and correctness of
   specifications; to identify specification activities with
   the related reasoning in order to provide consultation in
   the recommended specification strategy; to be able to show
   the user the reasoning used in the analyses.

The main features of the first Prospex prototype PrOspex include
the creation of specifications and formatted specification
documents, knowledge-based analyses of specifications to reveal
possible errors and poor quality, knowledge-based consultation in
specification strategies, explanations of the analysis reasoning
and a simple on-line HELP. In PrOspex, the creation activities
are supported by a graphics toolkit program called Analyst

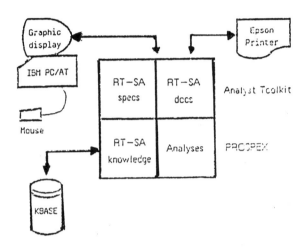

Figure 1 The structure of Prospex

Toolkit (which is a trademark of Yourdon Inc) (Analyst Toolkit Users Manual 1985), whereas the other functions belong to PrOspex (Figure 1). The latter is referred to as PrOspex in the rest of this paper.

The interface between Analyst Toolkit and PrOspex is based on so-called extract files which are specifications converted to ASCII coupling listings by the Analyst Toolkit´s command "dgsex". This feature of Analyst Toolkit makes it possible to manipulate further the specifications created by using it. In the case of PrOspex, the manipulation means a conversion to a set of Prolog facts and the analyses.

Specification Method Supported

PrOspex supports the Structured Analysis for Real-Time Systems (RT-SA) method and specifically its logical models:

1. an environmental model consisting of a context diagram and an event list;
2. a behavioural model consisting of data flow diagrams, state transition diagrams and entity-relationship (e-r) diagrams;
3. written specifications of the type textual specification, data composition specification and data element specification (Figure 2) (Ward and Mellor 1985a,b).

The Analyst Toolkit program has been developed to support the RT-SA method.

MODEL	SUB-MODEL	IMPLEMENTATION DEPENDENCE	OBSERVABILITY OF BEHAVIOUR	TOOL DESCRIPTION	DEVELOPMENT PHASE	CONTENTS
L O G I C A L	ENVIRON-MENTS	IMPLEMENTATION INDEPENDENT	NON-TRANSPARENT	CONTEXT DIAGRAM + EVENT LIST	ANALYSIS	SYSTEM SCOPE FOCUSING ON EXTERNAL EVENTS
	BEHAV-IORAL			NETWORK GRAPHIC (DFD, ERD, STD) + TEXTUAL SPECIFI-CATIONS		IMPLEMENTATION-FREE USER-OBSERVABLE REQUIREMENTS

Figure 2 The RT-SA models supported by PrOspex

The context of Analyst Toolkit consists of a graphics display including a mouse for inputting commands and RT-SA specifications and outputting the results. A local line printer is used to print out specifications and formatted specification documents, and a data dictionary that can be used to save, define and retrieve all names and data composition specifications is optional (Analyst Toolkit Users Manual 1985).

The Behaviour of PrOspex

The behaviour of Analyst Toolkit is not described in detail here; its properties are described in Analyst Toolkit Users Manual (1985). The main functions of Analyst Toolkit include the creation of RT-SA specifications and specification documents. A "warning-if-not-connected-or-named" type verification of the specifications created is also available, as well as on-line HELP windows. There are two operation types that can be used to create specifications: a free-formatted sketch mode and a formal RT-SA specification mode. Furthermore, data flow diagrams and state transition diagrams can be created by using the same methodology files, whereas e-r diagrams require their own.
  The functions of PrOspex are activated from a small menu system. The main menu is used to display the basic operations of "analyse", "consult in strategy", "explain analysis reasoning", "help", "return to the Prolog Interpreter" and "return to the DOS operating system". The selected functions are checked before they are activated (Figure 3).

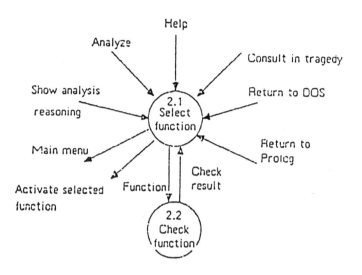

Dfd #: 2.1

Dfd Name: Select function

Author: VSe

Date: 30.01.86

Figure 3 The data flow diagram selected PrOspex function

Because return functions are trivial they are not described here.
Th HELP function is also very straightforward. Help texts can be
shown on the following topics: "tools available", "using Analyst
Toolkit", "using PrOspex", "RT-SA method" and "related
literature".
 The reasoning behind the knowledge-based analyses can in PrOspex
be shown either in connection with the analyses themselves or
separately, such that the knowledge in use is shown in its
external English-like production rule format.

Knowledge-based analyses

The analyses (Figure 4) are selected and checked from their own
menu.   The analyses supported are "communicability", "trace
ability", "scope", "completeness", "consistency", "redundancy",
"logical malfunctions", "naming" and "uniqueness" of the RT-SA
specifications. These are defined as:

1. communicability: a check of the quality of the object as far as its understanding is concerned, eg the number of subelements;
2. traceability: a check if the object can be traced via a tracing table to any named requirement in its charter;
3. scope: a check concerning cartain viewpoint limitations of a set of objects, eg whether the logical model also describes physical features;
4. completeness: a check whether the analysed object is complete in the sense that is described in the knowledge base;
5. consistency: an analysis to ensure that the object is in a balance with itself and other objects;
6. redundancy: a check to reveal redundant specifications;
7. logical malfunctions: a check to see that the object is free of some suspectable logical functions, eg data conversation errors;
8. naming: an analysis to check that the object is named and numbered according to the RT-SA conventions;
9. uniqueness: a check whether the object can be identified uniquely.

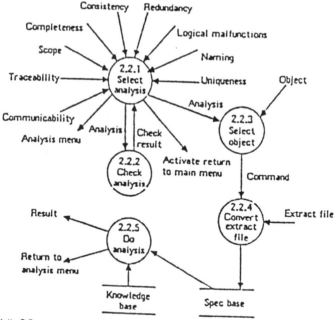

Dfd #: 2.2

Dfd Name: Select analysis

Authhor: VSe

Date: 30.01.86

Figure 4 The data flow diagram "selected analysis"

PrOspex is thus able to reveal mainly formal and logical defects
in the specification. The user has still his/her responsibility
for most of the stylistic aspects, as well as for the correction
of the erors revealed.

The extract files are converted to a set of Prolog facts to form
the current specification base to be analysed. The facts are
simple entities and relationships, such as "InputsTransformation
(TransformationName, TransformationId, FlowName, FlowType)". The
fact specifies that a named data or control flow is an input to a
named and numbered transformation in a data flow diagram. In the
second phase of development of PrOspex frames will be used for
the implementation of the specification base.

The analyses are performed after the conversion on the basis of
the RT-SA knowledge base, and their results are shown to the
user. The results are either analysis passed messages or error
messages of the three classes of a comment, a warning and an
error.

Consultation in strategy

A simple consultation of the RT-SA specification strategy is
available in PrOspex. The consultation is performed by displaying
the rules and facts concerning a specific topic from the three
viewpoints of "what", "why" and "how". Strategies related to
logical, environmental and behavioural models, as well as data
flow, state transition and e-r diagrams, can be consulted. The
consultation of the strategy of model levelling has also been
implemented.

Based on the event list, the data-transformation-driven, stored-
data-driven or state-transition-driven nature of the system can
be determined, and due to it the strategy of proceeding in the
development of the behavioural model proposed. The strategic
knowledge forms its own part of the knowledge base, different
from the analysis rules.

The knowledge in Prospex is organized to a couple of logical
substructures as described in Figure 5. The product knowledge
will, however, not be in use in the Prospex prototype. The
perceptual and conceptual knowledge is in the form of production
rules. The strategic knowledge exists currently only in its
external English-like form of production rules.

The rule database contains currently about 100 general rules but
can, however, easily be modified and extended.

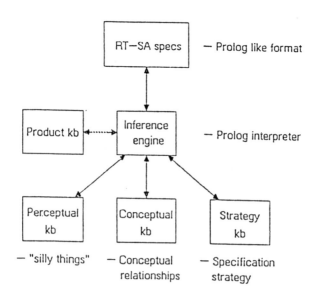

Figure 5 The knowledge types in PrOspex

Concluding Remarks

This paper has described a knowledge-based system Prospex, which supports the specification of embedded computer systems. A commercial toolkit has been used to assist in the creation of graphics specifications and formatted specification documents. The specification method in use has been selected on the basis of industrial requirements. The Prospex specification support system is capable of analysing specifications on the basis of its knowledge base, consulting in the specification strategy and explaining the analysis reasoning in use. These three basic functions are seen to meet the needs expressed by both the specification method developers and ordinary method users. The first prototype of Prospex has been implemented with IF Prolog. The knowledge-based nature of the system is claimed to enhance the usability of the original specification toolkit, while preserving its other useful features.

References

"Analyst Toolkit Users Manual" (1985) Yourdon Inc, New York.

ANSI/IEEE Std 729-1983 (1983) "Standard Glossary of Software Engineering Terminology", American National Standards Institute, The Institute of Electrical and Electronics Engineers.

Arango, G. (1984) "A Knowledge Engineering Perspective on Software Construction", Department of Information and Computer Science, University of California at Irvine.

Hayes-Roth, F. (1984) Knowledge based expert systems, "IEEE Computer" No. 17(10).

Huenke, H. (ed.) (1981) "Software Engineering Environments", North-Holland, Amsterdam.

Kowalski, R. (1984) AI and software engineering, "Datamation" No. 30(18).

Mizuno, Y. (1983) Software quality improvement, "IEEE Computer" No. 16(3).

Shaw, M. (1985) Scope and scale. The next challenges for software engineering, "Directions in Software Research", IBM-SISU Symposium, Stockholm, 16-18 September.

Ward, P.; Mellor, S.J. (1985a) "Structured Development for Real-Time Systems, Vol. 1. Introduction and Tools", Yourdon Press, New York.

Ward, P.; Mellor, S.J. (1985b) "Structured Development for Real-Time Systems, Vol. 2. Essential Modeling Techniques", Yourdon Press, New York.

A Plausible Inference Engine

J.P. Popchev and N.P. Zlatareva

Bulgarian Academy of Sciences, Sofia (Bulgaria)

RESUME: La conception d'un mecanisme plausible non-
monotone de sortie, qui pourrait fonctionner avec succes avec
des informations incompletes et incertaines, s'avere la tache
la plus importante a resoudre au cours de la creation des
systemes experts.

L'article examine une approche vers la conception d'un mecanisme de sortie semblable. Cette approche est developpee sur la
base des schemas d'inferences plausibles, proposes par G.Polya.
L'article examine aussi l'organisation des connaissances et
certaines fonctions principales, decrivant les schemas de
raisonnements plausibles les plus importants, ainsi que le
mecanisme de correction de la base de connaissances.

Mots cles: raisonnement plausible, schemas de raisonnement
                  plausible, systemes experts, systemes bases sur
                  des regles.

ABSTRACT: The building of nonmonotonic, plausible inference
mechanism, which would work successfully with incomplete and
uncertain information, is the most important problem, that must
be solved when creating expert systems.

The paper deals with an approach towards creating such an
inference mechanism. This approach is developed on the basis of
the human plausible reasoning schemes studied by G.Polya. Knowledge organization and some main functions, describing the most
important plausible reasoning schemes and debugging of the knowledge base, are presented.

Keywords: plausible reasoning, patterns (schemes) of
                 plausible reasoning, expert systems, rule-
                 based systems.

1.Introduction. The expert systems (ES) are a special
class of problem solvers which are characterized, most of all, by
the accentuating on the human style of reasoning in the
particular problem domain. This determines some specific requirements towards the inference engine by which they considerably
differ from the engines used in other types of problem solvers
(theorem provers, game programs,planning programs, etc.). Two are
the main reasons for this difference:
        (i) the problem domain-oriented knowledge (not only the
expert one, but most of all the conditions in which every
particular problem is solved) because of its incompleteness,
inconsistency, and even inaccuracy, does not allow the usage of
inference proving schemes;
        (ii) the accumulation and the modification of the know-
ledge base (KB) should be performed nonmonotonously. The mono-
tonicity and requirements for noncontroversity of the KB, characteristic for the classical logics (and the inference methods
based on them), do not allow adequate problem domain description.

Solutions to this basic for ES problem - building of nonmonotonic
plausible inference mechanism, which will work successfully with
incomplete, inconsistent and uncertain information - are seaked
in various directions. Reiter proposes a formalization based on
default logics (1), which works with rules of the type

        A(x1,....,xN):MB(x1,....,xN)

                C(x1,....,xN)

i.e. if A is true for particular value of the variables
x1,....,xN, and if B can be proposed (or in other words, it cannot
be prooved that B is false for them), then it can be concluded
that C is true for x1,....,xN.

McCarthy proposes another solution within the first-order logic
(2). He formulates the so called circumscription mechanism as a
rule which allows the program to "jump" to certain conclutions.

A detailed statement of several problems on the basis of the
model of endorsement is represenred in (3).

The paper deals with an approach towards creating a non-monotonic
inference mechanism, allowing work with incomplete and uncertain
information. This approach is developed on the basis of the human
plausible reasoning schemes studied by G.Polya (4). The general
structure of the knowledge used by the system, is described,
represented in the form of production rules and some main
functions, describing the most important plausible reasoning
schemes and debugging of the KB in the course of inference.

2. Patterns of plausible reasoning and their usage in the
inference engine. The most important condition for the arising of
nonmonotonicity in a given formal system is the principle impossibility to formulate a priori the whole information necessary
for solving a given problem. This means that the system from the
very begining works with incomplete and probably inaccurate
information which leads to the possibility that every new item of
knowledge could alter principally the course of reasoning, rejecting statements, true until this moment, and vice versa.
Generally the rejection of true statements is much more easier
than the contrary - to find the probability of a given statement
in the light of the new knowledge. The main reason for this, is
that the production systems controlling mechanism does not allow
activating of the rules, whose condition parts are not satisfied
in the KB. It carries out, to one or other extend the classical
proving schemes

$$\frac{A \rightarrow B, A}{B} \quad (1); \qquad \frac{A \rightarrow B, -B}{-A} \quad (2); \qquad \frac{A \rightarrow -B, B}{-A} \quad (3)$$

even when a probability mechanism is build-in (5). As such a
mechanism the most frequently used is the modified rule of Bayes,
which does not change at all the monotonous character of the
inference, because it supposes, that the given condition should
be unified with the particular statement in the KB. This is
carried out according to the scheme

$$\frac{A \rightarrow B, A \text{ is true with some degree of belief}}{B \text{ is true with value C, defined according to the rule of Bayes}}$$

If the value received for B is less than a defined tolerance
value, B is interpreted as false. In this way, it is not possible
to distinguish the cases when condition A is realy not satisfied,
because the KB is incomplete and part of its statements probably
are not enough reliable. This problem can be solved if the conditions are arranged accordingly using the input of new heuristic
information, for their role in the course of inference. Hence,
varying plausible schemes can be obtained.

$$\frac{A \rightarrow B, A \text{ is true with some degree of belief}}{B \text{ is propable}} \quad (1')$$

$$\frac{A \rightarrow B, B \text{ is true with some degree of belief}}{A \text{ is more propable}} \quad (2')$$

$$\frac{A \longrightarrow \lnot B, \ \lnot B \text{ is true with some degree of belief}}{A \text{ is more propable}} \qquad (3')$$

reaching the final one:

$$\frac{A \longrightarrow B, \ A \text{ is false or much less propable}}{B?}$$

Polya interpretes this scheme in the following way: when a probable reason for an assumption is destroyed, our confidence in this assumption can only diminish (4). Therefore, B becomes less propable. Is this scheme useful for an inference engine, though it is not controversial to the common sense reasoning? And if yes, under what conditions and when?

Further we will discuss the problem in the context of a particular realization, and we will study the possibility for developing an inference mechanism, using varying plausible inference schemes. We will also illustrate some of the main LISP-functions, realizing this schemes.

3. Knowledge organization. The KB organization is shown on fig.1. It consists of two parts - constantly changing (left) part, playing the role of working memory and containing all possible statements with their characteristics, and an unchanging (right) part, playing the role of constant memory and containing the inference rules. The structure of the statements describing the declarative knowledge is shown of fig.2. Every statement contains three sublists as follows:

     - sublist 1 is a predicate, describing the statement;

     - sublist 2 consists of identificators, showing as a result of what this statement is input in the KB. The identificators can have different meanings, as for example: T shows that the statement is input by the user, and is defined as a truth; F, the statement is defined by the user as false; N, the statement is input without defining its propability; I, the statement is a conclusion of an inference rule; D, the statement is obtained as a result of computations; A, the statement is a recommendation, received from the metacontrol and etc.;

     - sublist 3 contains the formalized information about the probability of a given fact. It consists of two parts (sublists). The first contains elements which are in favour of the probability of the fact, and the second - elements which are against it. This information is constantly actualized in the course of inference, which demands the probability of the statement to be

reevaluated before every usage. The realization of this process
is one of the most difficult elements of the inference mechanism.
In the system this problem is solved through arranging the
characteristics for and against the given statement and input of
additional heuristic information for their evaluation. At this
evaluation the statement is interpreted as a conclusion of some
"simple" rule, the conditions of which can be evaluated considerably easier. This is carried out in a specialized supporting KB
(fig.1). The supporting KB can contain facts and rules out of the
problem domain, but important for decision making in it. In
appendix 1 some basic functions of the KB debugging procedure are
shown.

The structure of the production rules describing the procedural
knowledge is given in fig.3. The indicator is an atom, which
determines the place of the rule in the chain of rules. It can be
evaluated in the process of inference on the basis of previously
formulated heuristics, according to the expert's preferences.

The conditional part of the rules has the form:

       <conditional part> := ((<name of identifying function>
                                (condition 1) <type>)

                        . . .

                               (<name of identifying function>
                                (condition n) <type>))

At this stage, in the inference mechanism three types of identifying functions are realized, processing   the following
conditions:

        - function for processing the conditions - facts. It
checks the type of condition and activates the probability check
procedure;

        - function for processing the conditions - negations. If
a given condition is defined as a condition - negation it is
interpreted according to the weak rule for the excluded third,
which has the form $T \rightarrow -A \lor - -A$ and is, that one statement is
true, if its negation is true, i.e. this statement is characterized with the identificator F, or in the KB no information
proving that its negation is not true is contained;

        - function for processing the conditions - questions. The
conditions - questions are unified with statements, which, at a
given moment might be not contained in the KB. Then they are
asked as questions to the user of the system.

The conditions themselves are predicates, which are unified with particular statements. Three types of conditions exist: obligitory, necessary and informative, these we will study bellow together with the inference schemes, according to which they are checked, and some of the main LISP-functions through which they are realized.

- Obligatory conditions. If the production contains obligatory conditions, they are the first to be evaluated and matched by the control, when studying the applicability of the production. The activating of the production is impossible, if the given condition does not exist in the KB (i.e. the list, characterizing the particular fact in the left part of the KB is NIL), or it is not supported by enough information for its probability. This can mean that the system, until this moment does not dispose with the information, necessary to term the fact true or probable enough. In this case the inference is carried out in accordance to the proof scheme (1), or its modification

```
A --> B, A is quite probable and therefore
         A can be accepted as true
----------------------------------------------
B is true with very high degree of belief
```

Further some of the most important functions for retrieval of obligatory conditions according to the above scheme are shown.

```
(DEFUN OBLF (LAMBDA (CL2)          *check the condition's
  ((AND                             reliability if it deals
     (MEMBER1 CL2 CHAR)             with the function for
     (EQ 'T (CAADR CH)) ) T)        processing facts*
  ((AND
     (MEMBER1 CL2 CHAR)
     (NOT (EQ 'T (CAADR CH)))
     (NULL (CAR (LAST (CAR (LAST CH)))))) )
   (SETQ IDEN 'I) )
  ((AND
     (MEMBER1 CL2 CHAR)
     (NOT (NULL (CAR (LAST (CAR (LAST CH))))))) )
   (PROG1
     (SETQ IDEN 'I)
     (SETQ NEG (CONS (CAR (LAST (CAR (LAST CH)))) NEG))
   ) ) ))
```

```
(DEFUN OBLN (LAMBDA (CL))          *check the condition's
  ((OR                              reliability if it deals
    (NOT (MEMBER1 CL CHAR))         with the function for
    (AND                           processing negations*
      (MEMBER1 CL CHAR)
      (NOT (EQ 'T (CAADR CH)))
      (NULL (CAR (LAST CH))) ) ) T) ))

(DEFUN OBLA (LAMBDA (CL)            *check the condition's
  (ASK CL)                         reliability if it deals
  ((OR                             with the functions for
    (NUMBERP ANSWER)               processing questions*
    (EQ 'YES ANSWER)
    (EQ 'NOT ANSWER) ) T) ))
```

where in the list CHAR the current content of the KB is
contained. The functions FACT, NOTF, ASK1 for retrieval of the
respective type of condition, distinguish the type of condition
and activate the respective procedure for check of the latter,
which is performed by the functions OBLF, OBLN and OBLA.

If the production is lacking obligatory conditions, it is
considered as a "week" one from information point of view. Its
conclusion is characterized as a newly inferred fact with
comparative probability. This means that if the production
conditions are satisfied, the conclusion will not be interpreted
as a truth, but only as a reliable fact. If the conclusion
already exists in the KB its probability considerably increases.
The production might be "weak" and due to the fact that it
describes a chunk of quite general knowledge or because it does
not characterize enough the case under consideration. In this way
the classical example can be interpreted:

$$\forall x(bird\ (x) \longrightarrow fly\ (x)),\ bird\ (penguin)$$

$$fly\ (penguin)$$

where the rule that every bird flyes is so general that the
degree of belief of its conclusion - the penguin flyes - is not
absolute.

   - Necessary conditions. The probability of the necessary
condition can considerably increase the "activeness" of a rule.
This corresponds to the probability scheme (1'). But, at the same
time the production can be activated, if the condition is not
reliable enough or even if it does not exist in the KB. The
latter means that it cannot be considered neither as a truth, nor
as a false one. The given production cannot be activated only, if

in the KB this condition is defined as a false one, i.e.

```
A --> B, -A, where A is a necessary condition
---------------------------------------------
              B is false
```

The function checking the reliability of the necessary conditions
has the form

```
(DEFUN NESF (LAMBDA (CL)
  ((AND
      (MEMBER1 CL CHAR)
      (EQ 'T (CAADR CH)) )
   (SETQ POS (CONS (LIST RULENAME CL) POS)) )
  ((AND
      (MEMBER1 CL CHAR)
      (NOT (EQ 'F (CAADR CH))) ) T)
  ((NOT (MRMBER1 CL CHAR))
   (SETQ NEG (CONS (LIST RULENAME CL) NEG)) ) ))
```

where the list CH contains the new statements obtained as a result from the application of a given rule; in the list POS information emphasizing the advantages of a given state is accumulated
and in the list NEG- information against its reliability. At this
stage this information is organized in the form of sublists with
the following structure

```
(<rule indicator> <statement>).
```

   - Informative conditions. If the informative condition is
satisfied, the reliability of the conclusion is increased. Simultaneously, if the KB does not contain a statement, with which the
latter can be unified, the reliability of the conclusion remains
unchanged. If the condition is not true, or it is much less
probable, the reliability of the conclusion only diminishes
according to the scheme

```
A --> B, -A, where A is informative condition
---------------------------------------------
              B is less probable
```

which is described by the following function

```
(DEFUN INFF (LAMBDA (CL)
  ((AND
      (MEMBER1 CL CHAR)
      (NOT (EQ 'F (CAADR CHAR))) )
   (SETQ POS (CONS (LIST RULENAME CL) POS)) )
  ((NOT (MEMBER1 CL CHAR)) T)
```

```
((AND
   (MEMBER1 CL CHAR)
   (EQ 'F (CAADR CHAR)) )
 (SETQ NEG (CONS (LIST RULENAME CL) NEG)) ) ))
```

The introduction of conditions ranging in importance and infor-
mativness is not controversial to the common sense reasoning,
used by a human being. Analysing a situation, one does not
consider equally important all its elements, and even does not
consider them simultaneously - in the begining one settles within
the bounds of those elements which he considers to be most
important for making a particular decision. Vice versa, the
absence of a fact can affect considerably the final conclusion,
while the absence of another one - might not affect it.

The production rule conclusion has the following structure:

```
<conclusion> := ( (<identificator>(statement 1))
                  ...
                  (<identificator>(statement n)) )
```

where the identificator shows which of all possible statements,
arising from the conclusion should be evaluated in the context of
the already performed analysis of the conditions reliability.

Further, some of the basic functions for the conclusion retrieval
are shown:

```
(DEFUN THENUSE (LAMBDA (THENPART)
  ((NULL (CAAR THENPART))
   (THENPR (CADAR THENPART)) )
  (LOOP
    ((EQ ANSWER (CAAR THENPART))
     (THENPR (CADAR THENPART)) )
    (SETQ THENPART (CDR THENPART)) ) ))

(DEFUN THENPR (LAMBDA (CONCLUSION)
  ((NULL CONCLUSION)
   (REMEMBER1) )
  ((PROSL (CAR CONCLUSION))
   (THENPR (CDR CONCLUSION)) ) ))

(DEFUN PROSL (LAMBDA (CONCLUSION)
  (EVAL CONCLUSION) ))
```

If the conclusion generates a new statement, it is recorded in
the respective type in the KB. But if an a priory information
about the reliability of this statement exists, the content of
the characterizing lists is changed, as the new components,

corresponding to the particular conclusion are added. This might
lead to considerable alteration in the statement reliability, and
to force the inference mechanism to "re-evaluate" its work (in
case that a true or enough reliable until this moment statement
becomes false in the light of the new knowledge).

Additional information, which is recorded in the list EXPLANE,
can be added to every rule. This information allows the user to
receive informal answer to the question why this particular rule
is preferred; wether there exist any restrictions which should be
taken into consideration, if the respective rule is used. This
information has significance for the explanation mechanism.

   4. Control organization. Several peculiarities of the
inference mechanism control were already shown in the previous
section, for this reason, in this section we will point out only
the general work scheme of the control. It includes three main
levels:

   - meta level, containing controlling heuristics,
represented in the form of production rules. The meta-rules
contain only obligatory conditions, i.e. they realize only
inference prooving schemes. Due to this reason their conclusions
are input in the KB as statements with meaning T. If such a
statement already exists in the KB, its sublists 2 and 3 are
modified, and it is interpreted further as a truth. This is
performed by function OBRCHAR (see Appendix 1).

   - main level,

   - supporting level.

All the necessary information - declarative and procedural - is
organized in the so-called main KB, which (provisionaly) consists
of two parts: constantly changing (left) part, containing the
information part of the inference schemes, and unchanging (right)
part, containing the implications themselves. The KB is
structured in the form of separate moduli, any of which
corresponds to some limited "subdomain" of the problem domain.
The activating of a particular module is performed by the meta-
control, where the problem is analyzed. The inference in the
general KB is forward chaining. The sequence for choice of the
rule is defined by the type of their conditions, as well as by
the corresponding to them indicators. If several rules have equal
chances to be activated, the rule which arises the strongest
conclusion, is chosen among them. The strenght of the conclusion
is defined by the fact wether the statement already exists in the
KB, and if yes, then what is its reliability. The more the
reliability of a given statement is proved or negated, the
stronger the conclusion is considered.

To each of the moduli in the general KB corresponds one supporting and one help KB (fig.1). The former contains information, which could render, if this is necessary, the conditions in the respective module, i.e. it plays the role of a learning subsystem for this module. The latter contains information rendering additionaly the solution obtained, and in this way the subsystem can be interpreted as explanatory subsystem to this module. The search in the supporting KB is backward chaining, while the search in the help KB is forward chaining.

5. Conclusion. The discussed plausible inference mechanism is realized in muLISP for IBM PC. Beside the described plausible inference schemes, modifications of the latter are intended to be implemented, which is aiming at extending the capabilities of the inference mechanism for distinguishing and manipulating with information differing in degree of reliability.

References:

1. Reiter, R. – A logic for default reasoning, Artificial Intelligence, 13, 1980.

2. McCarty, J. Curcumscription – A form of non-monotonic reasoning, Artificial Intelligence, 13, 1980.

3. P. Cohen, Heuristic Reasoning about Uncertainty: An Artificial Intelligent Approach, Pitman Publ.Inc., 1985.

4. G. Polya, Mathematics ans Plausible Reasoning, Princeton Univ. Press, 1968.

5. R. Duda, P. Hart, N. Nilsson – Subjective Bayesian method for rule-based inference systems. The information technology series, vol.VI Artificial Intelligence (ed. O. Firschein), AFIPS PRESS, 1985.

```
(DEFUN DEBUGKB (LAMBDA (A1 A)
  ((NULL A1)
    (SETQ CHAR1 NIL) )
  ((MEMBER1 (CAAR A1) A)
    (PROG1
      (DEBCH (CAR A1) A)
      (DEBUGKB (CDR A1) A) ) )
  ((NOT (MEMBER1 (CAAR A1) A))
    (PROG1
      (SETQ CHAR (CONS (CAR A1) A))
      (DEBUGKB (CDR A1) A) ) ) ))

(DEFUN DEBCH (LAMBDA (CL CHAR1)
  ((EQUAL (CAR CL) (CAAR CHAR1))
    (OBRCHAR CL (CAR CHAR1)) )
  ((DEBCH CL (CDR CHAR1))) ))

(DEFUN OBRCHAR (LAMBDA (CL B1CHAR)
  ((AND
      (EQ 'T (CAADR CL))
      (EQ 'T (CAADR B1CHAR)) )
    (SETQ CLCHAR (LIST (CAR B1CHAR) (CADR B1CHAR) (LIST (CONS
      (CAAAR (LAST CL)) (CAAR (LAST (B1CHAR))) NIL))) )
  ((AND
      (EQ 'T (CAADR CL))
      (NULL (CAR (LAST (CAR (LAST B1CHAR))))) )
    (SETQ CLCHAR (LIST (CAR B1CHAR) '(T) (LIST (CONS (CAAAR
      (LAST CL)) (CAAR (LAST B1CHAR))) NIL))) )
  ((AND
      (EQ 'F (CAADR CL))
      (EQ 'F (CAADR CL)) )
    (SETQ CLCHAR (LIST (CAR B1CHAR) (CADR B1CHAR) (LIST NIL (CONS
      (CAAR (LAST (CAR (LAST CL)))) (CAR (LAST (CAR (LAST
      B1CHAR)))))))) )
  ((AND
      (EQ 'F (CAADR CL))
      (NULL (CAAR (LAST B1CHAR))) )
    (SETQ CLCHAR (LIST (CAR B1CHAR) '(F) (LIST NIL (CONS (CAAR
      (LAST (CAR (LAST CL)))) (CAR (LAST (CAR (LAST B1CHAR)))))
      ))) )
  (PROG1
    (SETQ CLCHAR (LIST (CAR B1CHAR) (CONS (CAADR CL)
      (CADR B1CHAR)) (LIST (APPEND POS (CONS (CAAAR (LAST CL))
      (CAAR (LAST B1CHAR)))) (APPEND NEG (CONS (CAAR (LAST
      (CAR (LAST CL)))) (CAR (LAST (CAR (LAST B1CHAR)))))))))
      ) )).
```

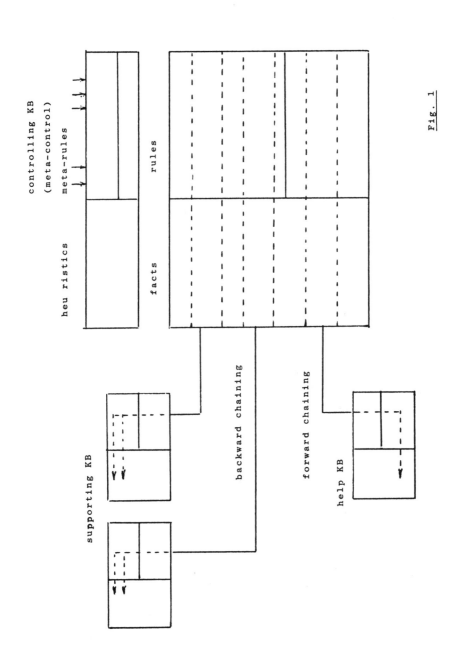

Fig. 1

statement i			
sublist 1	sulist 2	sublist 3	
predicate, describing statement i	identificator 1 .... identificator k	<element 1> .... <element n>	<element 1> .... <element n>
		<rule name> <statement>	

Fig. 2

rule j			
rulename	if-part	then-part	explane-part
<indicator>	<element 1> .... <element n>	<element 1> .... <element k>	<text>
	<function name> <condition> <condition type>	<identificator> <statement>	

Fig. 3

Analogies as a Case Study in Non Fregian Inference Strategies

J. Van Dormael and T. Tessier

State University of Ghent (Belgium)

ABSTRACT

Giving a description of reasoning by analogy in Logic and the Cognitive Sciences, we point at the difficulties created by reconstructing this 'reasoning process' on valid reasoning. Offering another perspective, based on counterfactual reasoning, we discuss some major differences concerning the constraints placed upon the representation of base and target situation by looking at some well known examples of reasoning by analogy in contexts of scientific discovery.

KEYWORDS: Analogy / Knowledge Representation / Inference strategies

1. The 'logic' of Reasoning by analogy.

One of the problems with the notion of analogy is understanding
exactly what it is.(2) At the most basic level an analogy is a
relation of resemblance between two things. These things may be
concepts, objects, properties of objects etc. Accordingly, an
analogy is often described as a statement of the following form:

   'x is to y as z is to w'

For which the mathematical or geometrical proportion:

$$\frac{x}{y} = \frac{z}{w}$$

serves as a paradigmatical example. Given this, and instead of
trying to formulate a concise summary of the entire field, we'll
give a general account of the different approaches in logic and
the cognitive sciences.

In logic and especially INFORMAL LOGIC, reasoning by analogy,
studied in contexts of argumentation,(3) is seen as an INFERENCE
RULE and its problem as a problem of validity. Basically we can
distinguish two different approaches: the induction-oriented and
the deduction-oriented approach.

In the **induction-oriented approach**, (4) reasoning by analogy is
treated as a kind of inductive reasoning and described as an
inference rule of, for example the following form:

   object 1 has the properties $(x_1 \ldots x_n)$
   object 2 has the properties $(x_1 \ldots x_{n-1})$

   (therefore) object 2 has the properties $(x_1 \ldots x_n)$

A characteristic of these inference rules (as well as of
inductive inferences) is the fact that even given the truth of
the premisses (statements about the number of properties in
common or about the degree of similarity between two
particulars), the conclusion isn't necessarily true. The
conclusion only states that there is an increase in similarity
between the two objects. Nothing justifies the inference that
they have a further property in common.

Side-stepping the problem of how to measure similarity, a
generally recognized difficulty with reasoning by analogy on this
account is the formulation of the conditions justifying the
conclusion. That is, under what conditions is the conclusion
justified given the truth of the premisses. For example consider
the following situation: Two cars are known to come from the same

assembly line at approximately the same time. They are known to be identical in structure and composition and one of them is black. Now as Weitzenfeld (1984) asks, 'does this justify the inference that the similar car is also black?' Suppose there is a third car, sharing the common properties of the other two, but known to be yellow. Does this justify that the unknown car is yellow? Clearly not! There must be a further link between the premisses and the conclusion. For example the fact that there is a relation between the colour of a car and the time it came from the assembly line.

Given this problem and its answer, reasoning by analogy is considered as a kind of deductive inference rule. In this **deduction-oriented** approach reasoning by analogy is seen as an inference rule in which the premisses are often uncertain but the form of the argument is seen as valid.(6)
Consequently the problem of validity is reduced to finding the implicit premisses which render the inference valid, better, deductively valid. These implicit premisses, seen as depending on general vague knowledge and normally tacit in the processes of drawing inferences, determine which conclusion can be drawn.

On this account an analogy is seen as a statement about **the structural similarity** , or even isomorphism, between two objects. Essentially two objects are taken to be structurally similar (using Gentner's terminology) if there is an overlap in attributive properties (one-place predicates) but also, and more importantly, an overlap in relational properties (multi-place predicates).
And an isomorphism is a relation between two structures, each of which consists of a set of elements (a set of elements is called a variable) and a set of relations defined on those elements. Two structures are then seen as isomorphic when there is a mapping of the elements of one structure onto the elements of the other such that all the relations are preserved. That is, every element, variable and relation in one structure is assigned a counterpart in the other in such a way that (1) an element is an element of the counterpart variable and (2) a relation holds between elements if and only if its counterpart holds between the counterparts of the elements.
Accordingly, reasoning by analogy is described as an inference rule of the following form:

object 1 has the properties (x1 ... xn)
object 2 has the properties (x1 ... xn-1)
There exists a relation R between (x1 ... xn-1) and xn.

(therefore) object 2 has the properties (x1 ... xn)

In this inference rule it is the third premiss which determines which valid conclusion to infer.

For example: Suppose you are trying to convince someone that cats can swim. Assume the person knows the fact that they have several properties in common and the fact that dogs can swim. Then you can convince your opponent by pointing at the relation between, for example, the structure of their legs and the swimming which determines the conclusion.

In the study of reasoning by analogy as a **psychological process** the central question takes the following form: what are the (computational) mechanisms underlying this reasoning process? Surprising as it may seem, it is the deduction-oriented approach, known as the **structure base account**, which is the dominant view in exploring the process of reasoning by analogy.(7)

In THE COGNITIVE SCIENCES, reasoning by analogy, predominantly studied in problem-solving contexts, is seen as a transfer of knowledge from a known situation - the base domain - to a novel, less known, situation - the target domain.

Reasoning by analogy is explained on the basis of a mapping process establishing structural similarity between the base and target domain. As in the foregoing the notion of analogy is seen as a statement involving structural similarity with functional import.(8)
Accordingly, reasoning by analogy is described as a process of constructing an initial partial mapping between the elements of both domains and 'deducing' an extension of the initial mapping. We must mention the fact that Cognitive Scientists often stress the non-serial character of the process of analogical problem-solving. For example "The use of analogy in problem-solving appears to be a complex and interactive process envoluing the retrieval of plausable base analogs, assessement of the causal relations in the base, reformulation of the target problem, tentative attempts at partial mapping, integration with other problem-solving heuristics" (Holyoak, 1982, p.225).

In explaining this process much attention has been given to the formulation and explanation of how the initial partial mapping relation is established.
At this point, cognitive scientists introduce the notion of a **scheme**. Such schemes are mental representations of both the base and target domains. Different options are taken concerning how knowledge is represented and which knowledge representation language is cognitively plausible. But given the fact that analogies are seen as statements about the structural similarity between objects of different domains, it isn't difficult to understand that the array of potential knowledge representation forms revolve around one fundamental representation structure: **a graph**.

Once a representation of the base and target domain **given** , an initial partial mapping between both domains is established by abstracting the identities. For this reason an **abstraction operator** is introduced. The function of this operator is to separate each concept into a "core meaning" which is identical across the mapped elements and a "residual meaning" specific to the particular analogue. Those meaning components common to both parts can then be translated into an independent scheme by a process of eliminative induction. This process involves deleting the differences between analogues while preserving their commonalities.(9) This scheme can then be seen as an abstract category of which the specific analogues are instances.
Often computational models assume, a priori, the existence of such an independent scheme. For a recent example see Welsch and Jones (1986), in which this scheme, called the background knowledge tree, serves as a means for determining the similarity between objects.

The central idea behind this approach (apart from the constraints laid upon "the representation language") is the fact that the process of finding similarities is essentially a process of establishing an identity at a higher level of abstraction (by comparison of the descriptions —often semantic representations of words — of the things between which an analogy is 'perceived'(10)) resulting in a more abstract representation of both situations or domains.
Side-stepping the problems generated by postulating another necessary representation and its abstracting operation (e.g. at what level of abstraction must there be an identity?) it can be said (as Weitzenfeld (1984) noted) that analogical reasoning is modelled on deductive reasoning in the sense that the analogical reasoning process is reconstructed as a process of finding 'arguments' (identities) to formulate the premisses (i.e. statements about the structural similarity of the two analogues) as true, on the basis of which a deduction (the extended mapping) is a valid deduction.

It is our view that given the importance of analogies in contexts of discovery, its problem isn't in the first place a problem of validity or justification. Instead of explaining analogical reasoning by giving a reconstruction of the process of **valid** reasoning, resulting in the postulation of different representations and operations, an account must be given of how analogies function as a means for (what Knorr-Cetina (1981) calls) a **'recontextualisation'** of objects.
In the following we'll try to formulate another description of analogical reasoning by giving an example, used by Gick and Holyoak (1982) as a typical illustration of analogical problem solving.

2. Analogical thinking, another perspective ?

In an experiment known as "Lori's Magic Carpet" a four-year-old girl was asked to solve a problem after being told a superficially dissimilar story describing the problem and its solution.
The story, told to Lori, was that a genie, who wanted to move his house from one bottle to another, moved his jewels from one bottle to another by commanding his magic carpet to roll itself into a tube and placing it as a hollow bridge between the bottles.
After being told this story, Lori was asked to move balls from one bowl to another (seated she couldn't reach the empty bowl; on the table with the bowls, other objects were placed, including a heavy sheet of paper).

According to Gick and Holyoak one of Lori's first reactions was to say "Let's pretend they are real jewels" (the balls, that is). After considering a couple of objects on the table, she looked at the sheet of paper and said, "that will be a magic carpet". She then laughed as she picked it up, rolled it, and asked the experimenter to help tape it. "That's the way the genie did it", she exclaimed as she rolled the ball through her newly constructed tube". "I did it like the genie". (Holyoak, 1982, p. 200).

Following Gick and Holyoak analogical problem solving involves four steps, which Lori's protocol illustrates.

1. A mental representation of the base and target problems must be constructed;

2. The potential analogy must be noticed; i.e., same aspects of the target must serve as a retrieval cue that reminds the person of the base;

3. An initial partial mapping must be found between the elements of the two analogues;

4. and finally, the mapping must be extended.

But on the basis of the protocol another description of analogical problem solving can be given (reducing the expression to its essentials, making things more clear without affecting our argument):

1. if the balls are the jewels then the genie moved the balls from one bottle to another by using his magic carpet.

2. if the paper is the magic carpet then the genie moved the balls from one bottle to another by using the paper.

3. if I (Lori) am the genie then I (Lori) move the balls from one bottle to another by using the paper.

Seen from this perspective, Lori solved the problem by formulating an identity between objects and substituting one for the other 'terms' (objects) in the respective sentences of the story. The formulated statements have the following characteristics:

1. they are a formulation of Leibniz's law of identity of indiscernibles (s=t ⊢ Y (s/t); if two terms are identical you can substitute s for t in the sentence Y) in a conditional form.

2. the formulated conditionals are conditionals having antecedents and consequents which are false giving the actual beliefs. Such conditionals are called counterfactuals.

For counterfactuals a semantics was given by Stalnaker (1968) and Lewis (1973) based on a possible world approach.
The central idea behind this approach is the fact that in evaluating a conditional we add the antecedent of the conditional to our set of beliefs and consider whether the consequent of the conditional would be true if the revised set of beliefs were all true.

Given the possibility of seeing this semantic procedure as a description of the argumentative structure of this 'thinking' process and without postulating this description as the underlying psychological mechanism we want to point at what according to us, is a central difference with the foregoing approach.

From our perspective, an analogy between a target domain and a base domain is the **result** of reasoning with counteridenticals by substituting the counteridentical in the actual set of beliefs.
From this perspective, there is no need to postulate an inference scheme or different inferential representations of analogical reasoning. But also, reasoning by analogy doesn't involve a process of comparing two mental representations of situations. There is no need to postulate, at an initial state, nor in the whole process, an extensive representation of both domains.

Firstly, concerning the extensive 'structured' representation of the BASE DOMAIN.
Although we are dealing with the same problems relating to the question of how identities are 'found', there is a difference between this approach and the structure base account concerning the role identities play in this reasoning process.
Reducing the differences between both approaches by describing

the mapping process as a process of substitution (as Wellsch and Jones noted, 1986) and looking at this process from a conditional perspective the difference between both approaches is a difference in constraints placed upon the antecedent.

As noted before, the structure base account is oriented towards finding identities making the substitution 'possible'. In other words, the process of finding identities, conceived as necessary, is a process of finding true antecedents.

From our perspective, the identicals aren't necessarily true. They are counteridenticals. Even if we take the semantic interpretation of the material conditional, the truth of the antecedent is not a necessary condition for making the conditional true. From this perspective the process of reasoning by analogy can be seen as oriented not towards finding identities, but towards the formulation of true consequences.

Given the fact that in finding true antecedents, precise knowledge of the base domain (the condition of base specificity, see Gentner 1982, Holyoak 1982) is a prerequisite, it is our view that this reorientation reduces the constraints placed upon the representation of the base domain and the process of finding identities.

Moreover, the history of science gives us various examples of useful analogies which are not based on those characteristics assumed by the structure base account.

To give an example: various scientists have used the priciples of thermodynamics as restructuring principles in their own field. At that period, very few scientists had a clear idea of the situation. The interpretation of the law and its concepts were under constant flux. Meanwhile, this vagueness was certainly not an obstacle for the invention to serve as a base domain. Following Lyttkens in his study on analogical reasoning in the work of Thomas Aquinas, we could even say that this is a typical feature of analogical reasoning.(see Lyttkens,1952)

By way of remark we want to mention that the same conclusions can be drawn from Boyd's paper on scientific metaphors in 'Metaphor and Thought' (Ortony, 1983, pp.356-408). In analyzing metaphorical language in science, Boyd starts from the influential analysis of Max Black (see Models and Metaphors(1972), see also Ortony(1983)). The characteristics that Black has mentioned for literary metaphors (open-endedness, interaction between primary and secondary subject) are also features of scientific metaphors. In particular, their success does not depend on their conveying quite specific aspects of similarity. Indeed their users are typically unable to specify precisely the relevant aspects of similarity. So we may conclude that neither base specificity nor a structured representation of the base domain is necessary for analogical reasoning. But more important, specific metaphors share their open-endedness with literary metaphors. This means that they cannot be reduced to a literal statement of an underlying similarity . Metaphors have the capacity to develop again and again new similarities between both domains (or between primary and secondary subjects) on the basis of the associated implicatures of the secondary subject. This is certainly not a comparison between two definite representations underlying analogical reasoning.

A last difficulty with the traditional view concerns the ultimate possibility of structured representations of the base domain. In his book "The Principles of Scientific Thinking", R. Harré offers a detailed classification of models with respect to their relations, their sources and their subjects. We won't go into detail, let us merely note that "broadly speaking, models belong in two great categories depending on whether the subject of the model is also the source of the model, the homeomorphs; or whether the subject and the source differ, the paramorphs"(1970,p.40).
We are interested here in paramorphs. The relation of a paramorphic model to its source is threefold. Harré distinguishes singly connected, multiply connected and semi-connected paramorphs, depending on the quantity of sources which are used. An example of multiply connected paramorphs is "Bohr's atom", since " to construct it in the imagination, one must draw on the sciences of mechanics and electromagnetism, and the principles of these sciences are not explicable one in terms of the other."(1970,p.45) In other words, "our conception of it is built up by drawing upon the concepts of electromagnetism and mechanics....(I)t contains a mechanical impossibility." (ibid.,p.44) But if this is true, then it poses a problem for the traditional view: the question is, how does one reconcile the fact of an inexplicable structure with a 'structured' internal representation of the base domain?

Secondly, concerning the representation of the TARGET DOMAIN.

Even if the foregoing is incorrect and assuming a representation of the base domain(whatever this may be), the target domain is 'structured' in progress. After finding a counterfactual another counteridentical is formulated on the basis of the first.
After formulating the counteridentical 'let's pretend that they are really jewels' and substituting 'jewels' for balls in the original sentence, Lori is looking for another possible identity, given the already changed set of beliefs.

This view is in accordance with the often made use of analogies in less defined problem contexts. It isn't often the case that the problem or goal state is explicitly specified. Consider the following general situation, fairly common in contexts of scientific discovery: a scientist is confronted with many observations in a specific field which seem particulary confusing: empirical generalisation is very hard, so the scientist has difficulties in stating what the problem is; so the

first thing is to explain in a clear way what exactly the problem
is.   Only afterwards can there be room for finding a solution.
In other words, an essential part of the context of discovery is
the recontextualisation (often restructuring) of the field of
observation   in   a   given   domain;   this   involves   the
conceptualisation of novel problems to be solved and of course
the solution of these novel problems.

Given this it seems implausible to assume a   well-defined
representation of the target domain. The function of an analogy
is precisely the reformulation of the problem space, inducing a
way of solving the problem. As such the results of reasoning by
analogy are instead of solutions to problems, reformulations of
ill-defined problems anticipating a possible 'testable' solution.

Let's consider for the second time the example of "Bohr's   atom",
which is again revealing for our purpose. Similar to what has
been said of paramorphic models in relation to their source, the
relation of a model to its subject may be of three different
kinds, depending on how and why the model is used in relation to
its subject.   Sometimes a model is resorted to because it is not
at all clear where to look for the mechanisms of the process, or
-even worse- when our ontological categorisations do not admit of
the 'things' being observed. In this case " the initial and
final states may only be similar, and that similarity may indeed
extend only to the similarity between numbers as for instance in
electrical simulation of hydraulic networks..."(1970,p.44).
These models are called   'partial paramorphic analogues',
exemplified by Bohr's atom. It is clear that this model, as a
multiply connected paramorph was " a jerry-built contraption, on
the basis of its incidently requiring a massy particle, as the
electron was then understood, to change position without
traversing the intervening space or perhaps worse to traverse it
in no time at all."(ibid.,p.45) This situation shows clearly the
relevancy which analogical reasoning can have for the way we
conceptualize the world. The Bohr atom at least raised the
question of the absoluteness of Newtonian criteria of existence,
i.e. our conceptions of what it is to be an object.   Perhaps
entities of a new kind should be admitted to exist alongside
these presently conceived possible entities.   Analogical
reasoning can really help us to undertake that ontological task,
even if it can not fulfil that task alone.

Given the plausibility of our introduced perspective concerning
uses of analogy in contexts of discovery, it is certainly not the
the case that all problems are cleared away. Of central
importance is of course the formulation of an explanation of how
counteridenticals, although less important than the structure
base account resumes, are 'perceived'. A question which will
decide, among others, the fruitfulness of this approach.

Notes

1. See for example Hesse (1966), Boden (1977), Knorr-Cetina (1981).

2. See for example the differentiation between analogy and its neighbouring concepts such as similes and methaphors.

3. For an explicit statement see Perelman (1953).

4. See for example Keynes (1929).

5. See for example Mauthner (1923) for an explicit statement of this view.

6. This view has been held explicitly by Weitzenfeld (1984).

7. For similar examples see: Moore and Newell (1973), Hayes and Simon (1975), Chouraqui (1981) and more explicitly, Gick and Holyoak (1983).

8. Different positions are taken concerning the mapping of attributive properties and the kind of object-relations existing between the mapped elements. For an overview see Gick and Holyoak (1983).

9. See Winston (1980), for a computer implementation.

10. The view that 'all' analogical thinking depends on the comparison of descriptions is stated by M.Boden (1977) p.319.

Bibliography

1. Boden, M. (1977) - Artificial Intelligence and Natural Man, New York, Basic Books.

2. Boyd, R. (1983) - Metaphor and Theory Change: What is "Metaphor" for Metaphor Fore. In Ortony (Ed.), Metaphor and Thought, pp.356-408.

3. Chouraqui, E. (1981) - Contribution à l'étude théorique de la réprésentation des connaissances, le système symbolique ARCHES. Thèse d'Etat, Institut Nationale Polytechnique de Lorraine.

4. Evans, D. and Palmer, E. (1983) - Understanding Arguments. Department of Extra-Mural Studies, University College, Cardiff.

5. Gentner, D. (1982)- Are scientific analogies metaphors ? In D.S. Miall (Ed.), Metaphor: Problems and Perspectives, Sussex, Harvester Press.

6. Harré, R. (1970) – The Principles of Scientific Thinking. London. MacMillan.

7. Hayes, J. and Simon, H. (1975) – Understanding tasks stated in natural language. In D.R. Reddy (ed.), Speech Recognition, New York: Academic Press.

8. Holyoak, K. and Gick, M. (1980) – Analogical problem solving. In Cognitive Psychology 12, 306-355.

9. Holyoak, K. (1982) – Analogical thinking and human intelligence. In R.J. Sternberg (Ed.), Handbook of Human Intelligence, Vol. 2, Cambridge University Press.

10. Hesse, M. (1966) – Models and Analogies in Science, South Bend, Ind., University of Notre Dame Press.

11. Keynes, J. (1928) – A Treatise of Probability, London, MacMillan.

12. Knorr-Cetina, K. (1981) – The Manufacture of Knowledge: An Essay of the Constructivist and Contextual Nature of Science, Pergamon Press.

13. Lewis, D. (1973) – Counterfactuals, Cambridge, Massachusetts, Harvard University Press.

14. Lyttkens, H. (1952) – The analogy between God and the World, Uppsala.

15. Mauthner, F. (1923) – Wörterbuch der Philosophy, Leipzig, Felix Meiner.

16. Moore, J. and Newell, A. (1973) – How can Merlin understand? In L.W. Gregg (Ed.), Knowledge and Cognition, Hillsdale, N.J., Lawrence Erlebaum Associates.

17. Perelman, Ch. and Olbrechts-Tyteca, L. (1958) – La Nouvelle Rethorique, Traite de l'argumentation, Paris, Presses Universitaires de France.

18. Stalnaker, R. (1968) – A theory of conditionals. In N. Rescher (Ed.), Studies in Logical Theory, American Philosophical Quarterly Monograph Series, Nr. 2, Oxford, Blackwell.

19. Weitzenfeld, J. (1984) - Valid reasoning by analogy. In Philosophy of Science, 51 137-140.

20. Wellsch, K. and Jones, M., (1986) - Computational analogy. In Conference Proceedings ECAI-86.

21. Winston, P. (1980) - Learning and reasoning by analogy. In Communications of the ACM, 23, 689 - 703.

Learning in Automate Networks

F. Fogelman Soulie

Université de Paris VI, Paris (France)

P. Gallinari et S. Thiria

CNAM, Paris (France)

Y. Le Cun

ESIEE, Paris (France)

RESUME:

Nous présentons un algorithme général d'apprentissage sur réseaux d'automates. Les poids des connexions du réseau sont progressivement modifiés de façon à incorporer la connaissance fournie par les exemples présentés au réseau.
Le principe de l'algorithme est le suivant: pour chaque exemple présenté au réseau, on calcule l'écart entre la sortie calculée par le réseau et la sortie désirée; les poids sont modifiés de façon à décroître cet écart.
Un tel réseau réalise donc un apprentissage à partir d'exemples, il est capable de généralisation et de résistance au bruit. Les connaissances sont représentées de manière distribuée dans les connexions du réseau.

Mots clés: réseau d'automates, apprentissage, propagation de gradient, connectionnisme, parallélisme.

ABSTRACT:
We present a general learning algorithm for automata networks. The connection-weights of the network are updated so as to progressively incorporate the knowledge of examples which are presented to the network.
The algorithm works by associating to each example an output computed by the network. This output is compared to a desired output and the weights modified so as to decrease the discrepancy between computed and desired outputs associated to each example.
The network thus performs learning from examples, it exhibits generalizing capabilities and fault tolerance.
The representation of knowledge implemented by such networks is distributed in the connection-weights.

Keywords: automata network, learning, gradient-back propagation, connectionism, parallelism

1- INTRODUCTION

Learning has been a major concern in Artificial Intelligence since the 50's: as McCarthy puts it «our ultimate objective is to make programs that learn from their experience as effectively as humans do» [10]. At the beginning, the learning capabilities of adaptive systems (e.g. the perceptron) were investigated. The relative failure of this line of research and the parallel development of the AI tools showed, in the 70's, the necessity to include knowledge, domain dependent, in learning systems. Very recently, the search for more efficient expert systems has induced research work on more sophisticated learning strategies (by analogy, instruction...).

In this paper, we will present a new method for learning, which origin can be traced back to the early work on perceptrons and which is actively developing in the US under the name of "connectionism". This method is based on the use of large sets of computing elements (automata networks) inter-connected through links with adaptable weights.
We will present a general algorithm by which a network can "learn" through examples: the connection-weights are progressively adapted so as to encode -"learn"- the examples.
Section 2 presents the general theory of learning on automata networks, section 3 gives the particular case of 2-layered networks and section 4 the general case of multi-layered networks.

2- LEARNING ON AUTOMATA NETWORKS

The general problem of learning can be simply modeled by the following scheme [2]:

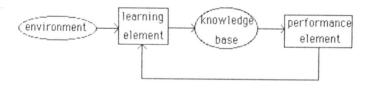

FIGURE 1: A SIMPLE MODEL OF LEARNING

The learning element is supposed to extract information from the environment so as to perform a given task. To do so, it makes use of a knowledge base which it progressively improves, both through new incoming information and from the results it obtains in performing the required task.

In the learning-from-examples situation, the system is provided with examples of how it should behave. It is then supposed to extract high level rules that will allow it to GENERALIZE these examples and perform correctly on cases never seen before. This view can be represented by the diagram shown in figure 2-1 [2].

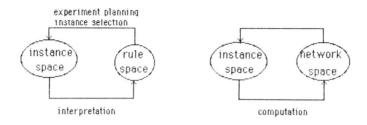

FIGURE 2-1   FIGURE 2-2

FIGURE 2: LEARNING FROM EXAMPLES

In the network-based approach to this problem, a network is presented with the examples and is supposed to extract the correct connection-weights that will allow it to further generalize. In fact, this approach consists in exploring a network space to select the network that will optimally generalize on the set of examples: this method can thus be depicted in a way very similar to the rule-based approach (see figure 2-2). The main difference here is that, instead of dealing with rules, logic-based representations and logical inferences, we use networks, distributed representation of knowledge in the connection-weights and computation.

Let us now present the general model of learning with automata networks.

An AUTOMATON is a computing element characterized by its internal state x and its transition function f. The state space will usually be $\mathbb{R}$ (not a finite space!) or $\{-1,+1\}$.

An AUTOMATA NETWORK (fig.3) is characterized by:
- the network architecture: number of automata, of layers and structure of connections.
- the transition functions of the automata.

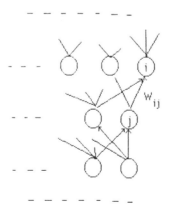

FIGURE 3: AUTOMATA NETWORK

In the following (for sake of simplicity), we will mainly use multi-layered networks with full connections between successive layers. Each automaton will use as its transition function a function of the weighted sum of its inputs, i.e. element i will compute its state x_i as a function of A_i, the weighted sum of the inputs x_j to i.

$$x_i = f(A_i) \tag{1}$$

where: $A_i = \sum_j W_{ij} x_j$ (2)

The coefficients W_{ij} are called the WEIGHTS of the connection from element j to element i. f will denote a smooth function, for example:

$$f(x) = a(e^{kx} - 1) / (e^{kx} + 1) \tag{3}$$

or a "step" function:

$$f(x) = \mathbf{1}\,[x] \tag{4}$$

where $\mathbf{1}\,[x] = 1$ if $x \geq 0$, -1 otherwise.

We will formalize the learning problem as follows: the examples are represented by vectors $\mathbf{x}$ in $\mathbf{R}^n$. We want the system to achieve the association between the examples $\mathbf{x}^1, \mathbf{x}^2, ..., \mathbf{x}^p$ and «correct» answers $\mathbf{y}^1, \mathbf{y}^2, ..., \mathbf{y}^p$, which are vectors in $\mathbf{R}^m$.

For example, in the problem of learning the tic-tac-toe game, the $\mathbf{x}^k$ will be the possible configurations of the game, and the $\mathbf{y}^k$ the corresponding outcome of the game (see [4]).

A network, with at least 2 layers, is used to compute, for each "input" vector $\mathbf{x}$, the ASSOCIATED output S. The "first" layer –the INPUT LAYER– has n automata, the "last" layer – the OUTPUT LAYER– m automata. S is computed as follows (fig.4):
- the states of the automata in the input layer are clamped in state $\mathbf{x}$.
- each automaton in the following layers computes its state by applying its transition function f as in equation (1).
All computations run sequentially from the second to the last layer ("propagation of states"), and in parallel in each layer.
The output S is then the state of the output layer.

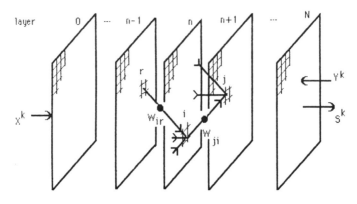

FIGURE 4: STATE DYNAMICS

Of course, for an arbitrary network -i.e. arbitrary weights W_{ij}- the computed output S associated to an example x^k will most probably be different from the desired output y^k. The network must hence be ADAPTED so as to realize the desired associations. The technique to achieve this adaptation is based on the minimization of a cost function, with a gradient algorithm.

- we start with a network where the architecture has been chosen according to the problem: for example, it will have a number of input cells that depends on the coding of the data, the structure of connections may help to encode some a-priori knowledge of the domain (for example, locality properties in images). The weights will initially be set at random, unless some previous experience has allowed to specify some convenient starting values. Let us denote $W(0)$ the initial weight vector. The learning session will consist in adapting the weights while keeping the network architecture fixed.

- examples are presented one at a time. Suppose example i is being presented at time t. The output S^k associated to x^k is computed by propagating x^k from the input to the output layer. Then S^k is compared to the desired vector y^k. The "error" function, which measures the discrepancy between S^i and y^k, is:

$$C[W(t)] = \sum_j [S^k_j - y^k_j]^2 \qquad (5)$$

The weight vector will be modified so as to decrease this cost, using an adaptive gradient method (Widrow-Hoff rule [16]):

$$W_{ij}(t+1) = W_{ij}(t) - \varepsilon(t) \, \partial C / \partial W_{ij} \qquad (6)$$

where $\varepsilon(t)$ is the iteration step at time t.

The problem is to compute the $\partial C / \partial W_{ij}$. Chain rule gives:

$$\partial C / \partial W_{ij} = \partial C / \partial A_i \, . \, \partial A_i / \partial W_{ij} = \partial C / \partial A_i \, . \, x_j$$

• for a cell i on the last layer and pattern x^k, we denote S^k_i the state of the cell in the associated output S. we then have:

$$\partial C / \partial A_i \ = 2[S^k_i - y^k_i] \, \partial S^k_i / \partial A_i$$
$$= 2[S^k_i - y^k_i]. \, f'(A_i)$$

Let us denote $g_i = \partial C / \partial A_i$. We thus have:

$$g_i = 2[S^k_i - y^k_i]. \, f'(A_i) \qquad (7)$$

• for the other layers:

$$\partial C / \partial A_i \ = \sum_h \partial C / \partial A_h \, . \, \partial A_h / \partial A_i$$

where h indexes the cells which receive their input from i. Hence, from (1) and (2):

$$\partial C / \partial A_i \ = \sum_h g_h \, . \, \partial A_h / \partial x_i \, . \, \partial x_i / \partial A_i$$
$$= \sum_h g_h \, . \, W_{hi} \, . \, f'(A_i)$$

i.e. $g_i = [\sum_h g_h \, . \, W_{hi}] \, f'(A_i) \qquad (8)$

Equation (6) thus becomes:

$$W_{ij}(t+1) = W_{ij}(t) - \varepsilon(t) \, g_i \, . \, x_j \qquad (9)$$

This algorithm has been proposed independently by several authors [7,8,13,14] and is known as the GRADIENT-BACK-PROPAGATION algorithm. It consists in updating the weights, through equation (9), where the g_i are computed sequentially from the last to the first layer, by successively applying equation (7) on the last layer, and then equation (8) to the previous layers. Thus the weights-dynamics runs backwards and the state dynamics forward (fig. 5).

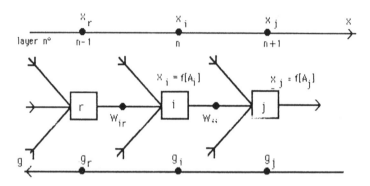

FIGURE 5: GRADIENT DYNAMICS

A learning session then consists in:
1● choose an initial network, i.e. a connection structure (which will remain fixed) and an initial weight vector $W(0)$
2● at time t, present an example x^k and
   - compute the associated output S^k (by forward propagation of states)
   - compute the gradient vector g by backward propagation
   - compute the weights modifications
3● reiterate step 2 as long as necessary
If the examples are presented to the system for long enough, the resulting network will successively encode the desired associations (x^i, y^i). The convergence problems of such algorithms are discussed in [4]. The performances of the system (success rate) and the rate of convergence heavily depend on the "learning pedagogy", i.e. the way examples are presented to the network.
We will illustrate this general method on a few examples.

3- TWO-LAYERED NETWORKS

The most simple example of a learning network is one where there are only two layers: the input and the output layers.

This case had been widely studied in the 50's with the work by Minsky-Papert on the perceptron [11] and more recently with the work on linear models of associative memories by Kohonen [6].

The algorithms developed above can be used to retrieve stored information from noisy data. The examples here may be letters [3], strings, images in multi gray-levels...

Figure 6 shows for example the case of a network where the elements have as transition function the identity. Auto-associations (x^k, x^k) are "taught" into the weights using equation (9), where the $\mathbf{x}^k$ are the letters of the alphabet. The resulting network correctly achieves the desired association $\mathbf{x}^k \mapsto \mathbf{x}^k$ and moreover is capable of generalization: when presented with an input $\mathbf{x}$ close to some $\mathbf{x}^k$, it can restore this $\mathbf{x}^k$. The figure also shows the results obtained by the same network when, during the retrieval process, a different procedure is used to compute the output $\mathbf{S}$ (see [3]).

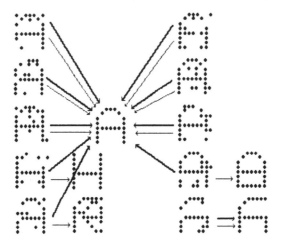

FIGURE 6: RECOGNITION OF LETTERS

4- MULTI-LAYERED NETWORKS

Networks with only two layers are limited. In fact, they have exactly the same limitations as the perceptron had: they can compute only predicates of order 1 [11]. In order to go beyond these limitations, it is necessary to provide the network with some feature extraction capabilities.

One way is to build by hand these feature extractors, or stated in different words to design an adequate coding of the data: it has been shown for example [4] that it was possible to use a 2-layered network (a perceptron) to compute a XOR function (a predicate of order 2) or even to learn the past tenses of english verbs from the infinitive (order of the predicate not known!).

Of course, it is not always possible to find the ad-hoc set of feature extractors and one would thus like to automatically derive them from the examples. This can be done through the Gradient Back Propagation algorithm (9) derived above in the case of a network that has MORE than just 2 layers.

This approach has been used to solve the following problems, that we present very briefly:

• automatic synthesis of boolean functions.
Suppose a function F is given through its table of values. We build the network which realizes the associations (**x**,F(**x**)) by algorithm (9).

This can be applied in the case where :
   - F is the Xor function: the algorithm thus provides automatically a decomposition of the function into more simple "building blocks". For example, the network may compute the decomposition of the Xor into linear boolean mappings of 2 variables (Or, And,...).
   - F is the product of two numbers. A network can be evolved, which by being shown some examples of the multiplication table generalizes the rule of the multiplication, i.e. computes the product of numbers not shown as examples.

• games
A network can be built to learn the outcome of a given configuration or to predict the next move in backgammon [1], Rambot [12], tic-tac-toe [9]. In game situations, the number of different "instances" is very large and it is impossible to present all the examples. The network thus extracts from a small set of examples the "rules" of the game. Note that this rule is never made explicit and no game-tree or evaluation rule is computed. After the learning session, the outcome is usually computed very fast – one pass through the network– where the usual methods are very long, since they involve heavy tree search.

• character-recognition
The problem of recognizing characters presented in multi-fonts can be solved by the same techniques. A network is evolved which memorizes in its weights the associations (**x**^{k},**y**^{k}) where **x**^{k} is a letter in any of 3 different fonts and **y**^{k} is a code of this letter. More fonts can be "added" to the network by presenting examples of the different letters in this font and running the learning algorithm from the previous weight configuration (learning here does not start from scratch). Note that the system also realizes fault-tolerance.

Such networks can also be taught to recognize translated characters: in a way, the network automatically derives a translation-invariant coding of the data.

• expert systems
We have used a data-base containing 5700 files of patients, consulting for abdominal pains. Each record contains a set of symptoms and there are 22 possible diagnostics. An expert system allows to give the diagnostic for an incoming patient. It is well known that experts can easily express the inference rules they use, but not the confidence weights with which they apply them. So the problem of estimating these weights must be solved with little help from the expert. We have derived a network which computes these weights so as to ensure the correct association patient symptoms-diagnostic.

Note that in all the cases sketched here, the learning algorithm is unique. However, the architectures are very different from one network to the other: it is in this architecture that the a-priori knowledge may be successfully used to improve performances.

Remark also that the knowledge contained in the examples is represented in a DISTRIBUTED way in the connection weights. This feature also explains the fault-tolerance ability of these networks. The elaboration of the network adequate for a given task realizes the decomposition of the problem into elementary predicates. These predicates play a role similar to the rules used to represent knowledge in most learning systems [5]. It is an open problem to transform one representation into the other.

5- CONCLUSION

The algorithm presented in this paper shows that it is possible to realize hard learning tasks through a UNIVERSAL learning algorithm. This technique makes use of automata networks where the knowledge is encoded in a DISTRIBUTED way in the connection weights.
This approach opens a new path for many problems in Artificial Intelligence. The results obtained so far are very promising and show that it will be possible to improve performances in hard problems by applying mixed procedures: a network may be used to extract from raw data the predicates which will then be used in logic-based systems...

6- REFERENCES

[1] J.R. BACHRACH: Connectionist learning in Backgammon. In «Connectionist models: a summer school», G. Hinton, T. Sejnowski, D. Touretzski org. Carnegie Mellon Univ., unpublished, 1986.
[2] P.R. COHEN, E.A. FEIGENBAUM: The Handbook of Artificial Intelligence. Vol III, **Pitman**, 1984.
[3] F. FOGELMAN SOULIE, P. GALLINARI, S. THIRIA: Learning and associative memory. In «Pattern Recognition, Theory and Applications », P.A. Devijver Ed., NATO ASI Series in Computer Science, **Springer Verlag**, to appear.
[4] F. FOGELMAN SOULIE, P. GALLINARI, Y. LE CUN, S. THIRIA: Automata Networks and Artificial Intelligence. In «Computing on Automata Networks», F. Fogelman Soulié, Y. Robert, M. Tchuente Eds, **Manchester Univ. Press**, to appear.
[5] Y. KODRATOFF: Generalizing and particularizing as the techniques of learning. **Computers and Artificial Intelligence**, 2, pp 417-441, 1983.
[6] T. KOHONEN: Self-Organization and Associative Memory. Springer Series in Information Sciences, vol 8, **Springer Verlag**, 1984.
[7] Y. LE CUN: A learning scheme for assymetric threshold network. In «Cognitiva 85», **CESTA-AFCET Ed.,** pp 599-604, 1985.
[8] Y. LE CUN: Learning process in an asymmetric threshold network. In «Disordered systems and biological organization», E. Bienenstock, F. Fogelman Soulié, G. Weisbuch Eds, **Springer Verlag**, NATO Asi series in systems and computer science, n°20, pp 233-240, 1986.
[9] Y. LE CUN, F. FOGELMAN SOULIE: Modèles Connexionnistes de l'Apprentissage. Special issue on "Apprentissage et Machine", **Intellectica**, to appear.
[10] J. MAC CARTHY: Programs with common sense (1958), reprinted in «Semantic Information Processes», M.L.Minsky ed., **MIT Press**, pp 403-409, 1968.

[11] M. MINSKY, S. PAPERT: Perceptrons, an Introduction to Computational Geometry. Cambridge, **MIT Press**, 1969.

[12] M.C. MOZER: Rambot: a connectionist expert system that learns by examples. In «Connectionist models: a summer school», G. Hinton, T. Sejnowski, D. Touretzski org. Carnegie Mellon Univ., unpublished, 1986.

[13] D.C. PLAUT, S.J. NOWLAN, G.E. HINTON: Experiments on Learning by Back Propagation. Carnegie Mellon University Technical Report, **CMU-CS-86-126**, 1986.

[14] D.E. RUMELHART, G.E. HINTON, R.J. WILLIAMS: Learning internal representations by error propagation. In «Parallel Distributed Processing: Explorations in the Microstructure of Cognition», vol.1, Foundations, D.E. Rumelhart, J.L. McClelland Eds: . **MIT Press**, 1986.

[15] D.E. RUMELHART, J.L. MAC CLELLAND: On learning the past tenses of english verbs. In «Parallel Distributed Processing: Explorations in the Microstructure of Cognition», vol.1, Foundations, D.E. Rumelhart, J.L. McClelland Eds: . **MIT Press**, 1986.

[16] B. WIDROW, M.E. HOFF: Adaptive switching circuits. **IRE WESCON Conv. Record**, part 4, pp 96-104, 1960.

An Approach to a Fuzzy Computer Hardware System

T. Yamakawa

Department of Electrical Engineering and Computer Science,
Kumamoto University (Japan)

Abstract

We have collaborated with L.A. Zadeh on how to manage fuzzy
information. However, we have no tools suitable for fuzzy
information processing available. We are forced to use low-speed,
expensive digital computers that are inefficient and have high-
power dissipation. We have to make a greater effort to get better
tools peculiar to fuzzy logic, not to Boolean logic. This would
satisfy the people who have been deterred by the unsuitability of
digital computers for handling fuzzy concepts. This paper
describes the electronic circuits (hardware systems) peculiar to
fuzzy information processing. They include fuzzifiers, fuzzy
logic circuits, defuzzifiers and fuzzy memories. Some of them are
implemented in the form of monolithic integrated circuits (IC). A
simple fuzzy computer hardware system employing MIN and MAX
operations is also described briefly, which facilitates fuzzy
inferences 10,000,000 times per second.

Introduction

Von Neumann's stored program concept and the monolithic
integrated circuit technology of stable binary digital hardware
have allowed a large data processing machine to be produced.
Therefore, these machines can be used not only for numerical
calculation but also for data matching. Updated expert systems
are based on data matching of "facts" and "rules" in knowledge
bases. Thus, a highly valuable expert system ought to possess a
very large knowledge base containing all possible rules and
inference is achieved by matching facts and rules.
A person's knowledge is derived from his accumulated experiences
and is reduced to linguistic information like the expertise of a
human expert. The linguistic information naturally contains
fuzziness, vagueness, uncertainty, incompleteness or
impreciseness. A key problem in the developemnt of an expert
system is how to represent the uncertain information in the know-
how of human experts. The MYCIN consultation system (Shortliffe
1976) employs a "certainty factor (CF)" to represent the
uncertainty. However, it is counterintuitive and thus has
occasionally led MYCIN to reach incorrect inferences.
L.A. Zadeh (1965) proposed fuzzy sets to handle uncertain
information included in natural languages and presented the
usefulness of fuzzy sets and fuzzy logic in expert systems (Zadeh
1983). Many papers (Gupta and Sanchez 1982, Zimmermann et al.
1984, Gupta et al. 1985, Sugeno 1985, Zimmermann 1985, Kandel
1986) have verified the use of fuzzy logic in expert systems by
using binary digital computers. In those systems, generation of
membership functions, which characterize uncertainty, and fuzzy
inference are achieved by binary codes in a serial manner
according to von Neumann's stored program concept. The fuzzy

inference employing a digital computer is slow and thus unsuitable for real-time use, especially in the case of a large knowledge base (Table 1A). Furthermore, it dissipates high power, is inefficient and expensive.

Table 1A Computer hardware systems and their functions

To realize a general purpose fuzzy information processing system at high speed, of low power dissipation, of high efficiency and of low cost, it is necessary to develop an intrinsic fuzzy hardware system of linear operation and parallel architecture (Table 1A). This paper describes intrinsic fuzzy logic circuits and fuzzy memory integrated in a monolithic silicon chip and the defuzzifier. A simple fuzzy computer employing MIN and MAX operations is also described.

What is a Fuzzy Computer?

A human brain very often makes inferences whose antecedents and consequences include fuzzy expressions. This type of inference cannot be achieved satisfactorily using classical Boolean logic. The following form of inference is considered:

        Implication: If x is A, then y is B
        Premise   : x is A′
        _____

        Conclusion : y is B′

where x and y are the names of the objects and A, A′ and B′ are fuzzy sets. This form of inference is called generalized modus ponens (Mizumoto and Zimmermann 1982). The concept was presented by Zadeh (1973).
Moreover, the following form of inference is possible:

        Implication: If x is A, then y is B
        Premise   : y is B′
        _____

        Conclusion : x is A′

This inference is called generalized modus tollens (Mizumoto and Zimmermann 1982) which reduces to modus tollens when B′=not B and A′=not A.
A fuzzy information A is denoted by a set of ordered pairs:

$$A = \left\{ (x_i, a_i) \right\} \qquad x_i \in X \qquad (1)$$

where X denotes a space of objects and a_i the grade of membership of x_i in A. a_i is assumed to be a number in the interval (0, 1)

for simplicity. The fuzzy set A can be regarded as a vector, so
that it is denoted as:

$$A = (a_1, a_2, a_3, \ldots, a_i, \ldots, a_m), \quad 0 \leqq a_i \leqq 1 \qquad (2)$$

when the number of its elements m is finite. Similarly, a fuzzy
informarion B is denoted by a vector as:

$$B = (b_1, b_2, b_3, \ldots, b_j, \ldots, b_n), \quad 0 \leqq b_j \leqq 1 \qquad (3)$$

Let R be the fuzzy relation from A to B. The compositional rule
of inference (Zadeh 1973, Kaufmann 1975) asserts that the
conclusion B´ can be deduced from the composition of A´ and R as
follows:

$$B' = A' \circ R \qquad (4)$$

or:

$$b'_j = \bigvee_i a'_i * r_{ij} \qquad (5)$$

where * is an operation which is associative and monotone non-
decreasing in each argument, eg minimum, product and so on. The
fuzzy relation can be derived from the fuzzy conditional
proposition "If x is A, then y is B". Zadeh (1975a, b) proposed
the following two types of fuzzy relations:

$$r_{ij} = (a_i \wedge b_j) \vee (1 - a_i) \qquad \text{Maximum Rule (6)}$$

$$r_{ij} = 1 \wedge (1 - a_i + b_j) \qquad \text{Arithmetic Rule (7)}$$

Mamdani (1977) proposed another type of fuzzy relation as:

$$r_{ij} = a_i \wedge b_j \qquad \text{Mini Operation Rule (8)}$$

and verified it in the application to industrial work.
Mizumoto and Zimmermann (1982) and Fukami et al. (1980) proposed
many types of fuzzy relations, examined them and suggested the
improved fuzzy relations which fit our intuitions under several
criteria.
In the updated fuzzy inferences employing a digital computer, a
generation of membership functions and an execution of some
operations included in the compositional rule of inference [Eqn
(5)] and in the fuzzy relation R are achieved in binary code.
Moreover, the execution is achieved in series by the stored
program concept but not in parallel.
In this paper, the fuzzy computer is defined as a hardware
system which accomplishes either generalized modus ponens
(forward inference) or generalized modus tollens (backward
inference) in a parallel manner with intrinsic fuzzy logic
circuits but not binary circuits. Fuzzy information is usually
given by the linguistic labels of membership, eg negative large
(NL), negative medium (NM), negative small (NS), approximately

zero (ZR), positive small (PS), positive medium (PM) and positive
large (PL) as shown in Figure 1.

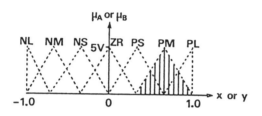

Figure 1 Expression of fuzzy information

For example, fuzzy grades (0, 1) are represented by (0 V, 5 V) or
(0 A, 5 μA) in voltage mode or current mode fuzzy computer,
respectively. The number of elements x_i or y_j is finite between

normalized values -1.0 and +1.0. Furthermore, the shape of the
membership function is represented with a piecewise linear
function in the fuzzy computer for easy handling without spoiling
fuzziness. Each grade a_i (or b_j) of membership of element x_i (or
y_j) is expressed by an analog voltage from 0 V to 5 V on the ith
(or jth) data line in a data bus A (or B) as shown in Figure 2.

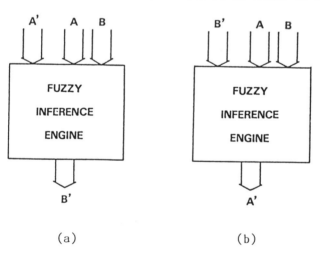

(a)   (b)

Figure 2 The fuzzy inference engine. (a) Generalized modus
ponens; (b) generalized modus tollens

Thus, fuzzy words (not binary words) A, B, etc imply fuzzy
information and are represented with sets of analog voltages a_1,

a_2, a_3, ..., a_i, ..., a_m and b_1, b_2, b_3, ..., b_j, ..., b_n, etc.
The fuzzy inference engine shown in Figure 2 is a central
processing unit and a fuzzy computer is constructed with fuzzy
inference engines, in parallel, as many as the number of
implication rules r. An useful fuzzy computer possesses a wide
variety of fuzzy logic functions for fuzzy inference and thus it
may be used as a fuzzy simulator.

Building Blocks of The Fuzzy Inference Engine

In this paper, nine fuzzy logic circuits in linear operation are
presented. These basic fuzzy logic functions are defined in terms
of membership functions μ_X and μ_Y ($0 < \mu_X$, $\mu_Y < 1$) in the following
where V, Λ, + and - denote max, min, algebraic sum and algebraic
difference, respectively.

Table 1   Functions of basic logic cell

FUNCTIONS	INPUT		OUTPUT
	I_{i1}	I_{i2}	I_o
BOUNDED-DIFFERENCE	μ_Y	μ_X	$\mu_X \ominus \mu_Y$
COMPLEMENT	μ_X	1	$\mu_{\overline{X}} = 1 \ominus \mu_X$
BOUNDED-PRODUCT	1	$\mu_X + \mu_Y$	$\mu_{X \odot Y} = (\mu_X + \mu_Y) \ominus 1$

Bounded-Difference

$$u_{X \ominus Y} \triangleq 0 \vee (\mu_X - \mu_Y) = \mu_X \ominus \mu_Y \tag{9}$$

Fuzzy Complement

$$\mu_{\overline{X}} \triangleq 1 - \mu_X = 1 \ominus \mu_X \tag{10}$$

Bounded-Product

$$\mu_{X \odot Y} \triangleq 0 \vee (\mu_X + \mu_Y - 1) = (\mu_X + \mu_Y) \ominus 1 \tag{11}$$

Fuzzy Logic Union (Max)

$$\mu_{X \cup Y} \triangleq \mu_X \vee \mu_Y = (\mu_X \ominus \mu_Y) + \mu_Y = (\mu_Y \ominus \mu_X) + \mu_X \tag{12}$$

Bounded-Sum

$$u_{X \oplus Y} \triangleq 1 \wedge (\mu_X + \mu_Y) = 1 \ominus [1 \ominus (\mu_X + \mu_Y)] \tag{13}$$

Fuzzy Logic Intersection (Min)

$$\mu_{X \cap Y} \stackrel{\Delta}{=} \mu_X \wedge \mu_Y = \mu_X \ominus (\mu_X \ominus \mu_Y) = \mu_Y \ominus (\mu_Y \ominus \mu_X) \tag{14}$$

Implication

$$\mu_{X \to Y} \stackrel{\Delta}{=} 1 \wedge (1 - \mu_X + \mu_Y) = 1 \ominus (\mu_X \ominus \mu_Y) \tag{15}$$

Absolute-Difference

$$\mu_{|X - Y|} \stackrel{\Delta}{=} \begin{cases} \mu_X - \mu_Y & (\mu_X \geq \mu_Y) \\ \mu_Y - \mu_X & (\mu_X < \mu_Y) \end{cases} = (\mu_X \ominus \mu_Y) + (\mu_Y \ominus \mu_X) \tag{16}$$

Equivalence

$$\mu_{X \rightleftarrows Y} \stackrel{\Delta}{=} \mu_{X \to Y} \wedge \mu_{Y \to X} = 1 \ominus [(\mu_X \ominus \mu_Y) + (\mu_Y \ominus \mu_X)] \tag{17}$$

All the basic fuzzy logic functions presented here can be expressed only with the Bounded-Difference and the Algebraic Sum, as described above. In current mode circuits, the Algebraic Sum is implemented only by connecting two lines to be summed (Wired Sum). Therefore, the Bounded-Difference arrays can be adapted to many kinds of fuzzy information processing hardware systems, the design of which should be directed only to wiring between the Bounded-Difference circuits (ie basic logic cells).

Figure 3(a) shows the circuit configuration of the basic logic cell where a MOS FET D acts as a diode. It has two input currents I_{i1} and I_{i2} and one output current I_0, which denote grades of membership. Figure 3(b) shows a microphotograph of the basic logic cell which is composed of three MOS FET. Figure 3(c) shows the input-output characteristics of the basic logic cell. It illustrates good linearity and introduces a very small error. This suggests that the basic logic cell can be appropriated to a binary logic and even to a 10-valued logic. The basic logic cell exhibits multiple functions according to the assignment of the input current I_{i1} and I_{i2} as shown in Table 1B.

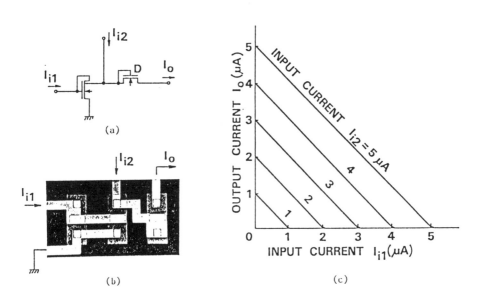

Figure 3 Basic logic cell in current mode circuit. (a) Circuit;
(b) microphotograph; (c) electrical characteristics

FUNCTION / HARDWARE	DETERMINISTIC PROCESSING [EXACT CALCULATION DATA MATCHING ETC.]	FUZZY PROCESSING [APPROXIMATE REASONING]
BINARY DIGITAL SYSTEM [VON NEUMANN'S CONCEPT]	UNIVERSAL USE	UNIVERSAL USE LOW SPEED LOW EFFICIENCY HIGH COST
INTRINSIC FUZZY SYSTEM [PARALLEL INFERENCE]	IMPOSSIBLE	GENERAL USE HIGH SPEED HIGH EFFICIENCY LOW COST

Table 1B Computer hardware systems and their functions

Adding only one input terminal to the basic logic cell brings it
to the Fuzzy Logic Union (MAX) circuit as shown in Figure 4. It
needs two identical input currents.

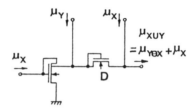

Figure 4 Union (Max) circuit

FUNCTIONS	INPUT			OUTPUT
	I_{i1}	I_{i2}	I_{i3}	I_o
BOUNDED-SUM	$\mu_X + \mu_Y$	1	1	$\mu_{X \oplus Y} = 1 \ominus (1 \ominus (\mu_X + \mu_Y))$
INTERSECTION	μ_Y	μ_X	μ_X	$\mu_{X \cap Y} = \mu_X \ominus (\mu_X \ominus \mu_Y)$
IMPLICATION	μ_Y	μ_X	1	$\mu_{X \to Y} = 1 \ominus (\mu_X \ominus \mu_Y)$

Table 2 Functions of cascade-connected basic logic cells

Figure 5 shows a cascade connection of two basic logic cells.   It
also   exhibits multiple functions according to the assignment   of
the   input currents I ,   I   and I   shown in Table 2.   In   this
                      i1   i2   i3
circuit, the diode D´ can be omitted.
  Wired Sum of two basic logic cells gives the Absolute-Difference
circuit shown in Figure 6. A cascade connection of this Absolute-
Difference   circuit   and   the   basic   logic   cell   implements   the
Equivalence circuit as shown in Figure 7.
  The   current mode basic fuzzy logic circuits presented   in   this
paper are ratioless circuits.   Therefore,   they can be fabricated
with a master slice of CMOS transistor array and thus the area of
active region is minimized.   Figure 8 shows a CMOS fuzzy chip for
testing,   which includes nine basic fuzzy logic circuits and test
devices   constructed with n-ch and p-ch MOS FET array of the same
dimensions.

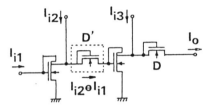

Figure 5 Cascade connection of the basic logic cell.   The diode D´
can be omitted

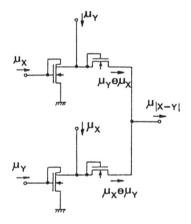

Figure 6 Absolute-Difference circuit

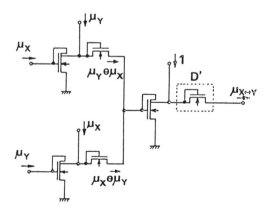

Figure 7 Equivalence circuit. The diode D´ can be omitted

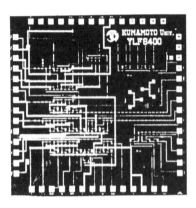

Figure 8 CMOS fuzzy chip for testing

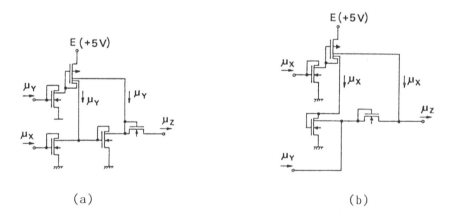

(a)   (b)

Figure 9 Circuit configuration of (a) MIN circuits and (b) MAX
        circuits for SPICE II simulation

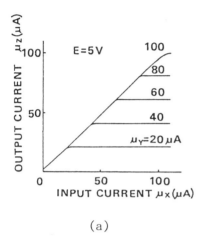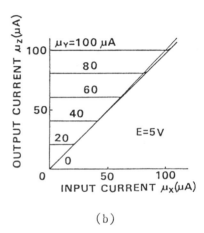

(a)

(b)

Figure 10 Input-output characteristics of (a) MIN circuits and (b) MAX circuits

It is very effective to make use of a digital computer for designing and estimating electronic circuit systems or integrated circuits. The most famous and authorized software system for circuit simulation is SPICE II which was developed at the University of California. Here MIN circuits and MAX circuits, which are typical building blocks of fuzzy systems, are examined by SPICE II simulation. The circuit configuration under test is shown in Figure 9(a) and (b) where two identical input currents are supplied by a multiple-fanout circuit. The input-output characteristics of MIN circuits and MAX circuits are shown in Figure 10(a) and (b), respectively. Fuzzy truth values or grades of 0 and 1 are represented by currents 0 A and 100 µA, respectively. These two figures show that output errors of MIN and MAX circuits are 5% FS (full scale) at most, ie the ratio of output error current to 100 µA (corresponding to 1) is within 5%. This error is permissible in designing fuzzy hardware systems.
  The dependence of input-output characteristics upon the supply voltage is examined and the results are shown in Figure 11(a) and (b). The fluctuation between 4 V and 6 V in supply voltage causes an output error of 3% FS in both cases of MIN and MAX circuits. If the signal error of 6% FS can be permitted, then the fluctuation of supply voltage between 4 V and 8 V is permissible. This insensitiveness to supply voltage is one of the distinctive features of the circuits described here, which cannot be achieved by an ordinary digital system or digital computer in voltage mode. It allows us to use noisy power supply or a decaying dry battery.

A temperature characteristic is also important because a hardware system should be able to operate normally anywhere in the world, eg in very cold places such as the polar regions and in very hot or heated environments. The military standard constrains hardware systems to operate normally in the temperature range -55°C ∿ + 125°C which is a very severe criterion. The MIN and MAX circuits described here pass the military standard admirably, which is easily understood by Figure 12(a) and (b). A change of temperature from -55°C to +125°C causes the output current deviation of only 0.74% FS which is not a problem in fuzzy hardware systems.

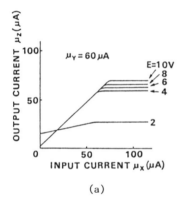

(a)

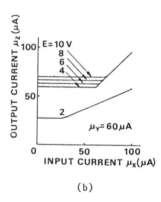

(b)

Figure 11 Dependence of input-output characteristics of (a) MIN and (b) MAX circuits upon the supply voltage

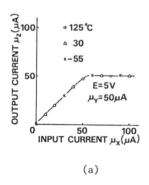

(a)

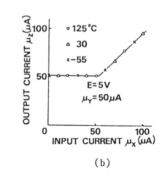

(b)

Figure 12 Temperature characterisitics of (a) MIN and (b) MAX circuits

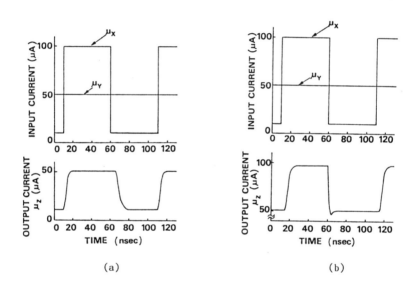

Figure 13 Operating speed of (a) MIN and (b) MAX circuits

The most significant point of hardware systems is the operating speed or response time described previously. Figure 13(a) and (b) shows the operating speed of MIN circuits and MAX circuits shown in Figure 9(a) and (b), respectively. In both cases, one input current μ_Y is a constant value (50 μA) and the other input current μ_X is a rectangular wave changing from 10 μA to 100 μA. Therefore, the output currents of MIN circuits and MAX circuits must change from 10 μA to 50 μA and from 50 μA to 100 μA, respectively.

Simulated results show that these circuits constructed with 10 transistors or more can respond sufficiently within 20 ns. It is very difficult to achieve using ordinary digital hardware systems, if not impossible. The MIN and MAX circuits shown in Figure 9 can be regarded as intrinsic fuzzy logic gates of linear operation.

The building blocks presented in this paper have the following
distinctive features:

1. The effect of the variation in V_{TH} and g_m on the electrical
   characteristics of the hardware systems can be cut off by
   adjusting the supply voltage to the appropriate value. Thus
   an expensive ion implanter is not needed.
2. The basic logic cell exhibits good linearity, robustness to
   thermal and supply voltage fluctuations and very high speed
   operation, which cannot be easily achieved in ordinary
   voltage mode circuits.
3. Since it does not need resistors nor isolation, it is
   suitable for a large-scale fuzzy hardware system.
4. Circuits presented here can be appropriated to a binary
   logic and even to a 10-valued logic.
5. The system has the advantage over fuzzy information
   processing by using binary circuits, which arise from the
   ability to provide much more "functions per unit area".
6. It is an inexpensive system and takes a short time to
   design and make.

Fuzzy Memory

In updated digital hardware systems, linguistics information of
uncertainty is represented as membership functions, and the
grades of membership are stored in binary code. This aspect is
quite different from human memory. In other words, a human does
memorize the label of membership but not the membership function.
Storing the membership function by label is more natural and
needs much less memory elements than storing by digitized grades
of membership (Yamakawa and Sasaki 1987). In this paper, a novel
fuzzy memory which stores fuzzy information by labels and is
indispensable for a fuzzy computer is described. The number of
distinguished and stored labels and the shape of membership
function can be chosen according to the complexity of implication
rules. Seven labels are adopted here as described above.
The architecture of fuzzy memory is shown in Figure 14. It
consists of a binary RAM, registers and membership function
generators (MFG) (Yamakawa 1986). The MFG consists of a PROM, a
decoder and a pass transistor array. A binary RAM and registers
can be realized by using standard IC technology. Seven labels and
an information "none" are denoted by a 3-bit binary code and
stored in the RAM and registers, such as 000(none), 001(negative
large), 010(negative medium), 011(negative small),
100(approximately zero), 101(positive small), 110(positive
medium), 111(positive large). MFG has the function to fuzzify the
3-bit binary signal. in PROM, distributed analog voltages
corresponding to grades of membership function of label=ZR are
programmed. The label is changed by shifting the distributed
analog voltages to the right or left through a pass transistor
array. A transistor array is driven by a decoder. For example, if
the distributed grades of membership function are shifted to the
right hand by 4 digits by activating pass transistor rows X and
3

X , the label changes into PS. If the distributed grades of
 5
membership function are shifted to the left hand by 8 digits by
activating pass transistor rows X and X , the label changes into
                                    2   4
NM. The row-activating word X X X X X X X is obtained from the
                            1 2 3 4 5 6 7
label word C C C through the decoder.
           1 2 3
 Figure 15 shows a microphotograph of the membership function
generator. Figure 16 shows a transient response of a test device
when the PROM is programmed to be 0 V, 1 V, 2 V, 3 V, 4 V and 5
V. The output waveform shows that the output error is too small
to detect from Figure 16. Though the pass transistor array
consists of PMOS FET, its function is very similar to that of a
CMOS inverter. Therefore, it exhibits low power dissipation.
Although the output signal of the fuzzy memory is analog, the
label is stored in binary code. Therefore, this fuzzy memory is
as robust as a binary RAM to the noise.

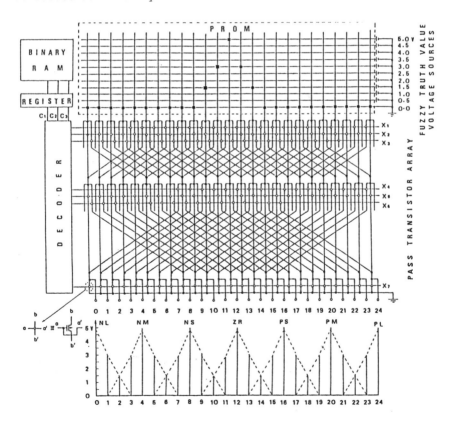

Figure 14 Fuzzy memory device constructed with binary memory and
        membership function generator (MFG)

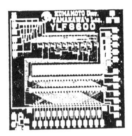

Figure 15 Microphotograph of membership function generator (MFG)

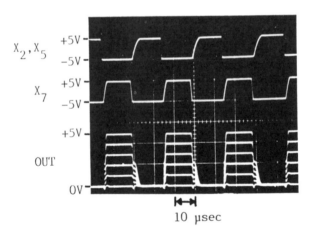

Figure 16 Transient response of a test device for MFG

Defuzzifier

A defuzzifier fufils two roles (Yamakawa 1986). One is a conversion of several parallel signal lines to a single line. The other is the induction of the essence of fuzzy inference results. A variety of defuzzification algorithms are proposed and they introduce inherent semantic errors. A centre of gravity method is adopted here. Figure 17 shows a defuzzifier employing a centre of gravity. It is composed of a resistive network for summation and weighted summation, a current mode divider and a level shifter with I-V conversion.

Logarithmic summation or subtraction followed by extraction of
the anti-logarithm gives the product or quotient, respectively.
Thus, if log A = log X + log Y - log Z, then A = X Y/Z. For an
emitter junction of a bipolar transistor the base-to-emitter
voltage is proportional to the logarithm of emitter current over
the range where the effects of series and shunt resistance and
reverse saturation current are negligible. This facilitates
multiplication and division. In other words, circuitry
implementing summation and subtraction of base-to-emitter
voltages gives multiplication and division of emitter currents.
Figure 18(a) shows a current mode divider employing PNP-NPN
transistor pairs Q_1, Q_2, Q_3 and Q_4. The resultant equation is
obtained as:

$$I_4 = K \frac{I_1}{I_2} \qquad (18)$$

scale factor $$K = \frac{I_{s2} \cdot I_{s4}}{I_{s1} \cdot I_{s3}} I_3 \qquad (19)$$

where $I_{s1} < I_{s4}$ represent theoretical emitter-junction reverse
saturation currents of $Q_1 \leq Q_4$, respectively. This equation means
that the circuit enclosed with a dotted line in Figure 18(a)
operates as a current mode divider whose scale factor K can be
assigned by an external current I_3.

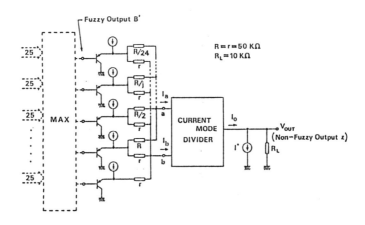

Figure 17 Defuzzifier employing a centre of gravity

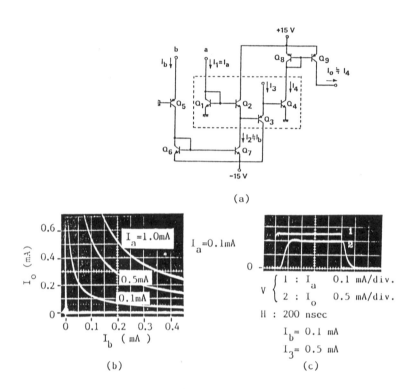

(a)

(b)   (c)

Figure   18(a)   Current   mode   divider;   (b)   its   static
         characteristics; (c) its dynamic response

While Ia is directly fed to the input of the current mode divider
($I_1 = I_a$), I is inverted through the current mirror Q_5, Q_6 and Q_7
to feed I_2 ($=I_b$). The flow-in output current I_4 is also inverted
through the current mirror Q_8 and Q_9 to obtain the flow-out
output current I_0 ($=I_4$). Thus, the following equations are
obtained:

$$I_1 = I_a = \frac{1}{R} \sum_{j=0}^{24} j \cdot V_j \tag{20}$$

$$I_2 \doteq I_b = \frac{1}{r} \sum_{j=0}^{24} V_j \tag{21}$$

$$I_4 \doteq I_0 \tag{22}$$

Equations (18), (20), (21) and (22) give:

$$V_{OUT} = R_L \cdot K \cdot \frac{\sum_{\ell=-12}^{12} \ell \cdot \mu_\ell}{\sum_{\ell=-12}^{12} \mu_\ell} \tag{23}$$

The current I_0 corresponds to the resultant value V_{OUT} in the normalized space of $0.0 \sim 2.0$ but not $-1.0 \sim +1.0$. Therefore, it

should be shifted by the amount of $I*$ which corresponds to $+1.0$ on the normalized space. Thus, we can get the final non-fuzzy output V_{out} expressed by:

$$I_o = K \cdot \frac{r}{R} \cdot \frac{\sum_{j=0}^{24} j \cdot V_j}{\sum_{j=0}^{24} V_j} \tag{24}$$

where μ_ℓ is the resultant fuzzy grade on the discrete conclusion

space.

A static characteristic and a dynamic response of the current mode divider are shown in Figure 18(b) and (c), respectively.

A Simple Fuzzy Computer Employing MIN and MAX Operations

In this paper, we consider a simple fuzzy computer which achieves only the generalized modus ponens in the inference engine constructed with voltage mode MIN and MAX circuits alone (Yamakawa 1987). We adopt minimum for * in Eqn (5) and Mamdani´s Mini Operation Rule [Eqn (8)] for the fuzzy relation. The hardware takes analog voltages ranging from 0 V to 5V, which correspond to grades of membership from 0 to 1.
From the compositional rule of inference we can get grades of membership on the element j in Conclusion B´ as:

$$\begin{aligned} b'_j &= \bigvee_i a'_i \wedge r_{ij} \\ &= \bigvee_i a'_i \wedge (a_i \wedge b_j) = \bigvee_i a'_i \wedge a_i \wedge b_j \\ &= b_j \wedge (\bigvee_i a'_i \wedge a_i) \end{aligned} \tag{25}$$

Equation (25) asserts that the MIN and MAX circuits are the fundamental building blocks for constructing the fuzzy inference engine.

Figure 19(a) and Figure 20(a) show novel fuzzy logic gates of MIN and MAX in voltage mode, respectively. Since all transistors in a comparator are coupled at emitters, the author named this type of electronic fuzzy logic circuit as an emitter coupled fuzzy logic gate (ECFL gate). 0.7 V across the emitter junction of the comparator and its thermal drift is compensated by rhe following stage, ie comparator. Figures 19(b) and 20(b) show the input-output static characteristics of MIN and MAX gates,respectively. They show an accuracy sufficient for fuzzy logic. ECFL gates (MIN and MAX) are considered as a cascade connection of two emitter followers which are driven by current sources I_{E1} and I_{E2}. Therefore, they exhibit very high input impedance and very low output impedance. This fact ensures that ECFL gates are able to drive many following stages (large fan-out). Since ECFL gates possess no storage effect of minority carrier in the base region they operate at high speeds. Figures 19(c) and 20(c) show the response time of less than 10 ns for each.

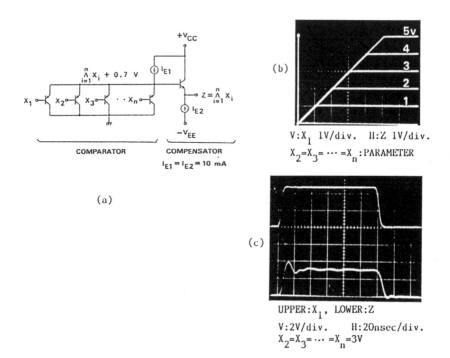

Figure 19 Emitter coupled fuzzy logic (ECFL) gate. (a) MIN circuit; (b) static characteristic; (c) transient response

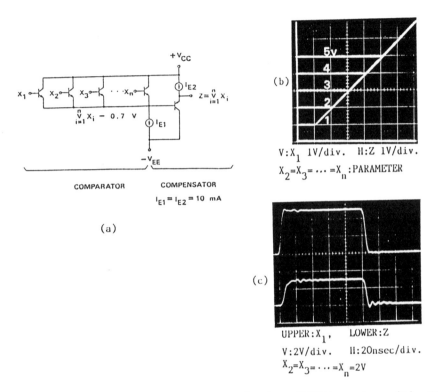

Figure 20 Emitter coupled fuzzy logic (ECFL) gate. (a) MAX circuit; (b) static characteristic; (c) transient response

The inference engine shown in Figure 21(a) carries out a fuzzy inference based on Eqn (25). The input fuzzy words A', A and B, which correspond to the fuzzy propositions, are implemented with distributed analog voltages on m or n signal lines which correspond to elements of the fuzzy sets, as described in previous papers. C-MIN is an array of m 2-input MIN gates and produces a fuzzy word whose ith signal line exhibits $a' \wedge a_i$. In other words, C-MIN makes anding of two membership functions A' and A. E-MAX is an m-input MAX gate as shown in Figure 20(a). Thus, the output of E-MAX is $(\vee a' \wedge a_i)$ and is fed to the truncation gate is a C-MIN whose one input data bus is commonly connected to the terminal "a". Input fuzzy word or membership function is truncated by "a" through the truncation gate. Accordingly, we can get the output fuzzy word B' whose jth signal line exhibits $b_j \wedge (\vee a' \wedge a_i)$, ie we can get the conclusion B'

as a set of analog voltages b_j ' distributed on n   output   signal
lines.

Figure 21(b) shows its electronic circuit implementation. This
inference engine needs (4m+5n+1) transistors. The operating speed
was obtained to be within 100 ns ($10-7$ s) by the experiment using
discrete bipolar transistors but not in the form of monolithic
integrated circuits. It means that this inference engine can
accomplish the fuzzy inference 10,000,000 times per second, ie 10
Mega fuzzy inferences per second (FIPS).
Finally, we realize a simple fuzzy computer which achieves   the
following forward inference:

Implication Rules
$$\begin{cases} \text{also} & A_1 \longrightarrow B_1 \\ \text{also} & A_2 \longrightarrow B_2 \\ \text{also} & A_3 \longrightarrow B_3 \\ & \quad \cdot \qquad \cdot \\ & \quad \cdot \qquad \cdot \\ \text{also} & \quad \cdot \qquad \cdot \\ & A_r \longrightarrow B_r \end{cases}$$

Premise   A'
                    _____
                           B'
Conclusion

where   r represents the number of implication rules. Aiming at
high speed operation we adopted a parallel architecture for the
fuzzy computer as described previously. The architecture is shown
in   Figure 22. Distinguishable linguistic information   is
represented with binary codes and stored at a binary RAM in a
fuzzy memory. They are transformed into fuzzy words through a
membership function generator in the fuzzy   memory.   Fuzzy
inference engines, the number of which is equal to that of
implication rules, are connected to the fuzzy memory in parallel.
A set of three fuzzy words, which correspond to the "fact" and
one "rule" (two fuzzy propositions) is fed to a fuzzy inference
engine to get each inference result, eg B_1', B_2', B_3', ...
These results are fed to a MAX block which works as connectives
"also" connecting implication rules. The MAX BLOCK (C-MAX)
produces a final conclusion C' which is a fuzzy output and
appears on the output data bus as a set of distributed analog
voltages. In some cases, eg fuzzy control, it is needed to obtain
a deterministic result or non-fuzzy output from this fuzzy
computer. An auxiliary defuzzifier accomplishes this process.
A   control unit and control buses which synchronize the
operation of the fuzzy computer are shown in Figure 22 for
simplicity.

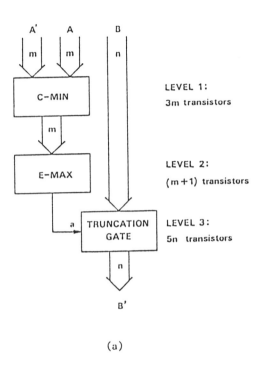

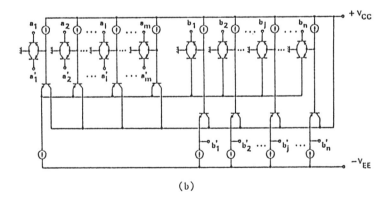

Figure 21 (a) Architecture of the fuzzy inference engine; (b) its electronic circuit implementation. $(4m+5n+1)$ transistors are necessary for this inference engine

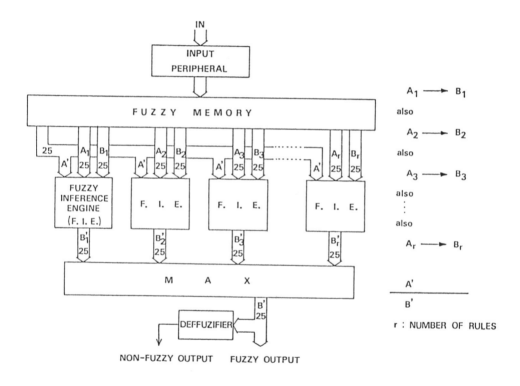

Figure 22 Architecture of a simple fuzzy computer employing MIN and MAX operations in voltage mode. A control unit and control buses are not shown

Conclusions

A fuzzy computer is defined as a hardware system which achieves either generalized modus ponens (forward inference) or generalized modus tollens (backward inference) in a parallel manner with intrinsic fuzzy logic circuits but not binary circuits.
Nine basic fuzzy logic circuits in linear operation are presented. These circuits can be easily implemented with a master slice of CMOS transistor array. They have the following distinctive features:

1. Electrical characteristics are insensitive to wafer process parameters.
2. The circuits exhibit good linearity, very high speed operation and robustness to thermal and supply voltage fluctuations. (MIN and MAX circuits can normally operate with a supply voltage of 4 V to 8 V under temperature range of -55°C to +125°C and respond enough within 20 ns.)
3. They are not in need of resistors nor isolation.

A fuzzy memory is presented, which is indispensable for a fuzzy computer. It consists of a binary memory and a membership function generator. It memorizes linguistic fuzzy information or membership functions by storing not binary-coded grades but binary-coded labels of membership. The membership function generator is implemented on a monolithic silicon chip by standard AI-gate pMOS technology to verify its utility. The fuzzy memory presented here ia as robust as a binary RAM against the noise.
A defuzzifier employing a centre of gravity method is presented. Finally, a simple fuzzy computer employing MIN and MAX operations is described. It achieves generalized modus ponens alone. Novel fuzzy logic gates of MIN and MAX in voltage mode, named emitter coupled fuzzy logic gates, are presented. A fuzzy inference engine is constructed with these gates. It can achieve the fuzzy inferences 10,000,000 times per second (10 Mega FIPS) and work normally even under the fluctuation amounting to 45 V of each supply voltage. Moreover, it is robust to changes in the ambient temperature, external noise and the variance of the transistors used. These features suggest that the use of the inference engine described here can be extended to a large-scale fuzzy computer which is our aim.

References

Fukami, S.; Mizumoto, M.; Tanaka, K. (1980) Some considerations on fuzzy conditional inference, "Fuzzy Sets and Systems" Vol. 4, No. 3, pp. 243-273.

Gupta, M.M.; Sanchez, E. (1982) "Approximate Reasoning in Decision Analysis", North-Holland, Amsterdam.

Gupta, M.M; Kandel, A.; Bandler, W.; Kiszka, J.B. (1985) "Approximate Reasoning in Expert Systems", North-Holland, Amsterdam.

Kandel, A. (1986) "Fuzzy Mathematical Techniques with Applications", Addison-Wesley, New York.

Kaufmann, A. (1975) "Introduction to the Theory of Fuzzy Subsets Vol. I, Fundamental Elements", Academic Press, New York.

Mamdani, E.H. (1977) Application of fuzzy logic to approximate reasoning using linguistic synthesis, "IEEE Transactions Comp" Vol. C-26, pp. 1182-1191.

Mizumoto, M.; Zimmermann, H.J. (1982) Comparison of fuzzy reasoning methods, "Fuzzy Sets and Systems" Vol. 8, No. 3, pp. 253-283.

Shortliffe, E.H. (1976) "Computer-Based Medical Consultations: MYCIN", Elsevier, New York.

Sugeno, M. (1985) "Industrial Applications of Fuzzy Control", North-Holland, Amsterdam.

Yamakawa, T. "Japanese Patent Kokai Publication" No. 60-199225, 60-199229, 60-199230, 60-199231, 61-20428, 61-20429, 61-20430, 61-65525, 61-65526, 61-141085, 61-141214, "European Patent Application" No. 0162225A1, 0168004A2, "United States Patents" (now pending).

Yamakawa, T. (1986) High-speed fuzzy controller hardware system, "Proceedings 2nd Fuzzy System Symposium, June 16-18, Tokyo, Japan", pp. 122-130.

Yamakawa, T. (1987) A simple fuzzy hardware system employing MIN & MAX operations, "Proceedings 2nd Congress of IFSA, July 20-25, Tokyo, Japan".

Yamakawa, T. (in press) Fuzzy hardware systems of tomorrow, " Artificial Intelligence: Applications of Qualitative Reasoning" (E. Sanchez, ed.), Pergamon, Oxford.

Yamakawa, T.; Miki, T. (1986) The current mode fuzzy logic integrated circuits fabricated by the standard CMOS process, "IEEE Transactions Comp", Vol. C-35, No. 2, pp. 161-165.

Yamakawa, T.; Sasaki, K. (1987) Fuzzy memory device, "Proceedings 2nd Congress of IFSA, July 20-25, Tokyo, Japan.

Yamakawa, T.; Miki, T.; Ueno, F. (1984) Basic fuzzy logic circuit formed by using p-MOS current mirror circuits, "Transactions IECE of Japan" Vol. J67-C, No. 12, pp. 1022-1029.

Zadeh, L.A. (1965) Fuzzy sets, "Information and Control" Vol. 8, pp. 338-353.

Zadeh, L.A. (1973) Outline of a new approach to the analysis of complex systems and decision processes, "IEEE Transactions Systems, Man and Cybernetics" Vol. SMC-3, No. 1, pp.28-44.

Zadeh, L.A. (1975a) Calculus of fuzzy restrictions, "Fuzzy Sets and Their Applications to Cognitive and Decision Processes", Academic Press, New York, pp. 1-39.

Zadeh, L.A. (1975b) The concept of a linguistic variable and its application to approximate reasoning I, II, III, "Information Sciences" Vol. 8, pp. 199-249, 301-357, Vol. 9, pp. 43-80.

Zadeh, L.A. (1983) The role of fuzzy logic in the management of uncertainty in expert systems, "Fuzzy Sets and Systems" Vol. 11, No. 3, pp. 199-227.

Zimmermann, H.J. (1985) "Fuzzy Set Theory - and Its Applications", Kluwer-Nijhoff Publishing.

Zimmermann, H.J.; Zadeh, L.A.; Gaines, B.R. (1984) "Fuzzy Sets and Decision Analysis", North-Holland, Amsterdam.

Applications to Social Sciences

TIPI, an Expert System written in Le-Lisp for a French Bank

J.M. Serre

Arthur Andersen, Paris (France)

R. Voyer

ACT Informatique, Paris (France)

Keywords: *Expert systems, Lisp, inference engines, banking, property loans, decentralisation, mortgages.*
Abstract: This paper describes TIPI, an expert system designed to aid a bank clerk process an application for a loan from a customer. Commissioned by the Caisse d'Epargne, the system was designed by Arthur Andersen. It is currently being tested in a number of branches of the bank in Paris and the Paris region. TIPI was developed using the expert system shell Antinea, using the implementation of Le_Lisp developed for use on microcomputers by ACT Informatique under license from the Institute National de Recherches Informatique et Automatique (INRIA). Its use is simple. The bank employee feeds into the system all the information necessary for a consideration of the application. TIPI automatically calculates the amount of money which can be offered by the bank, in accordance with the type of loan requested, the customer's resources and the security offered. The result is given immediately.

1. INTRODUCTION

The TIPI system was designed for a major French bank, tbe Caisse d'Epargne, which is currently engaged in the decentralisation of its system for processing requests for home loans. There is intense competition in this sector but, since most interest rates are controlled by the government through different mechanisms, a great deal depends on the quality of service offered to clients, who shop around for the loan which best suits their needs. In particular, much depends on the time which elapses between the first contact with the client and the bank offering a loan.

Home loans in France are organised on a different basis from the English system. In particular, the government subsidises one type of loan which is only available on low-cost properties and to lower income families. These are known as Prêts Conventionnés, which cannot be easily translated into English, so we will refer to them as "controlled loans".

Many people want a *controlled loan*, which carries a rate of interest lower than the rate on the ordinary property loan from a bank. The difficulty is that the granting of these loans is subject to numerous regulations, concerning both the home which is to be purchased and the financial circumstances of the borrower. In order to ensure that all the conditions have been met, every application had to be first processed at branch level and then sent to a central office for checking, before going back to the branch, often with requests for more information from the applicant.

This can lead to frustrating delays and the essential goal of TIPI was
to provide branch employees with a tool which would allow them to process
an application correctly even if they did not have any detailed knowledge
of the complex conditions and regulations applying to a particular tupe of
loan. It should be emphasised that the the system does not either refuse or
grant loans. It merely discovers whether all the conditions for granting a
particular type of loan to a particular client have been satisfied, and
calculates the required term of repayment, according to the borrower's
means, and the security to be obtained from the borrower.

The aim was to produce applications which are correct in 80 or 90 per
cent of all cases presented to the system, and to transfer responsibility
for granting or refusing loans to the branch offices. In the first phase,
TIPI works only on requests for *controlled loans* but it will soon be
applied to all the loans offered by Caisse d'Epargne. At present, TIPI
uses around 300 rules, and it has been estimated that even an enlarged
system, which can cope with all types of loan offered by the Caisse
d'Epargne, will require fewer than 600 rules, and will function on an IBM
PC with 256k of memory.

Already, executives at the Caisse d'Epargne say that the use of TIPI
allows an employee without any specialised knowledge of mortgages to
process an application for a loan. The original goal has been achieved.
The project required 9 man months of work spread over a period of 5 months.
The use of Le_Lisp on an IBM PC allowed the designers at Arthur Andersen to
build a powerful system at a relatively low cost.

The *controlled loans* were selected as the starting point as they are
more hedged about by conditions and regulations than the other types of
loan, and if TIPI could cope with them, it was felt that other types of
loan could be incorporated without major difficulties.

The project was not aimed simply at producing correct applications for a
loan. In many cases the client had to choose between different types of
loan and it was intended that TIPI should eventually enable bank employees
to advise clients on the type of loan which best matched their needs. With
this in mind it was essential that TIPI should not simply be a "black box"
spewing out answers. It had to be able to present the chain of reasoning
which led it to a particular answer.

This transparency was necessary for another reason. The bank wanted a
system which would not simply be an expert crutch for inexperienced
employees. It also had to contribute to their training. By working through
the questions asked by the system, and discovering the chain of reasoning
which led to those questions, employees would begin to understand the
obstacles to making a valid application for a controlled loan.

Using the system was to be a mechanism for transferring knowledge from
the "experts" at head office to the branch officials. It was also felt that
if a system could be devised to cope with the *controlled loans* it would be
relatively easier to apply the same techniques to other types of loan.

2. WHY USE AN EXPERT SYSTEM?

It would certainly have been possible to devise a classical procedural
programme, which would enable a branch official to process applications for
controlled loans without recourse to an expert system written in LISP.
Some of the reasons for taking the expert system route have been suggested
above. They can be expanded as follows:

a)   The expert system is able to explain the reasons for its decisions at each stage. This is important both from the standpoint of staff development, and in debugging the system and improving its performannce;

b)   The expert system can easily grow, with additional rules, to deal with many different types of loan. Once built, the tool has many applications;

c)   Because the expert system was designed to capture information from human experts, and then to modify its own performance in line with its newly acquired knowledge, it is relatively easy to upgrade its performance, and to test instantly the effect of adding new rules.

d)   Our analysis also showed that it would have taken a far larger conventional program to handle the problem, and this would have taken longer to develop and more expensive to develop.

The system was able to begin as a tiny nucleus of rules, around 20, which could handle the most routine requests for loans. In fact, it required less than a day to move from an empty shell to a system which could process trivial examples. One can imagine the time it would have taken to reach this point by conventional means. In the field we were working, which is highly subject to changes in regulation by the government , it was essential that we should have an operational system which could evolve, which would be readily subject to modification.

3.THE CHOICE OF DEVELOPMENT TOOLS
We chose an expert system shell called ANTINEA. This shell functions using propositional logic and is written in Le_Lisp, an implementation of LISP widely used throughout Europe. The system is highly interactive and has a range of debugging tools. As it is written in LISP, ANTINEA could easily be modified and we were able to tailor the system precisely to the client's needs. Le LISP was developed at the French National Institute for Research into Computing and Automation (INRIA) and is available on a wide range of computers, from mainframes down to micros.

ANTINEA is a general inference engine. That is to say, it has no knowledge of any particular domain or application built in. However, it is particularly well suited to support diagnostic activities, or to act as a decision support system. The program was originally designed to deal with this type of problem, and the control structures and the modes of knowledge representation are particularly appropriate for this type of work. ANTINEA is a complete interactive system. The programming environment makes it possible to customise the program to a high degree. It includes all necessary file handling utilities, an editor-compiler and decompiler of the database of rules and information.

The method of representing knowledge is based on a system of production rules, and the language allows the use of variables, the testing or comparison of objects, and the use of the following operators for this purpose: =, < , >, <=, >=, <>, included_in, belonging_to, not_included_in, and not_belonging_to.

The language also permits the expression of negative conditions, applied globally or locally, and to test for the   existence, absence or indetermination of a value for a particular property. Contradictions and breaks in the chain of reasoning are thereby detected at the time of execution.

The form of reasoning is forward chaining (deduction), backward chaining induction), and a mixture of the two. The engine itself can be modified by procedures written in the host language (Le_Lisp). The programming environment allows for a simple construction of the knowledge base and its revision by the expert charged with the education of the system, and ensures a convivial interface with the end user (explaining the chain of reasoning, and allowing further equiry to elucidate obscure decisions). The interface includes two modules, the dialogue module and the Editor/environment manager.

The Dialogue Module;
This takes care of the dialogue with the user, interpreting the statements and requests of the latter, permitting the insertion of new information, or the running of particular utilities;

The Editor and Environment Manager;
The editor verifies the syntax of the knowledge provided by the expert. The manager organises the knowledge into a form which makes it readily usable by the system, and controls access to the different files by the user.

The Data Structures
The knowledge acquired by ANTINEA is organised in the form of production rules and initial data. There are two forms of representing the same rule: One is in a form which can be readily understood by the human expert, who is assisting in the construction of the system. The other is a formalism more readily interpreted by the inference engine. Rules drafted in the first form can be compiled by the system into themore efficient, coded form. This mechanism allows for great readability at one level, and optimum speed and efficiency at the other. It has made it possible to build quite complex systems on an IBM PC.

The vocabulary includes
- alphanumeric identifiers represented as Lisp atoms;
- keywords: if, then, not, absent, append, remove, run, modify, included_in, belonging_to, not_included_in, not_belonging _to, etc

The Production Rules: Rules are used to express certain properties in the classical form:

IF <certain conditions are met> THEN <certain conclusions follow>

The conditions can be the truth or falsity of a "fact" or of an operator and its argument. There are some subtle distinctions here:

NOT <fact>
is "true" if and only if NOT <fact> appears explicitly in the database. This is the classical negation of a system without variables.

ABSENT <fact>
is true if <fact> is not present in the database.This is an essential operator if one is dealing with an evolvable system like ANTINEA in which it is possible to temporarily suppress a fact.

<fact> BELONGS_TO <expression>
is true if <fact> is an element of the result (which must be a list) of the
evaluation of <expression>.

The conclusions can also take a number of forms. For example:

APPEND <fact>
adds the element <fact> to the data base. This element could be in the form
of a negation.

APPEND /<expression>
adds to the data base the result of evaluating <expression>. This element
could be in the form of a negation.

REMOVE <fact>
removes the element <fact> from the data base. This element could be in
the form of a negation.

REMOVE /<expression>
removes from the data base the result of evaluating <expression>. This
element could be in the form of a negation.

MODIFY <fact> = <expression>
assigns a new value, the evaluation of <expression>, to <fact>

The Initial Data
These are the facts which will be loaded into the system every time it is
booted. In the course of its use, they can be suppressed, but they will
reappear on rebooting. These facts, together with the rule base, form the
knowledge of the system. For example the knowledge base concerning the
Fibonacci series contains four initial facts:

```
fibrank = 2     ;the highest Fib number whose value is known
fibval  = 1     ;the initial value of fibrank
fib1    = 1     ;an initial value of one Fibonacci number
fib2    = 1     ;the value of another Fibonacci number
```

Provided the system has been well thoguht out, the user can be guided
through the process of feeding it information with little prior training.

The Definitions
It is also possible to include a collection of Lisp definitions,
declarations and functionals in the rule base. A single Lisp function may
appear in a number of rules, and may be used in conjunction with the
knowlegde base. One can also attach to each "fact" two Lisp functions. One
is activated when inforation is requested (type DQ), the other when the
fact is inserted in the database (type DA). In ANTINEA functionals of the
type DQ are used to ensure precision in the text of a question, and to
remove any possibility of ambiguity. They can also be used to attract the
attention of the user at certain critical stages of the dialogue. The
functionals of the DA type are used to enable ANTINEA to give detailed
expression to the different stages of a chain of argument.

Examples of representation
The Fibonnaci function can be expressed as a rule.

```
IF fibrank <> fib?
THEN MODIFY fib = (+ fib1 fib2)
AND MODIFY fib1 = fib2
AND MODIFY fib2 = fib
AND MODIFY fibrank = (1 + fibrang)
```

```
Facts:
fibrank = 2
AND fib1 = 1
AND fib2 = 1
AND fib = 1
```

```
Definitions
   (DQ fib? (print "Give a number please")
```

The ancient problem of the monkey and the bananas can be resolved using
ANTINEA based on propositional logic. Here is an example of a rule from
the system:

```
IF place_of_object = place_of_monkey
   AND height_of_object = 'height
   AND monkey_is_on = 'ladder
THEN  execute ((print "The monkey has" monkey_has))
   AND modify monkey_has = monkey_has_solved
   AND problem_resolved
```

A final example may be drawn from the TIPI system itself:

```
IF own_finance
   AND percentage_personal_contribution belongs_to '(20 30)
THEN modify global_score = (+ global_score 2)
   AND remove own_finance
   AND APPEND modification_global_score
```

4. THE ORGANISATION OF THE TIPI PROJECT

The system was devised by a specialist in expert systems and an expert in the representation of knowledge, both from Arthur Andersen & Co in Paris, working closely with three experts from the bank. During the first four months of the project, we were taking up around 20% of these three bank officials' working day. During the final month of the project, when we were testing the system, two of the officials were spending all their time on the project. For the Arthur Andersen consultancy, the project represented 200 person-days spread over six months in three unequal tranches.

During the first phase, lasting about one month, we studied the different types of loan offered by the bank, with a view to choosing one which would be most appropriately be used as the basis for the initial building of the system. As we explained earlier, we chose the *controlled loan* because it presented the most problems for bank officials, and offered the greatest challenge to our system.

The initial feasibility study called for a system which could be implemented on an ordinary microcomputer (an IBM PC with no more than 512k memory) , and it was estimated at that time that we would require around 300 rules. This estimate has turned out to be correct in terms of the number of rules, but we underestimated the complexity of those rules, and this did not emerge fully until we began to implement the system. What would happen, for example, when there were several borrowers seeking a loan jointly?

During the second phase we actually begn to write the system and this took around 4 months. As we have seen, this was undertaken on an incremental basis, gradually adding rules and knowledge as we tested the limits of each level reached. This allowed us to build a system without a complete prior specification, so it was a very different process to the conventional analysis-specification-coding cycle. The rules can be broken down into three different modules:

a) The regulations peculiar to the type of loan (in this case *controlled loans*), accounting for 100 rules;

b) The borrower's needs and ability to repay the loan, accounting for 140 rules; and

c) The security required by the bank before making the loan, 70 rules.

It will be readily understood that this modularity makes it relatively simple to apply the system to other types of loan, governed by different regulations or requiring different types of security. The involvement of the experts increased dramatically in line with the level of expertise achieved by the system. We strongly encouraged this by writing the rules in a form which they could easily understand. As the development of the system progressed the problem,s became more complex and the distinctions more subtle, and the language used to express the rules was a major factor. We were able to provide the experts both with the information they had fed into the system, and the ways in which the system would use the information.

The last phase of the system consisted of a month of intensive tests. This was not just a matter of making sure the system worked satisfactorily for all types of application for a *controlled loan,* but also to convince the officers of the bank that it worked as we had promised it would, taking into account the fact that they had no previous experience of this type of

software. The ability of the system to explain its reasoning in each case
was a decisive factor in convincing them to accept the system for use in
the branch offices of the bank.

5. FUTURE EVOLUTION OF THE SYSTEM
The method of implementation, with the increasing involvement of the bank
officials, and their subsequent conviction that the system worked, will
have important implications for the future development of the system. At
present it is being tested in branches of the Caisse d'Epargne.

The first stage will be to extend the system to deal with applications for
other types of property loan. The next stage might be to allow the system
to consider different types of loan simultaneously, and to recommend one
rather than another to the bank's officers for the consideration of the
client. This goes well beyond the task of deciding whether a particular
borrower qualifies for a particular kind of loan on a particular property.

This will take time, but it will be far easier to achieve now that there
are members of the bank's staff who are beginning to understand this system
of representing knowledge and its limitations, and who will therefore be
able to initiate further developments, playing an active role from the
beginning in selecting suitable areas for "expert system" treatment.

6. CONCLUSION
With the advent of expert systems, a new era in computing is opening. It is
too early to say that these programs are a key stage in the development of
Artificial Intelligence, but it is already clear that the results obtained
with these programs in a wide variety of applications are very encouraging
for the future.
    In our specific area of concern, we are very satisfied with our
experience of expert systems, and can see many applications in the banking
industry, and the number is growing day by day. With legislation tending to
create new complexities, the use of evolvable, incremental, and interactive
expert systems offers an important decision support system for hard-
pressed bank officials. TIPI is just the first step, which demonstrates
the feasibility of the system in a wide range of applications.
    The inference engine ANTINEA was particularly well suited to the kinds
of problems we encounter in our work with banks, and should allow projects
to be completed very fast. TIPI is giving satisfactory results, even when
it is used by non-experts. This is worth emphasising as many expert systems
give good results in the hands of an expert, familiar with the relevant
domain of knowledge, but fail utterly in the hands of the non-specialist.
    Even on a machine with only 256k RAM, with a windowed operating system,
all 300 rules and 300 functionals (types DQ and DA) can be held in the main
memory giving almost instantaneous response times. The experience has
satisfied us that expert systems are no longer laboratory animals bred to
solve toy problems and have joined the real world of commercial data
processing.

An Overview of an Intelligent Language Tutoring System

C.B. Schwind

Groupe Représentation et traitement des connaissances,
CNRS, Marseille (France)

Abstract

In this paper, we present the theoretical background and the
conception and implementation of an intelligent tutoring system
(ILTS). Our research is based on natural language understanding
(NLU) by logic, and a prototype of an ILTS for the German
language has been implemented in Prolog.

Introduction

The crux of the system is a very fundamental and "objective"
knowledge base of the language taught (in our application,
German). This knowledge base ought to represent a structural and
semantic knowledge of German in a manner allowing use in very
different ways by very different access modes. This "grammar" of
German is used to:

1. analyse sentences;
2. produce sentences;
3. analyse and explain errors;
4. answer students´ queries.

On this grammar knowledge base we can construct a number of
different language learning exercises, for example:

1. sentence construction;
2. translation;
3. pronominalization;
4. transformation of sentences (from active to passive form,
    from present to past tense, etc);
5. composition of sentences (under causality, temporality,
    etc);
6. text understanding and conversation.

We have conceived and implemented prototypes for some of these
exercises. Each prototype is constructed around the German
language knowledge base and the dictionaries and semantics. Each
uses grosso modo the same error and analysis modules. We think
that there are many different ways to react to a student´s error,
for example to give him a description of what he has done or to
ask him leading questions. Our objective has been to provide the

tools needed to produce a required teaching strategy easily. In the next section, we present a sample tutor-student dialogue session which follows a very simple strategy. The student is asked to do an exercise. When he makes an error the system provides an explanation in three steps, which are pursued successively:

1. indication of the existence of an error at a certain place without any explanation;
2. leading question;
3. description of the error, ie description of what would have been required and what the student has done.

Generally, 1 is carried out first. If the student asks why there is an error, he gets a hint by a leading question, and if he still manifests misunderstanding, he gets given the description of his error. But we should like to point out that for us this is one example of how one could conceive a tutoring session based on a well-constructed knowledge base and we by no way pretend that this is "the" tutoring strategy.

There are very few papers on an artificial intelligence based approach to language teaching (Weischedel et al. 1978, Pulman 1984). The major difference between our approach and that of Weischedel is that in our system the student can communicate with the "tutor" at different levels. He can do the exercise but he can also ask questions about the tutor's explanations, the exercise and the properties of the German language in general.

Most of today's computer-aided language instruction systems are based on preprogrammed exercises (Ahmad and Rogers 1981, Araki et al. 1975, Frizot 1981, Montrigaud 1981). These systems do not themselves have the knowledge required to resolve the exercises intended for the students. Hence, they are not able to generate any individual or intelligent reaction to students' errors or questions during a language exercise. In the last few years, intelligent tutoring systems which really dispose of knowledge about the taught domain have been introduced. Such a system:

1. itself is able to perform all the exercises presented to a student;
2. understands what the student has done and analyses individually his answers instead of matching them to a list of predefined solutions;
3. can answer questions asked by students about the problems presented, the system's analysis and corrections and the taught language in general.

We have observed that the majority of research on ITS describes technically or mathematically oriented domains (electronic troubleshooting, Brown et al. 1982; algebra, Genesereth 1982; integration, Kimball 1982). We feel that this orientation towards "reasoning" domains is not simply accidental but is due to the expert system oriented approach to intelligent tutoring. It is possible to view a language instruction system as an expert

EXPERT SYSTEM	ILTS
Knowledge Base	Grammar Knowledge Base
Problem solving	Exercise Execution
"Natural" Interface	Natural Language or Graphic Interface
Explication module	Error Explication

Figure 1

system (Figure 1) but at the technical level it is not entirely clear how to conceive and implement it as an expert system. What kind of reasoning is used in learning language? If a person tries to formulate a sentence, does he use reasoning such as "I have to choose this verb, it has two objects. I have to employ the imperfect, it is of that form, etc"?

The construction of an ILTS is also a very interesting application of natural language understanding (NLU). It requires a language description at a very sophisticated and exact level. However, the problems generated by NLU in general, and this application in particular, are sometimes different. The treatment of ill-formed sentences, which has been widely studied during the last few years (Weischedel and Sondheimer 1983, Carbonell and Hayes 1983, Jensen et al. 1983, Granger 1983, Carberry 1984, Lesmo and Torasso 1984), is a good example of these differences. In our language teaching application, we have to represent a corpus of language knowledge which is complete with respect to the language student. One of our paradigms is that the system knows the subset of the taught language and the student has to learn it. So we deal only with students´ errors with respect to the language but not with the system´s errors with respect to a fluent speaker´s language knowledge. On the other hand, the student´s error analysis is crucial because it has to be worked out in more detail. Not only has our system to diagnose what error has occurred (and not just to understand the sentences in spite of errors) but it has also to explain to the student what has gone on. This presupposes recognizing what the student has done instead of what he was supposed to do. Natural language is

already highly ambiguous but errors in natural language are more
ambiguous.
In the next section, we give an overview of the entire system
and illustrate by a sample-commented exercise session the tasks
of the different modules and how they interact.
In the third section, we discuss the problem of error analysis
and we present our classification and treatment (ie analysis,
interpretation and correction or explanation) of student´s
errors. Due to limited space, we present only briefly our
treatment of errors. For a more detailed discussion see Schwind
(1986).
Our system is represented in logic and has been implemented in
Prolog.

Overview of the ILTS

Figure 2 is an overview of our ILTS for German. At the
theoretical level, the entire system is a conjunction of logical
formulae. Conceptually, we distinguish the following main parts:

1. German grammar knowledge base   KB
2. semantic laws about grammar concepts   GRA-SEM
3. error analysis modules   ERR
4. dictionaries   LEX
5. semantic laws for dictionary terms   SEM
6. dialogue managing module   DIA
7. exercise modules   UEB
8. editors   EDI
9. French interface to KB   FRZ

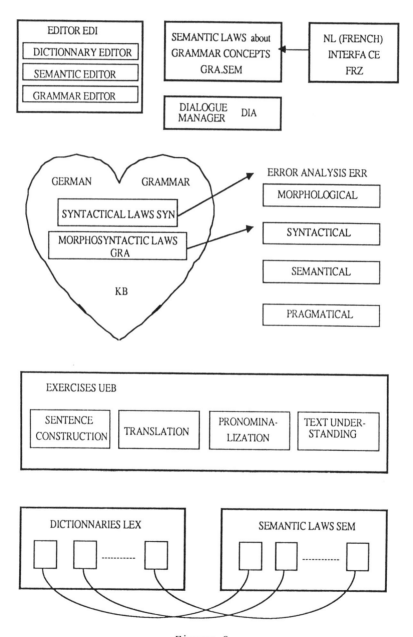

Figure 2

KB consists of grammatical laws for the construction of adjectives, nouns, articles and syntactic laws for the construction of sentences. The construction laws describe the morphological and syntactic properties of the different categories and their inflection groups and they can be used for analysis and for synthesis. The syntactic laws are formulated as an attributed feature grammar (Schwind 1978, 1986) which can be implemented immediately as a logic grammar (Colmeraurer 1978) and is enriched by morphological and semantic laws which are applied during sentence analysis. These laws also use the error analysis laws. KB is simultaneously used as a sentence analysis and synthesis module and as a knowledge base for German which can be interrogated. Grammatical knowledge is represented entirely descriptively and this allows different access types. When the grammar is used within an exercise for the analysis of students' sentences the error analysis modules are called by the syntactic analysis during sentence analysis. ERR is completely independent from SYN. This makes it very easy to suppress error analysis whenever this is required for some application of syntactic laws. For example, error analysis is naturally not applied for sentence generation.

We distinguish four types of error: morphological (agreement errors), syntactic (word order within a sentence is violated), semantic (semantic predicates are not true for tuples of concepts within a sentence) and pragmatic (pragmatic predicates are not true). Explanations of errors are given the following three steps:

1. When an error is diagnosed the system indicates only the noun phrase or verb phrase where the error was found without giving any more detail. It asks the student to correct his error.

2. If the student asks for further explanation or if he does not succeed in giving the correct construction, the system asks a leading question which points out the problem. For example, if the case of a whole noun phrase is wrong, the system would ask "Which case is required by the verb?". If only the case or number of an adjective or noun x is wrong, the question would be for example "What is the accusative singular of x?" (when x should be in the accusative singular). When it is not clear if the sentence (ie the verb) or one of the noun phrases should be in the singular or plural form the system tries to clarify that by asking which number the student wanted to choose.

3. If the student still does not succeed or understand, the system provides the violated grammatical rule and expains how it has been violated.

The dictionaries contain roots of adjectives, nouns and verbs, and proper names. To every dictionary belongs a set of semantic predicates (SEM) that represents semantic laws and semantic relations among concepts. The semantic predicates and their laws are the same as those described in Schwind (1985): isa, sup, mod, ref, verb-complement relations.

The exercise modules (UEB) are all organized in a similar way. Every exercise is of a certain type, for example, sentence construction, translation, transformations (from active to passive, from present to past tense, from noun to pronoun, etc). Every exercise type provides a teacher access and a student access. The teacher can then define a particular exercise of a certain type with the vocabulary he wants and with the semantics he wants. He can choose the verbs, adjectives, nouns and proper names he wants. When he uses unknown words he is asked if he wants to add them to the dictionary and if he does the system calls the lexical editor. The knowledge base and the dictionaries and their semantic predicates may be interrogated in French. In order to process French queries we have a French NLU understanding module (FRZ) and semantic predicates about grammar terms (GRA-SEM). Figure 3 shows how a student's sentence is processed by different modules.

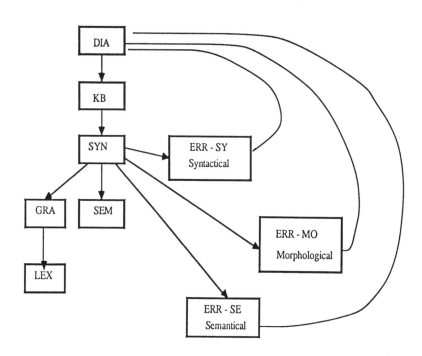

Figure 3

Example: "die Kind spielt" (the child plays)

DIA decides that this is a German sentence (by finding occurrences of German words). Then KB tries to parse the sentence by calling SYN. SYN calls GRA and GRA LEX for word analysis. In our example, "die" and "Kind" do not morphologically agree, hence ERR-MO is called and tries to find which error has been made. The result is memorized by DIA and the sentence analysis pursued. SYN calls SEM to verify if the noun phrase "die Kind" can be the subject of the verb phrase "spielt". The sentence is syntactically and semantically correct.

We now present a sample dialogue from an exercise session. The communication language used with this system is French or German. The taught language is German. The English translation is given in parentheses. This exercise is a simple sentence construction exercise. The student is given a list of verbs, nouns and adjectives from which he has to construct sentences. Now he can either construct a German sentence or he can ask questions about the exercise, the grammar or the system's error analysis. He asks these questions either in the taught language or in French. A dialogue is a sequence of dialogue sessions about different themes. Within every exercise the following themes can occur:

  i.   doing the exercise;
 ii.   asking questions about the grammar;
iii.   asking questions about the system's explanations;
 iv.   asking questions about word translations;
  v.   asking questions about word meanings.

The sample dialogue is:

(1) Sy: Formez des phrases à partir des éléments suivants (construct sentences from the following words):

lesen (read)	Lehrer (teacher)	faul (lazy)
schreiben (write)	Tafel (blackboard)	fleißig (diligent)
antworten (answer)	Schuler (pupil)	rot (red)
fragen (ask)	Heft (copybook)	groß (big)
	Bleistift (pencil)	

(2) St: j´aimerais voir la conjugaison de "schreiben" (I would like to see the conjugation of schreiben).

(3) Sy: Singular   Plural

1. Person ich screibe	wir schreiben
2. Person du schreibst	ihr schreibt
3. Person er schreibt	sie schreiben

(4) St: Quel est le pluriel de Tafel (What is the plural of Tafel)?

(5) Sy: Tafeln.

(6) St: Que veux dire "faul" (What is the meaning of faul)?

(7) Sy: paresseux.

(8) St: Der Lehrer fragt den faulem Schuler.

(9) Sy: **Erreur d´accord dans "den faulem Schuler" (Agreement error in "den faulem Schuler").

    réessayez (try it again)!
    La phrase est sémantiquement et syntaxiquement correcte.
    (The sentence is semantically and syntactically correct.)

(10) St: Quel cas demande "fragen" (what case is required by "fragen")?

(11) Sy: accusatif!

(12) St: den faulen schuler.

(13) Sy: Gut (good)!

    Mais "Schuler" s´écrit avec une majuscule (But "Schuler" begins with a capital letter)!

(14) St: Der Schuler antwortet den Lehrer.

(15) Sy: **Erreur d´accord entre sujet et objet.
    (Agreement error between the subject and the object).
    La phrase est sémantiquement et syntaxiquement correcte.

(16) St: Pourquoi (Why)?

(17) Sy: Quel cas demande antworten (Which case is required by antworten)?

(18) St: accusatif ou datif (Accusative or dative)?

(19) Sy: datif (Dative)!

(20) St: Quel est le datif de "der" (What is the dative of "der")?

(21) Sy: dem.

(22) St: Der Schuler antwortet dem Lehrer.

(23) Sy: Gut!

(24) St: Pourquoi est-elle sémantiquement correcte (Why is it semantically correct)?

(25) Sy: "antworten" demande un sujet et un objet vivant."Schuler" et"Lehrer" sont vivants.

    ("antworten" requires an animate subject and object.
    "Schuler" and "Lehrer" are animate.)

(26) St: Que veut dire "schreiben" en francais?

(27) Sy: écrire.

(28) St: et lesen?

(29) Sy: lire.

(30) St: et schnell?

(31) Sy: rapide. Mais cet adjectif n´est pas dans la liste des mots de l´exercice.

> (But this adjective is not within the word list of the exercise.)

(32) St: Der Lrehrer schreibt dem Heft.

(33) Sy: "Lrenrer" n´est pas dans la dictionnaire ("Lrehrer" is not in the dictionary.)

> **Erreur sémantique entre "schreiben" et "dem Heft".
> (Semantic error between "schreiben" and "dem Heft".)

(34) St: Why?

(35) "schreiben" demande un objet indirecte vivant. "Heft" n´est pas vivant.

> ("screiben" requires an animate indirect object. "Heft" is not animate.)

(36): Dem Schuler antwortet der Lehrer.

(37): Sehr gut (very good)!

The tutor-student dialogue around this exercise passes off as follows (Sy stands for the system and St for the student):

(1) The exercise is presented to the student. The system waits for a German sentence or for a question (in German or French).

(2) The student asks for the conjugation of one of the verbs.

(4) He has another question about a plural form. (German words within French sentences may be surrounded or not by quotes.) (2)-(5) are under theme (ii).

(6) He asks for the French translation of one of the adjectives. [Theme (iv).]

(8) The student tries a first sentence. [Theme (i).]

(9) The system has recognized an error. I: does not immediately correct or explain this error but indicates to the student where the error occurred and asks him to try again. Now the student can do any of the following:

      reconstruct the ill-formed noun phrase;
      reconstruct the whole sentence;
      ask for an explanation of the error;
      ask a question about the grammar;
      form another sentence.

(10) He asks a question about the object case of his sentence. DIA memorizes his last sentence (6) and its error analysis in order to always be able to present it to the student.

After the system's answer (11) the student succeeds in constructing the correct noun phrase (12). He only wrote tne noun "Schuler" beginning with a small letter instead of a capital letter, (10) is theme (ii), (12) is theme (i).

(14) The student forms another sentence. At this moment, the system will no longer remember the old sentence and its error analysis. This sentence contains an agreement error.

(16) The student asks for more explanation.

(17) Instead of directly explaining the error, the system asks a leading question from which the student could deduce that there is a problem with the case.

(18) The student really doesn't know. Hence, the system gives him the answer (19).

(20-22) After asking again for the dative form of the definite article, the student can finally correctly construct his sentence.

(24) But he has not finished. He would like more explanation about the system's semantic deduction.

(25) The system explains the main steps of its deduction within the semantic predicates.

(26-32) After some other questions about translation which may also be asked in elliptical form, the student forms another sentence (32). When he asks for a word which is in the dictionary but not in the word list the system gives him the translation but tells him that the word doesn't belong to the actual exercise. The same answer is given when the student uses a known word that does not belong to the exercise within a sentence construction.

(33) Sentence (32) contains an orthographic error. We do not correct these automatically. When a sentence contains a word which cannot be recognized the system is however able to process the other parts of the sentence. Here the unrecognized noun is before the verb. In this case, the syntactic analysis is pursued from the verb to the end of the sentence and this verb phrase can be completely analysed. There is another crucial problem with this sentence which is not treated at the moment. "schreiben" (write) requires an animate dative object and a prepositional object with the preposition "an", "in" or "auf" which is an object on which one can write (something which is made of paper

or a blackboard, etc). Hence sentence (32) could also be syntactically incorrect, the correct form being "in das Heft". We cannot analyse this error because we do not suppose that a whole preposition could have been omitted by the student. It will be very very complex to include considerations of this type.

(35) The system explains the main steps of its deduction and the point where it failed.

(36) is very good because the student has used a rather unusual syntactic form with the object at the beginning of the sentence. In German, every noun phrase within a sentence can be topicalized in this way. This is again a source of ambiguity because the accusative is very often identical to the nominative. In (36), it cannot be decided whether the student has made two errors one in the subject and the other in the object case of the sentence. But generally, whenever we can find one correct analysis we choose it.

Error Analysis and Explanation

There have been many papers on ill-formed or ungrammatical input in the last five years (Weischedel and Sondheimer 1983, Carbonell and Hayes 1983, Jensen et al. 1983, Granger 1983, Carberry 1984, Lesmo and Torasso 1984). In Weischedel and Sondheimer (1983), two types of ill-formed input are distinguished:

1. errors with respect to the language;
2. sentences which are correct but cannot be analysed by the system.

The second type of error contains errors of the system rather than errors of a user. The classification refers to users who generally know their language better than the system does but who sometimes produce ill-formed sentences. In our application however, we build on the following hypothesis:

1. the student knows less than the system;
2. the system knows what the student knows and what he has already learnt.

Later Weischedel and Sondheimer discuss four alternative approaches to the treatment of errors where grammar rules for well-formed and grammar rules for ill-formed sentences are used together (simultaneously) or one after the other. We think that any approach to the treatment of ill-formedness depends on the underlying grammar theory. We consider as a base for our grammar transformational theory. The reason is that we observe that most syntactic errors made by students of German result typically from the non-application of an obligatory transformation rule. A very frequent error is verb inversion: whenever a sentence begins with a part of speech other than the subject, eg an adverb or a subordinated sentence, the verb goes to the beginning of the sentence just behind the adverb. For example:

(1) Heute gehe ich nicht in die Schule.
    Today go   I   not   to school.

(2) Weil   Julia   so schrie   weinte Amandine.
    Because Julia cried so much, wept Amandine.

Typically French or English students of German would say:

*(3) Heute ich gehe nicht in die Schule.

*(4) Weil Julia so schrie, Amandine weinte.

It is self-evident to distinguish morphological, syntactic, semantic and pragmatic errors. The underlying grammar formalism is an attributed feature grammar where the features describe the morphological and semantic properties of categories (Schwind 1978, 1986). Every grammar rule is associated with morphological and semantic rules which treat the morphological and semantic agreements and errors.
  Syntactic errors are either by non-application of a grammar rule or are explicitly describable because word order has been violated.
  Semantic errors occur when concepts are related within a sentence which cannot be related in this manner.
  Pragmatic errors are errors of referring to a misconception of the real world context which underlies the text or the dialogue. We do not treat pragmatic errors in this paper.
  The treatment and even the definition of ill-formedness within a language tutoring context is very different to that within the context of NLU in general, eg of database access or the like. To formulate this concisely we could say: we try sensitive parsing rather than robust parsing. That is we aim at a system which is very sensitive to all kinds of error which could occur and moreover tries to find the "why" and the "how" of errors.

Agreement errors

The analysis of agreement errors in German is complex because the words are highly morphologically ambiguous. There are 24 different definite articles (4 cases, 3 genus and 2 numbers) but only 6 different words for them, each of which has between 2 and 8 interpretations (or meanings). In the same way, every noun has at most four different forms which again have 24 different morphosyntactic meanings. But the case and number of a noun phrase within a sentence depend on the verb, a case is required by a verb and the number is determined by it. Hence an error in the number of a noun phrase could also be an error of the number of the verb.
  We treat the following agreement errors:

    Agreement between:
      adjectives   within an adjective group
      adjective group-noun   within a noun group
      article-noun group   within the noun phrase

Agreement errors are treated along the following criterion:

  1. We take the error which is the highest possible within a syntax tree.

Example: Er glaubt an der Gotter

"an" is a preposition which requires the accusative case, "der Gotter" is in genitive. Hence the error is signalled for the whole noun phrase "der Gotter".
2. Criterion 1 is not applied when a subject noun phrase, which should be in nominative case, could be analysed as having another case, whereas parts of it are in the nominative. The reason is that we assume that people would not really make mistakes about the nominative of the subject of a phrase, ie they would not try to form another case for a subject noun phrase.

Example: der Gotter glaubt

According to criterion 1 the noun phrase "der Gotter" is entirely analysed as a genetive but it is the subject of the sentence. Hence it has to be in nominative case, "der" and "Gotter" can both be in nominative case but "der" is singular and "Gotter" is plural. Hence this error interpretation (error in number between the article and the noun) is chosen instead of the first one (error in the case of the noun phrase) although this situates the error deeper down the syntax tree.

Syntactic errors

We consider two sources for syntactic errors:

1. non-application of obligatory transformational rules;
2. application of "false" rules usually derived from the native language of the student.

In Schuster (1985), she claims to use systematically (and automatically) this relationship between errors made by second language studying students and the grammar of their mother tongue for error handling. We will show by two examples how errors can be treated in Prolog very clearly:

1. In German, adjectives precede the noun group, in French, they frequently follow it. This is described by the following rules (formulated as Prolog clauses):

```
np(X,X0):- art(X,X1), ng(X1,X0,F),F.
ng(X,X0,correct):- ag(X,X1),noun(X1,X0);
                   noun(X,X0).
ng(X,X0error(noun,ag)):- noun(X,X1), ag(X1,X0).
ag(X,X0):- adj(X,X0);
           adj(X,X1), ag(X1,X0).
art("das".Y,Y).
noun("Auto".Y,Y).
adj("blaue".Y,Y).
correct.
error(noun,ag):- error-message.
```

In order to be more understandable, we simplified these
rules by suppressing all terms describing the morphological
and semantic analysis and properties of the categories. The
noun phrase "das blaue Auto" would be analysed correctly as
np("das"."blaue"."Auto".nil,nil,correct) whereas the
incorrect noun phrase "das Auto blaue" is analysed as
np("das"."Auto"."blaue".nil,nil,error(noun,ag)). The np-rule
treats the error predicate F, which is a Prolog term, by
calling it.

2. In German, verb groups in the perfect tense are frequently
split off. The auxiliary takes the place of the verb, and
the participle goes to the end of the sentence, eg:

"Ich habe dem Baby Milch gegeben"
"I   have to the baby milk given"

French (and equally English) students of German would say

"Ich habe gegeben dem Baby Milch"

This transformation rule, as well as its erroneous omission, is
represented in Prolog as follows:

```
vp(X,XE,correct):-
      verb(X,X1,t,XH), compls(X1,X0),eq(X0,XH.XE).
vp(X,X0,error(verb,part-perf)):-
      verb(X,X1,perf,XH),freeze(X2,compls(X2,X0)),eq(X1,XH.X2).
verb("fahrt".Y,Y,pres,0).
verb("ist".Y,Y,perf,"gefahren").
```

Again, this description is simplified in order to make clear how
these transformation rules function in Prolog. freeze is a
predefined predicate of Prolog II [PrologIA]. freeze(X,P) delays
the evaluation of P until X takes a value. compls analyses the
verb complements of the sentence. The order of the sentence parts
is produced by the equations between them (predicate eq).

Semantic errors

All concepts described on the natural language level by either
nouns, verbs or adjectives are described semantically by
predicates and rules about these predicates (Schwind 1985): isa,
sup, mod, ref, verb-complement relations.

   sup(x,y) holds if x is a concept superordinated to y,
            eg: sup(town,chief-town)
   ref(x,y) holds if the adjective x can modify the noun y, eg
            ref(red,car)
            objl(x,y) is a verb-object relation and holds if
            the concept y can be an indirect object of the verb
            x.

sup is transitive and all the other relations are transitive with
sup, eg:

objl(x,y)∧ sup(y,z)∧ ‾| contra(x,y) -> objl(x,z)

Contra(x,z) is true whenever the concept x has properties which
contradict properties of the concept z. These semantic predicates
are evaluated during syntactic analysis in order to treat
semantic agreement.   In Prolog, these rules are formulated in the
following way:

vp(X,X0,V):- verb(X,X1,V), np(X1,X0,N), agree-sem(V,N).
agree-sem(V,N):- objl(V,N)!;
                      sem-err(V,N).

When a verb phrase vp is formed by a verb V and a noun N which is
not a possible object for V a semantic error is diagnosed and the
appropriate explanation is presented to the student.

Conclusions

Within this paper we only present a very short overview of our
ILTS. Our experiments with language students and teachers have
shown that it is possible to do interesting language learning
exercises with a computer.

References

Ahmad, K.; Rogers, M. (1981) Development of teaching packages for
undergraduate   students of German,   "Computer Simulation in
University Teaching" (D.   Wildenberg,   ed.),   North-Holland,
Amsterdam.

Araki, J.; Tanabe, Y.; Falt, B.; Johnson, W.R.; Hayashi, H.
(1975) CAI in language education, "Computers in Education" (O.
Lecarme and R.Lewis, eds), IFIP, North-Holland, Amsterdam.

Brown, F.; Schwind, C. (1978) Outline of an integrated theory of
natural language understanding, "Natural Language Communication
with Computers" (L. Bolc, ed.), Lecture Notes in Computer Science
No. 63, Springer Verlag, New York.

Brown, J.S.; Burton, R.R.; De Kleer, J. (1982) Pedagogical,
natural language and knowledge and engineering techniques in
SOPHIE I,II, and III, "Intelligent Tutoring Systems" (D. Sleeman
and J.S. Brown, eds), Academic Press, London.

Carberry, S. (1984) Understanding pragmatically ill-formed input,
" Proceedings of Coling 84".

Carbonell, J.G.; Hayes, P.J. (1983) Recovery strategy for parsing
extragrammatical language, "American Journal of Computational
Linguistics" No. 9 NR 3-4.

Carbonell,   J.G.;   Hayes,   P.J.   (1984)   Coping   with
extragrammaticallity, "Proceedings of Coling 84".

Colmeraurer, A. (1978) Metamorphosis grammars, "Natural Language Communication with Computers" (L. Bolc, ed.), Lecture Notes in Computer Science No. 63, Springer Verlag, New York.

Frizot, D. (1981) Teaching English with computer assisted learning, "Computers in Education" (R> Lewis and D. Tagg, eds), IFIP, North-Holland, Amsterdam.

Genesereth, M.R. (1982) The role of plans in intelligent teaching systems, "Intelligent Tutoring Systems" (D. Sleeman and J.S. Brown, eds), Academic Press, London.

Granger, R.H. (1983) The NOMAD system: expectation-based detection and correction of errors during understanding of syntactically and semantically ill-formed text, "American Journal of Computational Linguistics" No. 9 NR 3-4.

Jensen, K.; Heidorn, G.E.; Miller, E.A.; Ravin, Y. (1983) Parse fitting and prose fixing: getting a hold on ill-formedness, "American Journal of Computational Linguistics" No. 9, NR 3-4.

Kimball, R. (1982) A self-improving tutor for symbolic integration, "Intelligent Tutoring Systems" (D. Sleeman and J.S. Brown, eds), Academic Press, London.

Lesmo, L.; Torasso, P. (1984) Intepreting syntactically ill-formed sentences, "Proceedings of Coling 84".

Montrigaud, A. (1981) Automatic generation of exercises on Italian Grammar, "Computers in Education" (R. Lewis and D. Tagg, eds), IFIP, North-Holland, Amsterdam.

Prologia (1985) "Prolog II, Version 2.2, Reference Manual".

Pulman, S.G. (1984) Limited domain systems for language teaching, "Proceedings of Coling 84".

Schuster, E. (1985) Grammars as user models, "IJCAI 85, Proceedings of the Ninth International Conference on Artificial Intelligence" No. 1, pp. 20-22.

Schwind, C. (1978) A formalism for the description of question answering systems, "Natural Language Communication with Computers" (L. Bolc, ed.), Lecture Notes in Computer Science, No. 63, Springer Verlag, New York.

Schwind, C. (1985) Logic based natural language processing, "Natural Language Understanding and Logic Programming" (V. Dahl and P. Saint-Dizier, eds), North-Holland, Amsterdam.

Schwind, C. (1986) "An Intelligent Language Tutoring System", Research Report GRTC 105.

Weischedel, M.; Sondheimer, N.K. (1983) Meta-rules as a basis for processing ill-formed input, "American Journal of Computational Linguistics" No. 9, NR 3-4.

Weischedel, R.M.; Voge, W.M.; James, M. (1978) An artificial intelligence approach to language instruction, "Artificial Intelligence" No. 10, pp. 225-240.

Implementing Programming Consultation System LISP-PAL: Framework for Handling Frame-Based Knowledge in Object-Oriented Paradigm

S. Uehara, R. Nishioka, T. Ogawa and T. Mohri

Fujitsu Laboratories Ltd, Kawasaki (Japan)

abstract

LISP-PAL is a consultation system for teaching LISP programming skills through natural language conversation. As its knowledge base, the system integrates a frame system and a production system in an object-oriented paradigm. In this paper, we argue that an object-oriented paradigm is not sufficient to handle such a basic operation as knowledge retrieval on the frame system model. By implementing LISP-PAL, we introduce the idea that the nested frame expression plus associated operations becomes a very powerful tool for handling such a knowledge base. The tool is implemented with an object-oriented LISP-based language, and enables us to handle knowledge more flexibly than an object-oriented paradigm. The framework represented here is general, and a summary comparison with other related work is given.

Keywords: knowledge representation, frame system, object-oriented paradigm, production system, consultation system.

1. Introduction

The primary objective of our research is to build a system that intelligently transfers or teaches expert knowledge from the knowledge base to users, and to develop a framework that accelerates the production of knowledge-based application systems.

Our long-term target is software engineering. It is recognized that education is a very important factor in improving software productivity. Large numbers of consultation or advising systems in this area are expected to emerge in the near future. Currently, our focus is on a LISP programming consultation system.

Our application requires a natural-language interface for the following reasons:
(1)Many users are casual users and/or newcomers.
(2)In on-line documents, the user searches by using keywords. In a consultation system, the user should be able to use any expressions to obtain information. Only natural language enables a user to truly express a purpose or indicate what is to be done.
(3)A natural language interface is a flexible tool if it supports the context process and augmentation of omitted words.

The requirements for LISP-PAL are summarized as follows:
(1)Displayed knowledge should meet the user's need: anything beyond one's interest is noise. In contrast, related and refined knowledge displayed at the appropriate time plays an important role in his knowledge building.
(2)System response should vary in different contexts and in accordance with the user's skill or interests: what he knows and what he wants to know.
(3)The system should have a tutoring component because skills, such as writing program schemas, are more effectively taught in the course of programming.

Under the above conditions, the technical elements provided to support LISP-PAL are:

(1)Japanese-language processing

(2)framework for knowledge representation and handling

(3)context management

(4)a user model

A prototype system has been developed. A sample interaction with an English translation is shown in the appendix.

This paper concentrates on our approach to item 2 above. We discuss the knowledge structure of the system, and a new framework for handling knowledge, which is implemented on an object-oriented, LISP-based language.

2. Structure of the System and Knowledge Base

The fundamental part of domain knowledge can be acquired and systematized from text books such as [9,10]. We observed that the frame system is appropriate for forming inter-related knowledge elements to be included in a knowledge structure. Heuristic knowledge, such as question-answering, problem solving, or BUGGY problem solving strategy can be properly represented in production system (IF-THEN rules).

The implementation language we chose is a multi-paradigm language, integrated with LISP functional/procedural oriented, data oriented, rule-oriented, and object-oriented paradigms, which is inspired by LOOPS [2,8]. An object-oriented paradigm is suitable for implementing a frame system because of the ability to define: (1)object hierarchy, (2)object's method, and (3)demon.

The structure of the current system is depicted in Figure 1. Questions from a user are translated by the Japanese translator into an internal representation, called SEM (semantic representation), which expresses the essential meaning of an input sentence. The Japanese Translator is implemented with a portable natural language interface [7], which requires a world model and a word-dictionary customized in the LISP programming domain.

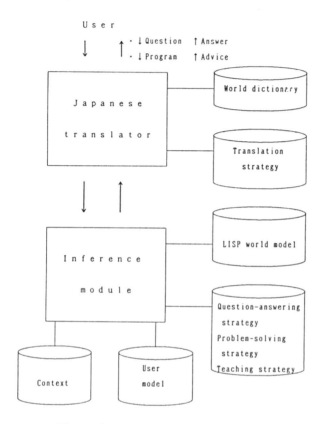

Figure 1. Overview of LISP-PAL system

Given the SEM input, the inference module applies the
question-answer rules to fetch appropriate knowledge from the
LISP world model, then generates a response in SEM. In this process, a question and a response both in SEM are added into the
context and the user model is modified. The modified context and
user model are used later for production-rule execution.

The system supports a tutoring function which chooses an appropriate problem to a user request, and advises the user if he
makes a mistake, in a fashion similar to LISPtutor based on the
study of [1]. Our approach differs in that the subgoals are
represented in SEM uniformly in the system and, after completion

of practice, the system teaches more elegant skills which were not used in the practice.

The knowledge base is made up of frame-based and production rules as illustrated in Figure 2. The core of the knowledge base is the LISP world model, in which knowledge of LISP functions consists of the following slots: name, syntax, function/purpose, usage-example, side-effect, caution, dependency. The important point is that a function/purpose slot contains a pointer to the descendant of a purpose object which specifies the very meaning of LISP functions, like "concatenate lists" of function APPEND.

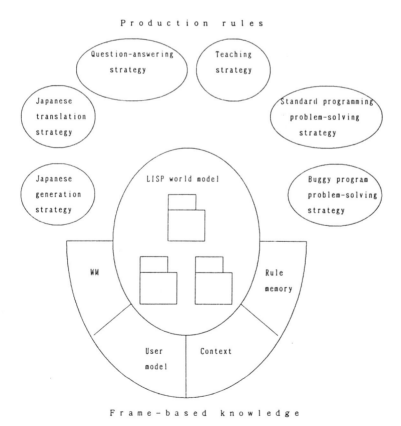

Figure 2. Structure of LISP-PAL knowledge base

Most other slots contain a string of Japanese words for display to the user.

The following memories constitute subworlds of the LISP world model: working memory (WM) for question-answering, user model, context, and rule memory used during rule execution. Various strategies such as for question-answering, the other part of the knowledge base, are implemented with production rules.

3. Problem in Handling the Knowledge Base

Does an object-oriented paradigm, such as realized by LOOPS, provide us with sufficient features to handle a frame-based knowledge base? Our experience says "no." The main features object-oriented languages provide are defining or using methods for only a single object or a hierarchy of objects. In other words, the framework of the object-oriented paradigm only allows us to traverse networked objects in sequence.

However, a set of networked objects rather than a single object is usually the target when an inference is made or a knowledge base is searched. Conditionals in production rules concern a fact represented by networked objects.

We concluded that a new type of framework is necessary, one which greatly improves the writability of networked objects. Without such a framework, the complex strategy for handling the user model or the context cannot easily be embedded into a program and maintained.

Another problem concerns the management of separated world models under the LISP world model, such as WM, the user model, etc. Most of these consist of instances of class objects in the LISP world model. The mechanism needed must distinguish between objects in different world models when accessing with production rules; we need a framework for management of several interrelated world models.

4. Proposed Framework

Our solution to the problem of handling networked objects is: (1)the extension of SEM to allow nested frame descriptions, and (2)the introduction of knowledge-based operations on SEM expressions. The design of the SEM representation is based on frame-theory and predicate calculus, as is CD [3]. This framework enables writing of networked objects directly in conditions of production rules. We called the tool implemented on this framework, SEMtool.

Our principal idea in designing the consultation system is that we should be free to choose an appropriate paradigm or notation at different places. This idea is illustrated in Figure 3. The idea that we should not be confined to a single notation is advocated in [3].

Figure 3 shows different representations of the same input sentence in the ovals, "make a list from elements of list A, which satisfy a certain condition." The frame-based networked knowledge is at the abstract level; there are one instance of the class "make-from," and three instances of the classes "list" and "element." These instances are networked by an instance-of and an attribute relation.

In the concrete representation, B (meaning basic representation), supported by our implementation language, each instance object must be described separately. A slot, such as "super" or "object" of an object "make-from-1", contains an instance object name, in a fashion similar to that of a pointer.

In SEM, the same knowledge can be described in a compact and a frame based form, where a pointer slot of little interest is suppressed. In this nested frame representation, an object name and a slot name appear alternately, that is, (make-from (object (list))...). It should be noted that an instance name does not appear because the SEM represents a meaning of the sentence rather than an internal representation or instances.

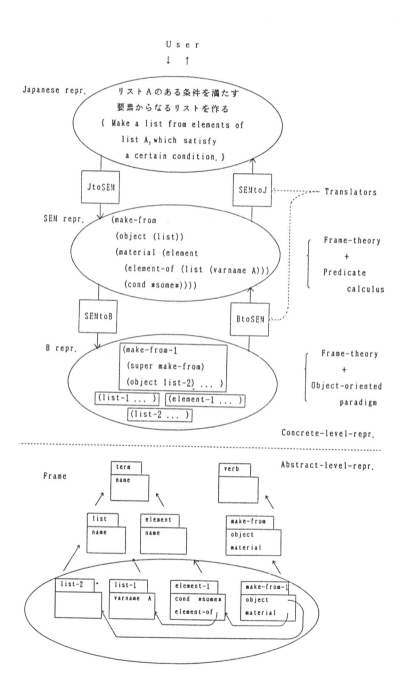

Figure 3. A view of frame-based knowledge in LISP-PAL

These different representations including Japanese can be mutually translated by JtoSEM, SEMtoB, BtoSEM, and SEMtoJ translators. The knowledge retrieval is usually done by the B representation translated from the SEM representation, because SEM is the more appropriate representation to be written in production rules, and the target to search is the knowledge in B. The retrieved knowledge in B is translated into SEM for making the next processing easy.

Table 1 compares SEM and the network representation of the frame system. Each has advantages and disadvantages, but SEM is superior in knowledge handling.

Table 1. Comparison of SEM and the frame system

	S E M	F r a m e s y s t e m (from the network viewpoint)
Understandability	G o o d	G o o d
Indexing schema	N o n e	G o o d
Program writability	G o o d	B a d (Hard to express)
Extendability on logic-based concept	G o o d (Extension such as AND or OR is easy)	B a d (Difficult to extend)

Figure 4 shows how SEMtool works, using a simple example of answering a LISP programming schema. The Japanese translator, JtoSEM, converts an input sentence into an inner representation in SEM. An appropriate question-answering rule performs the next task: understanding the user's question by pattern matching, fetching the desired schema from the knowledge base using a SEM-

```
リストAのある条件を満たす要素からなるリストを作る方法は？
(How can I make a list from elements of list A, which satisfy a certain
condition.)
          ⇩ * applying the JtoSEM translator
(question
  (exp (skill (plan *unknown*)
             (purpose (make-from
                      (object (list))
                      (material (element (element-of (list (varname A)))
                                (cond *some*)))))))))
```

```
           * applying the Question-answering rule :

              if
                (MATCH question
                 (question (exp (skill (plan *unknown*)
                                      (purpose ?purpose)))))
              then
                (CREATE (query-result
                         (purpose ?purpose)
                         (plan (FETCH (skill (plan *any*)
                                            (purpose ?purpose))))))))
```

```
(answer
  (exp (skill (plan scheme-for-filtering)
             (purpose (make-from
                      (object (list))
                      (material (element (element-of (list (varname A)))
                                (cond *some*))))))))
          ⇩ * applying the SEMtoJ translator
リストAからある条件を満たす要素を取り出しリストを作るには，以下の
スキーマを使います。
(To make a list from elements of list A, which satisfy a certain
condition, use the following scheme :)
    (mapcan A (function (lambda (x) (if <condition> '(, x) '()))))))
```

Figure 4. SEM representation in basic question-answering process

tool operation, FETCH, and using CREATE to form a response in SEM with the retrieved knowledge. The point here is that "a pattern of networked objects" plays an important role as meaningful knowledge in this process; this representation in the production rule is exactly what we want to express. Finally, the response in SEM is translated into Japanese by applying the Japanese genaration rules of the SEMtoJ translator.

In the actual LISP-PAL, the fetching procedure and response-forming rules are more complex so that all relevant descendant objects of the matched object are processed. According to certain criteria, some of the fetched knowledge is displayed to the user; the rest is displayed on request.

Our solution to the other problem of managing different world models is the introduction of a world name with knowledge-based operations. For example, the target world to be searched must be specified in a fetching operation, but the default is set to the LISP world model, as in the example.

5. SEMtool

This section describes the SEMtool features. SEMtool handles networked objects as meaningful knowledge. In SEMtool, a world model is managed under a world name. The current implementation is done by using methods and LISP functions.

FETCH

Syntax: (FETCH <search-pattern> <return-items> <world-name>)

FETCH searches networked objects (or simply an object) and their slots specified by <search-pattern>, in which the value-don't-care slot is marked by *any* and the matching variable is prefixed by a question mark. Items to be fetched are specified by <return-items>, which is a list of * (for networked objects) and matching variables. <world-name> is the target to search. When no matched objects are found, <u>nil</u> is returned. This FETCH operation can be used as a predicate to test if <search-pattern>

is satisfied in the current knowledge base.

FETCHSTRM and NEXTITEM

   Syntax: (FETCHSTRM <stream-variable> <search-pattern> <return-
       items> <world-name>)

   Syntax: (NEXTITEM <stream-variable>)

    A pair of these operations is a variant of FETCH. The
difference is that only one item is searched by NEXTITEM. This is
useful when not all items are necessary or the search space is
too large to process all matched objects at once.

CREATE

   Syntax: (CREATE <frame-expression> <world-name>)

    CREATE creates networked or single objects; a new object
name may be specified in <frame-expression>.

Others

    Other operations include INSERT, which inserts objects into
a world model, and REMOVE, which is the opposite of INSERT.

Knowledge Base Demon

    Methods or LISP functions associated with FETCH, INSERT, and
REMOVE operation can be specified to operate before or after the
operation is performed. This type of demon is of the knowledge
base level, in contrast to demons associated with an object in an
object-oriented paradigm. This type of demon becomes an interesting tool for backward or forward reasoning.

6. Comparison with Other Related Work

    A frame-based AI language, Pearl, uses a fundamentally equal
concept of SEMtool [5,6]. The difference is that our environment
permits a multiparadigm, and frame handling can be more easily
implemented because the knowledge base is organized in an
object-oriented paradigm. One example is that in our system the

user need not supply an explicit hashing designation.

The basic technique in the question-answering process of LISP-PAL is pattern-matching, so one may argue that PROLOG may be a better tool. It is not, however, because a pattern in the fetching operation of SEMtool may match any descendant of the related object whereas PROLOG strictly matches the same data structure.

The Unix Consultation system [4], which inspired our strategy in the question-answering process, requires the existence of answer instances beforehand. Our approach is more general in the sense that such existence is not needed: "instance" objects generated by the user's question can even match "class" level objects in the LISP world model.

7. Conclusions

In this paper we argued that the object-oriented paradigm is not sufficient to handle such a basic operation as knowledge retrieval on the frame system model. Through the application of LISP-PAL, we showed that the nested frame expression plus associated operations becomes a very powerful tool to handle such a knowledge base. This does not mean the object-oriented paradigm is poor, but the current features usually provided are not sufficient. Another solution to our problem may be possible by extending an object-oriented paradigm.

We are currently improving the features of SEMtool and are exploring ways of achieving faster implementation of SEMtool operations. We are also embedding a variety of question-answering and context process strategies using SEMtool, and are evaluating the practical use of the system.

References

[1] J. R. Anderson, R. Farell, and R. Sauers, "Learning to Program in LISP," Cognitive Science 8, pp. 87-129, 1984.

[2] D. G. Bobrow and M. Stefik, "The LOOPS Manual," Xerox PARC, Knowledge-based VLSI Design Group Memo, 1983.

[3] E. Charniak and D. McDermott, "Introduction to Artificial Intelligence," Addison-Wesley, 1985.

[4] D. N. Chin, "A Case Study of Knowledge Representation in UC," IJCAI, pp.388-390, 1983.

[5] M. Deering, J. Faletti, and R. Wilensky, "Using the PEARL AI Package," University of Calf. Berkeley, 1982.

[6] J. Faletti and R. Wilensky, "The Implementation of PEARL: a Package for Efficient Access to Representations in LISP," University of Calf. Berkeley, 1982.

[7] H. Ishikawa, et al., "A Knowledge-Based Approach to Design a Portable Natural Language Interface to Database Systems," IEEE Int. Conf. on Data Engineering, pp.134-143, 1986.

[8] M. Stefik, A. G. Bell, and D. G. Bobrow, "Rule-Oriented Programming in LOOPS," Xerox PARC, 1983.

[9] R. Wilensky, "LISPcraft," W.W.Norton&Company, 1984.

[10] P. H. Winston and B. K. P. Horn, "LISP," Addison-Wesley, 1984.

Appendix: an example session

(JAPANESE)

（ユーザ）
「属性リストとは何ですか？」
（LISP-PAL）
⇒属性リストとは，属性と値のペアからなるもので，通常，シンボルに関連した種々の情報をシンボルに対応付けて管理するものです。属性リストを操作する関数には，GET，PUTPROP，DEFPROP，REMPROPなどがあります。

「リストをつなぐ関数は？」

⇒リストをつなぐ関数はAPPENDです。

「その使用例は？」

⇒Xが（白い），Yが（馬　は）のとき，
（APPEND　X　Y　X）→
（白い　馬　は　白い）となります。

(ENGLISH Translation)

(user)
"What is a property-list?"
(LISP-PAL)
⇒A property-list consists of pairs of a property and value, and usually used for managing various information on a symbol by relating it to the symbol. Among functions to handle it are GET, PUTPROP, DEFPROP, and REMPROP.

"What function concatenates lists?"

⇒Function APPEND concatenates lists.

"Its example?"

⇒When X is (SHIROI), Y is (UMA HA),
(APPEND X Y X) → (SHIROI UMA HA SHIROI)

「他の関数は？」

⇨リストをつなぐ関数はNCONCです。副作
用が有るので注意が必要です。

「副作用？」

⇨引数はコピーされず，それぞれのリストの最
後のセルが変更されてつながれるため，引数が
変化してしまいます。

「リストを処理する方法は？」

⇨リストLをDOで処理する方法は，
```
(DO ((L L (CDR L)))
    ((ATOM L)  <返却値>)
    <処理> ... )
```
例えば，リストLを反転させるには，
```
(DO ((RESULT NIL)(L L (CDR L)))
    ((ATOM L) RESULT)
    (PUSH (CAR L) RESULT))
```

・ ・ ・ ・

"Any other function?"

⇨Function NCONC catenates lists. Take care
this has a side-effect.

"Side-effect?"

⇨Because arguments are not copied to catenate
the last value of the lists are changed.

"How can I process a list?"

⇨To process a list L with function DO, use:
```
(DO ((L L (CDR L)))
    ((ATOM L) <RETURN-VALUE>)
    <TRANSACTON> ... )
```
For example, to reverse a list L, use:
```
(DO ((RESULT NIL)(L L CDR L)))
    ((ATOM L) RESULT)
    (PUSH (CAR L) RESULT))
```

・ ・ ・ ・

Learning

Learning as Search: a Logical Approach

J. Nicolas

IRISA, Rennes (France)

Résumé : Cet article présente une formulation logique du problème de la "généralisation en tant que recherche" introduit par Mitchell. Un nouveau système, ALLY, a été conçu dans ce cadre. Les caractéristiques principales d'ALLY reposent sur trois idées: une représentation logique uniforme des informations, une définition originale du critère de consistance des généralisations produites, traitant symétriquement exemples et contre – exemples, et enfin une stratégie de contrôle adaptée à la complexité du problème, combinant avantageusement les approches classiques descendante (dirigée par les données) et ascendante (dirigée par un modèle).

Mots clés : Apprentissage symbolique automatique. Logique.

Abstract : The purpose of this paper is to present a logical formulation of the "generalization as search" problem first studied by T.Mitchell, and to describe a new system, called ALLY, built upon this model. The main characteristics of ALLY are : a uniform logical representation of information, a new definition of consistent generalizations with a symmetrical processing of positive and negative instances, and a mixed control strategy which closely combines the data – driven and the model – driven approaches. A general concern of this work is to keep the whole process within a logical frame.

Keywords : Machine Learning. Logic.

1 INTRODUCTION

The seventies saw the birth of a wide variety of symbolic learning programs, which used many different techniques, yet which were more or less tailored to a given application. The eighties have given rise to great efforts to formalize the concepts underlying these programs, with attempts to provide a "universal" terminology as well as to develop an "AI" methodology of the domain. The publication of two books [MIC 83b] [MIC 86] fully devoted to these problems is seen to be significant in this respect. One of the most promising ideas which has evolved in the past ten years is to consider generalization (that is, the central concern of learning) as a search in a partially ordered space [MIT 82]. Points in this space correspond to statements of the generalization language used to describe concepts.

In the next section, we will recall the main results obtained by Mitchell for representing and exploring this space. Afterwards, we present a criticism of these results and we give a revised formulation of the generalization paradigm, based on a logical view of the problem. Section 3 describes the main characteristics of an original system, ALLY (for Automated Learning with a Logical Yoke), conceived within this framework. We deal with the difficult problem of the design of an efficient control strategy for ALLY in section 4. The generality of our approach has enforced us to devise a new strategy, highly constraining the search but allowing the system to start from any arbitrary model of the concept to be learned. The end of this section exhibits an example of an output of ALLY. We conclude in section 5 with a recall of main contributions and a study of limitations of this approach.

2 LEARNING AS LOGICAL SEARCH

This section introduces our view of the generalization paradigm. Many authors have presented their own definition of this problem. The most famous one is certainly Mitchell's definition and we summarize it first. Then, we emphasize some limitations of this characterization and we illustrate with a new formulation how we can go beyond these limitations.

2.1 The problem

In [MIT 82], Mitchell states the generalization problem as follows :

"Given   1) A language in which to describe instances
        2) A language in which to describe generalizations
        3) A matching predicate that matches generalizations to instances
        4) A set of positive and negative training instances of a target to be learned

Determine Generalizations within the provided language that are consistent with the presented training instances."

Mitchell has devised an algorithm, called the Version Space approach, to implement a solution to this problem for which he makes two other important assumptions [MIT 78]:

5) The generalization language (call it G for convenience) is provided for each new application. Let L be the general language of all possible generalizations, given any set of instances. G is a subset, a "biased" version of L. It means that the user of the learning system carefully chooses the set of allowed expressions in the general language L in order to build a "narrow" convex search space, with a low branching factor. This restriction is one way to obtain a tractable exploration of the search space. Indeed, this space may be then represented with a small number of points, two for each set of generalizations consistent with the data (each set is a convex subspace fully determined by its lower and upper bound). The search in the Version Space is reduced to the study of these particular points.

6) A generalization is consistent (i.e. has to be kept) iff it matches every positive instance and no negative instance in the set. Most of the time, the unformal "matching predicate" between a generalization G and an expression E amounts to looking for a substitution σ such as $\sigma G = E$.

Most of the existing systems may be formulated within this framework. They mainly differ in the control strategy they use to explore the Version Space. We argue now as to explain why it is not fully adequate.

2.2 Criticism of Mitchell's formulation

The aim of the next section is to propose a logical formulation of the "search" view of learning. In this framework, the previous statement require to be precised and suffers, in our opinion, from three drawbacks :

– The use of two different languages to describe instances and generalizations : this is epistemologically groundless and increases the difficulty of building a formal model of the system behaviour. The need for each application to define a matching process for the comparison of instances and generalizations becomes a major issue if they are expressed in two different dialects, especially if the attributes involved are not independent. In fact, learning is made up of two components to be clearly distinguished : (1) The generalization component, aimed at the generation of correct general descriptions. It does not require any new language. (2) The display component, using "reformulation" rules to achieve a suitable form of the description for the user. It is just a translation step from an internal to an external form.

- The introduction of a bias in the generalization language to prune undesirable branches in the space : here lies one of the major assumptions of most studies in Machine Learning. This bias is a kind of compiled prior knowledge; it is very effective in directly constraining the search but too specific to be really useful. In order to obtain a "narrow" space, one must overprune the original space, thus removing from it plausible generalizations. Then a special algorithm must be defined to retrieve descriptions that have been lost (see for example the Refocusing algorithm to retrieve disjunctions in [BUN 85] or the methodology suggested by UTGOFF [UTG 83]). Furthermore, bias seems to be a rather rough tool to specify coherently prior knowledge. We need a better mechanism, founded on general syntactical or semantical considerations to express this knowledge.

- A definition of valid generalizations too restrictive. Acceptance of a generalization is based solely on its ability to describe what IS the concept to be learned. There is no place for describing what IS NOT the concept. For example, if two positive instances are considered :

$$P \quad \text{and} \quad Q$$

with one negative instance : $(P \lor Q) \land R$

It is not possible to find a consistent generalization, although the information $\neg R$ seems to be worthy of some consideration to characterize the concept. Naturally, we apply in this case a form of non monotonic reasoning. To be precise, we assert : if R may be deduced from negative instances and R may not be deduced from positive instances, then infer $\neg R$ is part of the concept.

2.3 Reformulation of the problem

We have elaborated upon two ideas :

- Choosing a unique language to describe instances, generalizations, and prior knowledge. The language should be general enough to cope with any application. Furthermore, this language should be provided with a symbolic manipulation system well enough formalized to yield results that makes it able to compare and transform expressions of the language.

 — Extending the concept of consistency in such a way as to allow generalizations describing what IS NOT the concept. We will see in section 3.2 the consistency criterion chosen in ALLY. It derives directly from the remark evolved in the previous example and seems to be relevant for all learning problems involving negative instances. However, we will just give in the statement below a very general framework for consistency criteria.

As in many domains in AI, the choice of the language is straightforward : logic provides highly suitable languages for representation and strong mechanisms for manipulation of symbolic data. Many authors use more or less a subset of first order logic as a representation language with good results (e.g. APC [MIC 83b] or AGAPE Language [KOD 83]). The new fact here is to systematize this point of view and to consider the whole learning process as a logical issue. We will see in section 3.2 the great significance of this assumption on the concept of generalization. The new "learning as logical search" problem may be summarized as follows:

Given   — A logic.
            — A theory made up with known facts (background knowledge, learned facts).
            — Two sets of formula (positive and negative instances, input facts).
            — A consistency criterion founded on the validity relation of the considered logic which expresses necessary properties of any potentially learnable formula.
            — A preference criterion founded on this validity relation and/or an interpretation of the considered logic (semantic criterion) which expresses properties of "suitable" consistent formulas (i.e potentially interesting formulas).

Determine — Formulas of the logic satisfying the consistency and the preference criteria

We have devised a new learning system in this framework, called ALLY. We present it below.

3 ALLY : A NEW LEARNING SYSTEM

This section presents the main characteristics of ALLY. It is composed of three parts. First we determine the chosen subset of predicate language. Then we specify the meaning of the results produced by ALLY. We end by the description of the basic transformation rules of the system.

3.1 Representation Language

 — We use a subset of first order logic, namely the Bernays–Schoenfinkel restriction

[ACK 54], in which terms using function symbols are prohibited. [1] Our choice is motivated by the learning domain we intend to focus on: real world applications in need of knowledge acquisition tools. In these domains, the need for **universally** defined functions seems highly improbable. Learning in other domains like mathematics may require more sophisticated decidable subsets of logic. Our conviction is that the defined language is already powerful enough to deal with a great diversity of applications. Also, this restriction permits a decidable and tractable language to be obtained.

– The system uses the conjunctive normal form of formulas. A reformulation module transforms the results of the algorithm into formulas of the original ALLY language. This module depends on the application selected and has to be redefined for each new domain whose language does not fit ALLY language (for example in the task of learning networks).

3.2 Our definition of generalization

Before asserting our definition of consistency for generalizations, it is necessary to have a look at what is to be learned.

With a broad meaning, an event F1 is said to be more general than another one F2 if the context in which F1 may appear is larger than the context in which F2 does.

– Usually, in a logical frame, a formula F1 is said to be more general than F2 if F2 "describes" a subset of F1, i.e. F2 is valid whenever F1 is valid. A classical example of this fact is to assert that "this crow is black" is less general than "all crows are black". Learning in this framework is a very hard task, because the only link between a formula F and its generalization G is an inductive one: $G \Rightarrow F$. It results there is no truth–preserving way to infer G from F. A deductive system is of no help here and one has to develop a special system to define a validity criteria of G. Such formal attempts have been run by Plotkin [PLO 71]. It leads to develop an inductive system in a dual way of the deduction one (The main point lays in the substitution of the concept of "most general unifier" with the concept of "least general generalization").

– Kodratoff contrasts in [KOD 86] this "theorem learning" approach, with the "concept learning" one (what Michalski, in a more general way, calls "descriptive generalization" versus "concept acquisition" issue). In the following paragraph, x is a set of variables, denoting a set of objects involved in the description of a concept. Learning a concept C corresponds to learning a recognition function R(x) true iff x belongs to the concept. There are three logical ways to do that.

---

[1]   This language is not reduced to Horn clauses as in PROLOG language.
We allow existential quantifiers, negation and disjunction of literals.

One of these is to define a deductive function, that is, to learn a property P such as for all set of objects x, characterized with the property X(x), R(x) iff P(x) ⇒ X(x). In this case, P has to be inferred inductively from properties of instances. It suffers from exactly the same drawback as the previous method. One has to build a new system, giving up the strong results achieved by the widely developed deductive approach.

The second way is to directly build the recognition function R, that is, to learn a formula R(x), x being a set of free variables, each possible instantiation of x giving necessary properties of instances of the concept. This approach, followed by Kodratoff involves an essential complication: occurence of free variables forbids the application of the deduction theorem.

At last, R may be defined as an inductive function. In this case, we look for a formula P such as for any set of objects x, characterized with the property X(x), R(x) iff X(x) ⇒ P(x). In this case, P may be deduced from properties of instances.

– Following these observations, our methodology has been purely deductive. To learn from a set of instances is now equivalent to look for a formula P that symbolizes what is common to all the elements of the set. We say a formula P1 is more general than a formula P2 if it is implied by P2: P2 ⇒ P1. For example, from the two facts (instances): "this crow is black" and "that crow is black", we deduce the new common fact (generalization): "there is a black crow" (thus introducing an existential quantification).

It is a generalization in the sense that the new formula is valid in a greater number of models than the original one. To decide if a new instance belongs to the concepts described with the formula P, we use the associated recognition function R. In our example, given any new black crow, say jack, we are able to recognize it belongs to the concept since :   crow (jack) ∧ black (jack) ⇒ ∃x crow (x) ∧ black (x)

So, as in theorem learning, we recognize all black crows as normal objects of the universe and it establishes the important fact we want to learn. However, we never assert such unverifiable formulas as "All crows are black". Taking into account these remarks and the last observation of section 2.2, we may give now our definition of consistency for generalizations.

Definition 1 : Consistency

A description P is **consistent** iff

(1) It is implied by all the positive instances E and is implied by none of the negative instances C
We note this assertion as   (E / C) I ~ P   (for E |— P and C |≁ P).

or

(2) Its negation is implied by all the negative instances C and is implied by none of the positive instances E
We note this assertion as   (C / E) I ~ ¬P   (for C |— ¬P and C |≁ ¬P).

The consistency criterion is universal but not strong enough to limit the spectrum of possible formulas. One needs another criterion, more suited to a certain class of applications. We have called this criterion a preference criterion. In our system, it is founded on the search for "extremal" formulas (an extension of the classical notion of most specific generalization). We are giving now a definition of "extremality".

Definition 2 : Extremality

We call **most specific learnable set** of a set of formulas F_1 against another set of formulas F_2, the set :

$$S(F_1 / F_2) = \{ P : (Q \mid— P) \Rightarrow (F_1 / F_2) \mid\not\vdash Q \}$$

We call **most general learnable set** of a set of formulas F_1 against another set of formulas F_2, the set :

$$G(F_1 / F_2) = \{ P : (P \mid— Q) \Rightarrow (F_1 / F_2) \mid\not\vdash Q \}$$

A description P is **extremal** iff

$$P \in S(E / C) \cup G(E / C) \quad \text{or} \quad \neg P \in S(C / E) \cup G(C / E)$$

We say that a consistent formula is the most specific one when there is no other consistent formula Q implying P. The set of all the most specific formulas is called the most specific learnable set. The "most general learnable set" is defined in a dual way. "Extremal" formulas rely to most specific or most general formulas deriving from both sets of positive or negative instances. To make clear our purpose, we compare now this definition with results provided by the Mitchell's Version Space approach [MIT 82] which may be considered as a particular case of our specification. Indeed, Mitchell constructs in a similar fashion two sets : a S–set made up of the most specific generalizations covering the examples and a G–set, built up from counter–examples and containing the most general generalizations covering the examples. The S–set represents the necessary properties of the concept to be learned. With regard to the G–set, Mitchell makes use of a not too "branchy" space to obtain an interesting positive characterization of sufficient properties of the concept from what is not the concept. We propose to generalize the definition of these sets, according to our consistency criterion. The idea is to maintain a S–set (noted S(C / E)) (resp. a G–set noted G(C / E)) for negative instances C . Now, part of the final G–set (resp. S–set) describes the negation of the most general (resp. specific) generalizations covering the counter–examples (and none of the examples) and reveals what is necessarily not the concept. It may be noticed that this approach is easily extendable to any number of classes of instances C_i by computing a S(C_i / E) set and a G(C_i / E) set for each C_r

3.3 Generalization and particularization rules

The algorithm proceeds by elementary steps, modifying a formula with rules of generalization or particularization that effect "atomic" changes in this formula. The purpose of this section is to describe the set of rules that ALLY applies. We will show in section 4.3 how it is possible to constraint the triggering of these rules during the learning process. All examples in this paper are given in a classical blocks world. In our opinion, even if it does not form at all a good validation test for a learning system, it permits to clearly illustrate the handled concepts.

There are four types of rule. For each type, there are two possible orientations : generalization or particularization.

   – **Alteration of a conjunct :**

>   Generalization: It is the well known dropping condition rule.
>   Example: Square(A) ∧ Small(A) may give two generalizations, Square(A) and Small(A).

>   Particularization: Adds a single term to a conjunction.
>   Example: Square(A) may give, taking into account a negative instance Square(A) ∧ Large(A) the particularization Square(A) ∧ ¬ Large(A).

   – **Alteration of a disjunct :**

>   Generalization : It is the Michalski's adding alternative rule. Its application requires a carefull control (See algorithm) but it is essential to introduce exceptions and inherently disjunctive facts.
>   Example: Yellow(A) may give the generalization Yellow(A) ∨ White(A) which in this case represents the hidden knowledge Light(A).

>   Particularization: Suppresses a disjunct.
>   Example: Sup(Weight,10) ∨ Inf(Weight,5) gives two particularizations, Sup(Weight,10) and Inf(Weight,5).

   – **Alteration of a quantification :** (What Michalski calls "turning constraints into variables")

>   Generalization: Introduces existential quantification. To be precise, transforms everywhere in the formula a constant or a universal variable by an existential variable.

Example: Triangle(A) ∧ On(A,B) gives two generalizations, ∃x Triangle(A) ∧ On(A,x) and ∃x Triangle(x) ∧ On(x,B).

Particularization: Introduces universal quantification.
Example: ∃x Black(x) gives as a particularization ∀x Black(x).

– **Application of an axiom** : It means use background knowledge to infer new interesting facts (i.e not equivalent), either deduced or induced from the current formula.

Generalization: Deduction.
Example: Assume the system knows the following axiom:
∀x Small(x) + Medium(x) + Large(x), where " + " represents exclusive or.
Then Small(A) gives two generalizations, ¬Medium(A) and ¬Large(A).

Particularization: Induction.
Example: Assume the system knows the following axiom:
∀x Square(x) ⇔ Rectangle(x) ∧ Equal – Sides(x).
Then Rectangle(B) gives one particularization, Square(B).

4 THE CONTROL STRATEGY

Although it does not seem as a learning problem but rather as a classical search problem, the definition of the exploration strategy plays a leading part in the design of pratical systems because it directly acts upon the generalizations produced. We describe first the strategy of ALLY. A study of other existing technics may be found in [NIC 86]. This strategy takes advantage of basic explanations provided by the prover : it is the subject of the second part of the section. We end with an example of an output of ALLY to enlight the general behaviour of the system.

4.1 Architecture and Exploration Strategy of ALLY

ALLY may be functionally viewed as consisting of three components, as shown in figure 1.

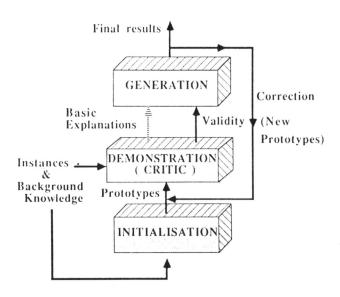

Figure 1. Architecture of ALLY

The initialisation block provides initial models (built from the examples or the user knowledge) that are refined by other components. The central block is a prover. The main idea is that the prover not only furnishes a validation result, but also gives basic explanations on this result which are based on the track of the proof.

The generation module contains general transformation rules (See 3.2) that may be considered as models of correction. The application of rules is ordered and each rule is preceded by a guard to fire it as in expert systems. This way, we are able to prune unpromising or forbidden rules (as the "add a disjunct" rule). Furthermore, these models of correction are "instantiated" during the learning process in light of the basic explanations furnished by the prover. Explanations are listed in the next paragraph and their use is illustrated with an example. These explanations come either from the background knowledge (thus, the strategy is typically model – driven) or from instances and in this case, strategy is data – driven. So, the elaborated control uses not only a mixed strategy but also a real blend (an "alloy") of both strategies.

4.2 Basic Explanations

In the current version of ALLY, basic explanations are made of :

(1) The list of variable instantiations.
(2) The list of valid literals.
(3) The list of axioms and auxiliary hypotheses used.
(4) The number of unifications.

Point (4) is merely a measure of complexity to sort the generated formulas. Other explanations serve to control the search by "instantiating" general correction rules described in section 3.3. An example of correction process is given below for each type of basic explanations :

(1) Variable instantiations Assume we are at step 1) of the algorithm with

a complete formula	F =	$\exists x \ \exists y$ Square(x)$\wedge$Size(x,y)
a negative instance	C =	$\exists x$ Square(x)$\wedge$Size(x,5)
We have	C $\vert$—F	and then, F must be specialized

A general specialization rule for this purpose is "add a conjunct". Instead of adding a randomly selected term, the generation module chooses a term based on the variable instantiations and builds the new description F' = $\exists x \ \exists y$ Square(x)$\wedge$Size(x,y)$\wedge$dif(y,5)

(2) Valid literals Assume we are at step 1) of the algorithm with

an initial formula	F =	$\exists x$ [Square(x)$\Rightarrow$ White(x)] $\vee$ [Square(x)$\Rightarrow$ Yellow(x)]
a negative instance	C =	$\exists x$ Square(x) $\wedge$ White(x)
We have	C $\vert$— $\neg$F	and then F must be specialized

A general specialization rule for this purpose is "suppress a disjunct". Instead of removing a randomly selected term, the generation module chooses a term among the valid literals and builds the new formula F' = $\exists x$ Square(x) $\Rightarrow$ Yellow(x)

(3) Unused axioms Assume we are at step 2) of the algorithm with

a current generalization	F =	$\exists x$ Square(x) $\wedge$ [Small(x)$\vee$White(x)]
a positive instance	E =	$\exists x \ \exists y$ Square(x) $\wedge$ Triangle(y) $\wedge$ Small(x)
We have	E $\vert$— F	and we test if F may be specialized

A general specialization rule for this purpose is "add a conjunct". Instead of appending a randomly selected term, the generation module chooses a term derived from an axiom not employed and builds the new description F' = $\exists x,y$ Square(x) $\wedge$ [Small(x)$\vee$White(x)] $\wedge$ Triangle(y).

4.3 A complete example

The purpose of this section is to provide an overview of the behaviour of the system. So, the selected example is not representative of the actual domain of learning of ALLY (which is learning in speech recognition) but is just a didactic one.

Assume the system knows the following axioms (where " + " means exclusive or):

A_1 $\forall x$ Polygon(x) $\Leftrightarrow$ Rectangle(x) + Triangle(x)
A_2 $\forall x$ Square(x) $\Leftrightarrow$ Rectangle(x) $\wedge$ Equal – sides(x)
A_3 $\forall x$ Circle(x) $\Rightarrow$ Ellipse(x)
A_4 $\forall x$ Small(x) + Medium(x) + Large(x)

Assume there are two positive instances of the concept to be learned :

E_1 $\exists x$ $\exists y$ $\exists z$ Square(x)$\wedge$Small(x)$\wedge$Circle(y)$\wedge$Small(y)
$\wedge$Circle(z)$\wedge$Small(z)$\wedge$On(y,x)$\wedge$Inside(z,x)
E_2 $\exists x$ $\exists y$ $\exists z$ Rectangle(x)$\wedge$Medium(x)$\wedge$Circle(y)$\wedge$Small(y)
$\wedge$Circle(z)$\wedge$Small(z)$\wedge$On(y,x)$\wedge$On(z,x)

Assume there are two negative instances of the concept to be learned :

C_1 $\exists x$ $\exists y$ Square(x)$\wedge$Small(x)$\wedge$ Triangle(y)$\wedge$Small(y)$\wedge$Red(y)$\wedge$On(y,x)
C_2 $\exists x$ $\exists y$ Circle(x)$\wedge$Large(x)$\wedge$ Triangle(y)$\wedge$Small(y)$\wedge$Inside(y,x)

We describe now results of the algorithm.

Step 1.1 : The system asks for an initial description of both positive and negative instances. It is an optional step. If the user has no idea about the form of the result, ALLY provides an initial formula taken from one arbitrary selected instance. In our example, suppose the user fixes only the initial description for negative instances. So, ALLY starts from the formulas :

$$F_E = E_1, \quad F_C = \exists x\ \exists y\ On(y,x)\vee Inside(y,x)$$

Step 1.2 : The system checks for weak consistency of initial descriptions. It fails for F_C since E_1 implies F_C. In order to correct this formula, ALLY uses an axiom not employed in C_1. Now:

$$F_E = E_1, \quad F_C = \exists x\ \exists y\ [\ On(y,x)\vee Inside(y,x)\ ]\wedge Triangle(y)$$

Step 1.3 : The system looks for completeness. It applies first a very efficient heuristic to constrain the search for suitable generalisations. It tries only generalization of conjuncts c_i for which there exists an instance not implying c_i (In our example, terms Square(x), Small(x) and Inside(x) for F_E). ALLY applies axioms A_2 and A_4 to the formula F_E and we obtain the sets:

$$T_E = \{\ \exists x\ \exists y\ \exists z\ \text{Rectangle}(x) \wedge \neg\text{Large}(x) \wedge \quad \text{Circle}(y)\wedge\text{Small}(y) \wedge \text{Circle}(z)\wedge\text{Small}(z) \wedge \text{On}(y,x)\ \}$$
$$T_C = \{\ F_C\ \}$$

Step 1.4 : The system looks for consistency. T_E and T_C remain unchanged.

Step 2 : Building of the S–set. S(E/C) and S(C/E) are made of a single element:

$$S(\ E/C\ ) = T_E$$
$$S(\ C/E\ ) = \{\ \exists x\ \exists y\ \text{Triangle}(x)\wedge\text{Small}(x) \wedge[\ \text{Inside}(x,y)\vee\text{On}(x,y)\ ]\ \}$$

Step 3 : Building of the G–set. From T_E, ALLY computes the G (E/C)–set composed from three elements. The last one derives from a specialization of the literal On(x,y), using the negative instance C_1.

$$\exists x\ \exists y\ \text{Ellipse}(x) \wedge \neg\text{Large}(y)$$
$$\exists x\ \exists y\ \text{Ellipse}(x) \wedge \text{On}(x,y)$$
$$\exists x\ \exists y\ \neg\text{Red}(x) \wedge \text{On}(x,y)$$

From T_C, ALLY computes the G (C/E)–set composed from two elements:

$$\exists x\ \exists y\ \neg\text{Circle}(x) \wedge[\ \text{Inside}(x,y)\vee\text{On}(x,y)\ ]$$
$$\exists x\ \text{Triangle}(x)$$

5 CONCLUSION : First critique of the system

The goal of our study has been to define a new deductive paradigm for automated learning. We have described a new system, ALLY, elaborated within his framework. ALLY is implemented in PROLOG II on a VAX 750. We are working on a transfer of the program in Quintus Prolog on a SUN 2. The system is too young to furnish valuable measures about this approach. We are currently studying the applicability of ALLY in the domain of speech recognition which has a great need for automatic acquisition tools.

What we intend to do in this section is to emphasize some of the intrinsic properties of the system (qualities or drawbacks) with respect to the classical issues of the domain:

* **Use of background knowledge** : the contextual knowledge of learning is handled in a

natural way, represented as axioms of the theory. For example, the taxonomy : polygon = {square, triangle, rectangle} is included in the knowledge of the system by adding the axiom (+ means exclusive or) : polygon ⇔ square + triangle + rectangle to the theory. In fact, an axiomatic representation is much more powerfull than a taxonomic one. For instance, using previous axiom, we are able to generalize **square** not only in polygon but also in polygone ∧ ¬triangle and in polygone ∧ ¬rectangle. To forbid replacing of an expression with a logically equivalent expression is the only precaution to take in order to avoid loops in the generalization or particularization process.

* **Generalization and particularization rules** : ALLY is a very flexible tool owing to its ability to move on both sides of an inference link. The set of correction rules may be extended by retaining more basic explanations from the prover. We have not adressed the very important problem of defining **constructive** rules. It involves detection of relevant links of variables and automatic generation of new predicates (and so, it is a second order logic problem).

* **Classification of a new instance** : ALLY generates more precise answers than Mitchell's Version Space does. It asserts one of five possible answers, when given a new instance X to classify :

positive instance :   iff $\forall G \in S_E$ $X \vdash G$

negative instance :   iff $\forall G \in S_C$ $X \vdash \neg G$

plausible positive instance :   iff $\exists G \in G_E$ $X \vdash G$ and $\forall G \in G_C$ $X \nvdash G$

plausible negative instance :   iff $\exists G \in G_C$ $X \vdash \neg G$ and $\forall G \in G_E$ $X \nvdash \neg G$

unclassable instance   in other cases

* **Complexity** : the algorithm is "greedy" in its use of proofs. Each time a correction is tried, the system tests if weak consistency or completeness is preserved. This requires the current formula be checked against all positive or negative instances. This seems to be unescapable, due to the generality of the representation language and the extension of the consistency criterion. Our hope is to establish the practicability of ALLY in applications with a great amount of background knowledge where time is not a critical issue.

To conclude, this work represents just one step in a potentially very large and fascinating research area which would be to define a logical system suited to the learning system. In Section 2, we have laided out learning as a logical problem. We have developed a consistency criterion directly linked to the validity relation of the first order logic. However it is only an approximate model and we need a new formalism better tailored to the learning problem. We have emphasized two directions to overcome limitations of our formalization. The first one is to use a non–monotonic logic. Classical logic seems to be insufficient in this case. Indeed, one of the principal characteristics of the learning problem is that we are faced with two kinds of information : one about positive facts of the world (E), and another one dealing with negative facts (C) that embodies what is necessarily false. The validity of a formula P in this logic depends on both sets. The second one deals with the introduction of second–order mechanisms. The aim is to introduce constructive rules of generalization, creating new predicates, thus giving the system some discovery capabilities.

Acknowledgements

I wish to gratefuly acknowledge a number of people for their remarks and useful comments on a first draft of this research. R. Allen, P. Besnard, L. Trilling, M. Habib, X. Marie and W. Buntine have all contributed to improve the form of this paper.

REFERENCES

[ACK 54]   W.ACKERMANN
            Solvable Cases of the Decision Problem
            North Holland Publishing company. Amsterdam. 1954

[DIE 83]   T.DIETTERICH R.MICHALSKI
            A comparative review of selected methods for learning from examples
            Machine Learning: an Artificial Intelligence approach Tioga 1983

[KOD 86]   Y. KODRATOFF, J.G. GANASCIA
            Improving the generalization step in learning
            Machine Learning II Morgan Kauffmann Los Altos CA 1986

[MIC 83a]   R.MICHALSKI J.CARBONELL T.MITCHELL
            Machine Learning: an Artificial Intelligence approach
            Tioga Palo Alto CA 1983

[MIC 83b]   R.MICHALSKI
            A theory and methodology of inductive learning
            Machine Learning: an Artificial Intelligence approach
            Tioga 1983

[MIC 86]   R.MICHALSKI J.CARBONELL T.MITCHELL
            Machine Learning II
            Morgan Kauffmann Los Altos CA 1986

[MIT 78]   T.MITCHELL
            Version Spaces: an approach to concept learning
            PHD thesis Standford University Dec. 1978

[MIT 82]   T.MITCHELL
            Generalization as search
            Artificial Intelligence 18, pp203 – 226, 1982

[NIC 86]   J.NICOLAS
            Les stratégies de contrôle dans l'apprentissage à partir d'exemples.
            Journée Francaise sur l'Apprentissage. Orsay Feb. 1986

[PLO 71]   G. PLOTKIN
            A further note on inductive generalization
            Machine Intelligence 6. Metzer and Michie eds. Edimburgh University Press 1971

[UTG 83]   P.UTGOFF
            Adjusting Bias in concept learning
            Proc. of the International Machine Learning Workshop June 83 Monticello

[YOU 77]   R.YOUNG G.PLOTKIN R.LINZ
            Analysis of an extended concept learning task
            IJCAI 77 MIT Cambridge Aug.1977

Decision-Tree Network Representation of Knowledge for Expert Systems

D.M.G. Mc Sherry

The Queen's University of Belfast, Belfast (Northern Ireland)

ABSTRACT

Representation of knowledge as a network of decision trees can reduce considerably the work involved in building expert systems. Knowledge can be acquired by a simple method which enables the domain expert to interact directly with the computer from the outset, thus reducing the need for lengthy interviewing of the expert by the knowledge engineer. Expert systems based on decision-tree networks share most of the advantages of rule-based expert systems, including the ability to explain their reasoning and ease of knowledge base maintenance. Alternatively, decision-tree networks can provide a method of intermediate representation of knowledge for rapid prototyping of rule-based expert systems.

A working expert system based on a decision-tree network has been developed by reconstructing the knowledge base of a rule-based medical expert system.

Keywords : knowledge representation, knowledge acquisition, knowledge engineering, production rules, decision trees, inference strategy, explanation of reasoning

Decision-tree network representation of knowledge for expert systems

1. Introduction

Knowledge acquisition is now generally recognised as a major bottleneck in expert system development.   Commonly in expert systems, knowledge is represented as a set of production rules.   But experience has shown that experts do not find it easy to express decision-making knowledge directly in this form.   Thus the development of a preliminary set of rules is usually undertaken by a knowledge engineer, who first must gain a sound understanding of the domain through lengthy interviews with the expert.   Apart from its obvious inefficiency, this approach can be very unrewarding for the expert because of the lack of feedback in the early stages.   Attempts to simplify knowledge acquisition have included the development of intelligent rule editors such as Teiresias [1], which enable experts to extend or edit the knowledge base interactively.   The difficulty of transferring expert knowledge to the computer ultimately depends, however, on the method used to represent knowledge in the computer.   The method of knowledge representation proposed here is based on decision trees.

The idea of using decision trees to represent knowledge is not new, but the method has been rejected in favour of the rule-based and other approaches because of its apparent limitations [2-3].   Existing programs which are based on decision trees are difficult to modify, unable to explain their reasoning, unable to deal with incomplete information, and unable to reach multiple conclusions. These limitations can largely be overcome, however, by explicitly representing knowledge, not as a single complex decision tree, but as a *network* of decision trees.   Many of the advantages of production rules which have led to their wide-spread use in expert systems arise from the use of subgoals to reduce complex reasoning to a series of simple steps.   In the decision-tree network (DTN) approach, subgoals play a similar role.   The network contains a decision tree corresponding to each subgoal.

A shell for building DTN-based expert system has been implemented in BASIC on the Apple II microcomputer.   A working expert system based on a DTN has been implemented by reconstructing the knowledge base of a rule-based medical expert system.   This expert system was designed originally to standardise the diagnosis of perceptual disorders in stroke for research purposes [4].   One of the major perceptual disorders in stroke is *neglect,* in which the hemiparetic patient may tend to ignore his surroundings on the affected side of his body.   (Hemiparesis, a muscular weakness or paralysis of one side of the body, is common in stroke patients).   Four of the decision trees in a DTN for the diagnosis of neglect are shown in figures 1 and 2.

2. Structure of a Decision-Tree Network

Each decision tree in the DTN represents a subgoal.   Two different types of subgoal [5] are used in rule-based expert systems.   A *contextual* subgoal serves to classify the object to be identified or narrow the context of the problem. In a medical application, it may be a clinical hypothesis which would account for all the findings which have been reported on reaching an intermediate stage of the consultation, or a revised statement of the objectives of the consultation in the light of these findings.   Typically in the course of the consultation, a series of successively stronger contextual subgoals is established, any of which could be an alternative starting point for the consultation.   In the diagnosis of chest pain, for example, an appropriate contextual subgoal might be *chest pain of cardiac origin*.   An *incidental* subgoal summarises a group of related findings reported in the course of the consultation and is used typically to avoid asking a question which may be difficult for the user to answer by reducing it to a

serie of simpler questions.   For example, positive responses to the questions
(i) female? (ii) age more than 15 years? (iii) age less than 50 years? may be
sufficient to establish *female of reproductive age* as an incidental subgoal.

Corresponding to these two types of subgoal, there are two types of decision tree
in the DTN, contextual and incidental.   Each decision tree also takes its name
from the subgoal which it represents.   A contextual decision tree is invoked by
name during the consultation if and when the corresponding subgoal has been
established.   Normally there is a *top-level* contextual decision tree which
represents the broadest possible description of the problem (e.g. equipment fault
to be diagnosed or patient's presenting complaint) and this is invoked at the
beginning of the consultation.   In the DTN for the diagnosis of neglect, the
top-level contextual decision tree is *Hemiparesis* (figure 1).

The purpose of an incidental decision tree is to determine the truth or falsehood
of the subgoal from which it takes its name.   Thus each terminal node of an
incidental decision tree is labelled either *true* or *false*.   An incidental
decision tree is invoked by name during the consultation if and only if the need
arises.   One of several incidental decision trees in the DTN for the diagnosis
of neglect is *Evidence of neglect on Albert's test* (figure 1).

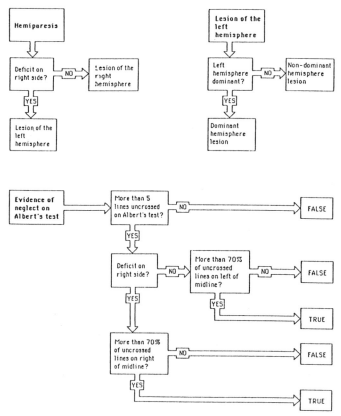

Figure 1   Part of a decision-tree network for diagnosis of the perceptual
           disorder of neglect

3. Inference strategy

The architecture of a DTN-based expert system is similar to that of a rule-based expert system, knowledge being explicitly represented and stored separately from the inference engine which applies it.   At the beginning of the consultation, the top-level decision tree (or other contextual decision tree selected by the user) is invoked, and its branching logic is followed until a terminal node is reached.   Each non-terminal node is labelled by a proposition, the truth or falsehood of which is determined in one of three ways:

(a) by recognising it to be a fact which has already been established;
(b) by invoking an incidental decision tree corresponding to it in name;
(c) by asking the user.

In the case of (b), the incidental decision tree which is invoked becomes the current decision tree.   When a terminal node of an incidental decision is reached, the subgoal from which it takes its name is established as being either true or false, and the decision tree which invoked the incidental decision tree (which may itself by incidental) becomes the current decision tree.

When a terminal node of a contextual decision tree is reached, the proposition which labels the node is established as true.   The network is searched for a contextual decision tree corresponding in name to this proposition.   If one is found, the proposition is interpreted as a subgoal, the corresponding decision tree is invoked, and the consultation continues.   If none is found, the pro- position is interpreted as the final conclusion, and the consultation ends.   In the former case, the subgoal may have also the status of a conclusion;   if so it is added to the list of conclusions to be presented at the end of the consultation.

The inference strategy cannot appropriately be described as either forward chaining or backward chaining.   Two inference mechanisms are in fact simul- taneously at work.   Progression through the contextual decision trees in the network, as increasingly stronger contextual subgoals are established, resembles forward chaining, and matches its efficiency.   The mechanism produces more pertinent dialogue, however, than rule-based forward chaining.   Activation of the incidental decision trees as they are needed is similar to backward chaining. On the whole, however, the system is more efficient than a typical rule-based expert system with backward chaining, as less time is wasted in fruitless searching of the knowledge base.

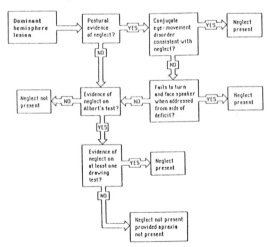

Figure 2   Contextual decision tree corresponding to the intermediate goal *Dominant hemisphere lesion* in the diagnosis of neglect

4. Explanation of reasoning

The DTN-based expert system can explain its reasoning both during and after the
consultation. Like a rule-based expert system, it relies on subgoals to reduce
complex reasoning to a series of simple steps. Before answering any question,
the user may ask why it is relevant. The program's response depends on whether
the current decision tree is contextual or incidental. In the former case, the
program generates an explanation by navigating from the current node forward
through the current decision tree, assuming to be true all undecided propositions
it encounters at non-terminal nodes, until a terminal node is reached. This
enables it to construct a statement (resembling a rule) explaining what further
evidence, together with a positive response to the current question, would enable
the subgoal or conclusion at the terminal node to be established. If not satisfied, the user may request further explanation. Provided the proposition at the
terminal node is a subgoal (i.e. if there is a contextual decision tree in the
DTN corresponding to it in name), a statement explaining why it would be useful
to establish this subgoal can be generated. As many levels of explanation can
be provided as there are decision trees in the network which must be navigated
to reach a conclusion.

The first level of explanation provided when the current decision tree is
incidental is just a statement of the subgoal which the program is attempting to
establish. If the user requests further explanation, this is generated as if
the decision tree which invoked the incidental decision tree were the current
decision tree.

At the end of the consultation, all conclusions which have been reached are
listed, and the user is invited to review the steps involved in the chain of
reasoning which led to these conclusions. The program generates a step-by-step
explanation in natural language from a record of its traverse through the network
of decision trees. Each step in the chain of reasoning corresponds to a
decision tree which has been invoked.

5. Knowledge acquisition

The first step in building a DTN-based expert system is to identify appropriate
subgoals through careful analysis of the application domain. Then the domain
expert (or knowledge engineer) develops a decision tree corresponding to each
subgoal. Because links between decision trees are implicit, a top-down
approach to building the DTN can be adopted. To create a new decision tree,
the expert specifies its name (the subgoal or presenting problem it is intended
to represent) and enters the most likely conclusion. If the expert enters
either *true* or *false* as the most likely conclusion, the decision tree is designated as incidental; otherwise it is designated as contextual. As soon as at
least one contextual decision tree has been created, the expert system is ready
to be consulted, although it will always reach the same conclusion until it
acquires further knowledge. Knowledge is acquired through teaching sessions
conducted by the expert. The expert teaches through examples and the program
learns by discovering its own ignorance. At each stage of the teaching process,
the expert challenges the program with a new case which (in a medical context)
he knows it will diagnose incorrectly by overlooking some important symptom or
test result. When the program has committed the anticipated error, it requests
the expert to reveal the correct diagnosis and the crucial symptom which is has
overlooked. In future the program will always ask about this symptom whenever
it encounters a similar case.

Teaching sessions focus on individual decision trees and any links to other
decision trees in the network are not activated.   A typical teaching dialogue
is shown below.   The expert creates and begins to develop a contextual decision
tree corresponding to the subgoal *Dominant hemisphere lesion* in the diagnosis of
neglect.   The completed decision tree is snown in figure 2.   (The expert
appends an exclamation mark to the name of the likeliest conclusion to indicate
that it is to retain the status of a conclusion when it later becomes also a
subgoal through the creation of a contextual decision tree of that name).

    Enter name of new decision tree: *Dominant hemisphere lesion*
    Please enter likeliest conclusion: *Neglect present!*

    Conclusion: Neglect present
    Do you agree?   *No*
    Please enter your conclusion: *Neglect not present*

    Please construct a YES/NO question which would distinguish between:
    1) NEGLECT PRESENT
    2) NEGLECT NOT PRESENT

    Postural evidence of neglect?

    If the answer to your question is YES which conclusion does this
      indicate: 1 or 2?   *1*
    Another case to discuss? *yes*

    Postural evidence of neglect? *No*

    Conclusion: Neglect not present
    Do you agree?   *No*
    Please enter your conclusion: *Neglect present!*

    Please construct a YES/NO question which would distinguish between
    1) NEGLECT NOT PRESENT
    2) NEGLECT PRESENT

    Evidence of neglect on Albert's test?

    If the answer to your question is YES which conclusion does this
      indicate: 1 or 2?   *2*
    Another case to discuss? *no*

The decision tree grows dynamically as each new case is presented, and its
development need not be completed in a single teaching session (or by a single
expert).   Skill and judgement is needed in choosing the best question to discriminate between the computer's conclusion and the 'correct' conclusion at each
stage in the development of the decision tree.   Especially in the early stages,
there may be several other (less likely) conclusions which would account for the
reported findings.   In general, a good question is one which will not only discriminate between the two most likely conclusions but also will divide the set
of all possible conclusions into two subsets which are roughly equal in size
(or likelihood) in the sense that a positive response would favour one subset
and a negative response the other.

The development of incidental decision trees is similar, but involves less effort,
since the expert has only to enter a question to distinguish between *true* and
false for each new case he presents.

6. A typical consultation

Before the consultation begins, the user is invited to select from a list of all
the contextual decision trees in the network.   In the DTN for the diagnosis of
neglect, an inexperienced user typically would select the top-level decision tree
Hemiparesis (figure 1), which makes no assumption about cerebral dominance or
side of deficit.   The more knowledgeable user, aware for example that the
hemiparesis is due to a lesion of the dominant hemisphere, could save time by
selecting instead the contextual decision tree *Dominant hemisphere lesion*
(figure 2) as a starting point for the consultation.

    Decision tree: Hemiparesis

    Deficit on right side? *why*

    Because if the following are true:
    1) HEMIPARESIS
    2) DEFICIT ON RIGHT SIDE
    then we can deduce: LESION OF THE LEFT HEMISPHERE

    Deficit on right side? *why*

    Because if the following are true:
    1) LESION OF THE LEFT HEMISPHERE
    2) LEFT HEMISPHERE DOMINANT
    then we can deduce: DOMINANT HEMISPHERE LESION

    Deficit on right side? *yes*
    Left Hemisphere dominant? *yes*
    Postural evidence of neglect? *no*
    More than 5 lines uncrossed on Albert's test? *why*

    Trying to establish: EVIDENCE OF NEGLECT ON ALBERT'S TEST

    More than 5 lines uncrossed on Albert's test? *why*

    We have established: DOMINANT HEMISPHERE LESION
    Therefore if the following is false: POSTURAL EVIDENCE OF NEGLECT
    and the following are true:
    1) EVIDENCE OF NEGLECT ON ALBERT'S TEST
    2) EVIDENCE OF NEGLECT ON AT LEAST ONE DRAWING TEST
    then we can deduce: NEGLECT PRESENT

    More than 5 lines uncrossed on Albert's test? *yes*
    More than 70% of uncrossed lines on right of midline? *yes*
    Relative lack of detail on right of copy of house? *yes*

    Conclusions:
    1) Neglect present
    2) Refer patient to an occupational therapist.   Encourage activities
       which focus attention on the right side.   Encourage patient to
       turn towards the right side.

    Would you like to review the 6 steps in the chain of reasoning which led
    to these conclusions? *yes*

Step 1
Since the following are true:
1) HEMIPARESIS
2) DEFICIT ON RIGHT SIDE
we can deduce: LESION OF THE LEFT HEMISPHERE

Step 2
Since the following are true:
1) LESION OF THE LEFT HEMISPHERE
2) LEFT HEMISPHERE DOMINANT
we can deduce: DOMINANT HEMISPHERE LESION

Step 3
Since the following are true:
1) MORE THAN 5 LINES UNCROSSED ON ALBERT'S TEST
2) DEFICIT ON RIGHT SIDE
3) MORE THAN 70% OF UNCROSSED LINES ON RIGHT OF MIDLINE
we can deduce: EVIDENCE OF NEGLECT ON ALBERT'S TEST

Step 4
Since the following are true:
1) DEFICIT ON RIGHT SIDE
2) RELATIVE LACK OF DETAIL ON RIGHT OF COPY OF HOUSE
we can deduce: EVIDENCE OF NEGLECT ON AT LEAST ONE DRAWING TEST

Step 5
Since the following is true: DOMINANT HEMISPHERE LESION
and the following is false: POSTURAL EVIDENCE OF NEGLECT
and the following are true:
1) EVIDENCE OF NEGLECT ON ALBERT'S TEST
2) EVIDENCE OF NEGLECT ON AT LEAST ONE DRAWING TEST
we can deduce: NEGLECT PRESENT

Step 6
Since the following are true:
1) NEGLECT PRESENT
2) DEFICIT ON RIGHT SIDE
we can deduce:
REFER PATIENT TO AN OCCUPATIONAL THERAPIST. ENCOURAGE ACTIVITIES WHICH FOCUS
ATTENTION ON THE RIGHT SIDE. ENCOURAGE PATIENT TO TURN TOWARDS RIGHT SIDE.

Another case to discuss? *no*

As the typical consultation illustrates, DTN-based and rule-based expert
systems are comparable in their ability to explain their reasoning. Reference
to the *Dominant hemisphere lesion* decision tree (figure 2), however, reveals the
program's inability to recognise redundancy in the explanations it generates.
In Step 5 of the explanation provided at the end, for example, the second premise
(absence of postural evidence of neglect) is unnecessary. This limitation of
the simple explanation strategy currently implemented could be remedied. The
quality of explanations generated by the program would benefit also from a
mechanism for forward propogation of deductions (for example *not* deficit on the
right side implies deficit on the left side) as provided by forward chaining
rules in a rule-based system. A combination of knowledge representation
methods (decision trees and rules) would provide this capability and also would
enhance the program's reasoning strategies.

The typical consultation illustrates the program's ability to reach multiple conclusions, provided the conclusions are reached in the course of pursuing a single line of reasoning. At present, however, the program cannot match the ability of a rule-based expert system to pursue, and draw conclusions from, several independent lines of reasoning in a single consultation.

A further limitation of the DTN-based system currently implemented is its inability to cope with incomplete information. Most rule-based expert systems do not insist that the user answers every question *yes* or *no*. If the information requested is not available to the user, typically he may answer *unknown*, and the system will search for an alternative rule which may enable it to establish its current goal. At the expense of some increase in complexity, the ability to deal with incomplete information could be provided in a DTN-based expert system by increasing the branching factor of the decision trees from two to three. A modified dialogue for knowledge acquisition would enable the expert to indicate appropriate conclusions for *unknown* as well as for *yes* or *no* answers to each new question.

7. Knowledge base maintenance

The knowledge base of a DTN-based expert system is as easy, if not easier, to maintain as that of a rule-based expert system. Several facilities for know-ledge base maintenance are provided in the current implementation. A text editor is available for immediate use during both teaching sessions and con-sultations to enable the designer to modify the text of questions and conclusions. Decision trees can be renamed or deleted, and since links in the network are implicit, there is no need to remove links to deleted decision trees. The program's ability to explain its reasoning in teaching sessions, as well as in consultations, facilitates debugging. The program also can detect the presence of circular reasoning.

At any stage of its development, the DTN (or selected decision trees) can be printed out for graphic representation as a collection of flow charts (which must, at present, be constructed manually). It is relatively easy to check the logic of the DTN in this form and to identify areas of weakness or predict the global effects of proposed changes in the knowledge base. Structural changes within decision trees are facilitated by reversal of the knowledge acquisition process. Each decision tree in the DTN implicitly contains a record of all the examples from which knowledge has been acquired, and the order in which they were presented. The program can be instructed at any stage to 'forget' the most recent example. By repeating this instruction several times, the designer can prune back the tree to the node at which restructuring is to begin.

8. An intermediate method of knowledge representation

Weiss and Kulikowski |6| have emphasised the importance of building a prototype model early in the development of an expert system. Because of the ease with which knowledge can be elicited directly from the expert, the DTN model is potentially valuable as a means of rapidly producing prototypes for rule-based expert systems. Production rules derived from the knowledge base of the DTN-based prototype would provide a preliminary knowledge base for the rule-based expert system. For, example, production rules which can be derived from the DTN for the diagnosis of neglect include:

If the following are true:
1) MORE THAN 5 UNCROSSED LINES ON ALBERT'S TEST
2) DEFICIT ON RIGHT SIDE
3) MORE THAN 70% OF UNCROSSED LINES ON RIGHT OF MIDLINE
then we can deduce: EVIDENCE OF NEGLECT ON ALBERT'S TEST

If the following are true:
1) DOMINANT HEMISPHERE LESION
2) EVIDENCE OF NEGLECT ON ALBERT'S TEST
3) EVIDENCE OF NEGLECT ON AT LEAST ONE DRAWING TEST
then we can deduce: NEGLECT PRESENT

Any redundancy in rules derived from the DTN should be eliminated to enable the
rule-based expert system to reach a conclusion whenever possible, even if some of
the relevant information is not available.   In the second rule, for example, no
reference to postural evidence of neglect is necessary.

Intermediate representation of domain knowledge in the form of a DTN reduces the
reasoning process to a series of simple steps corresponding to the decision trees
it contains.   The generation of rules from the DTN, in which appropriate subgoals
are explicitly represented, could therefore be automated.   (If the domain knowledge were represented instead in the form of a single large decision tree, on the
other hand, the translation process could not be fully automated because a single
decision tree would not contain the knowledge necessary for the identification of
appropriate subgoals |5|).

CONCLUSIONS

DTN-based expert systems share many, though not all, of the advantages of rule-
based expert systems.   The behaviour of a DTN-based system is more predictable
than that of a rule-based system because the greater connectivity of the DTN
knowledge base permits the designer tighter control of the reasoning process.
This could be advantageous in the design of large-scale systems since, as
Winston |7| has observed, *bequeathing control generally means losing control.*
The main advantages of the DTN approach to knowledge representation, however,
are the ease with which knowledge can be elicited directly from the expert and
the immediacy of computer feedback available to the expert.   In many applications
these advantages may outweigh the greater functionality of the rule-based
approach.

Alternatively, the DTN model is potentially valuable as an intermediate method
of knowledge representation in the development of rule-based expert systems.

ACKNOWLEDGEMENTS

I wish to thank Dr K. J. Fullerton, clinical author of the original perceptual
disorder knowledge base, for permitting its use here as a source of examples.
I am grateful also to Mrs Joy Lewis for typing the manuscript.

REFERENCES

1   Davis, R.   'Interactive transfer of expertise: acquisition of new inference rules", *Artificial Intelligence*, 12, 1979, pp. 121-157.

2   Shortliffe, E.H., Buchanan, B.G., Feigenbaum, E.A.   'Knowledge engineering for medical decision making: a review of computer-based clinical decision aids', *Proc IEEE*, 67, 1979, pp. 1207-1224.

3   Szolovits, P.   'Artificial Intelligence and Medicine', in P. Szolovits, Ed. *Artificial Intelligence in Medicine* (Colorado, Westview Press, 1982), pp. 1-19.

4   McSherry, D.M.G. and Fullerton, K.J.   'PRECEPTOR: a shell for medical expert systems and its application in a study of prognostic indices in stroke', *Expert Systems* 2; 1985, pp. 140-147.

5   McSherry, D.M.G. and Fullerton, K.J.   'Intermediate representation of knowledge in the development of a medical expert system', *Biomedical Measurement, Informatics and Control* 1, 1986, pp. 75-82.

6   Weiss, S.M. and Kulikowski, C.A.   'A practical guide to designing expert systems'.   New Jersey: Rowman & Allanhead, 1984.

7   Winston, P.H.   'Artificial intelligence'.   Addison Wesley, 1984.

Speech Recognition

Logic Programming for Speech Understanding

D. Snyers and A. Thayse

Philips Research Laboratory - Brussels (Belgium)

RESUME

Nous décrivons la réalisation au moyen du langage Prolog d'un module de compréhension de la parole. Ce module reçoit une séquence de phonèmes éventuellement entachée d'erreurs à l'entrée. Par un accès au lexique guidé par la syntaxe, ce module reconstruit une phrase syntaxiquement correcte qui peut alors être traduite en une série de commandes exécutables par un automatisme. Dans l'exemple qui nous occupe il sagit d'un éditeur de texte.

Nous verrons comment représenter tout ce module dans le formalisme DCG moyennant quelques extensions ou dans le formalisme $DCTG$ plus concis et plus lisible.

Mots clés:
Programmation déclarative, grammaires, compréhension de la parole, ...

ABSTRACT

A grammar has been devised which describes a speech understanding algorithm for a voice command of a text editor. This algorithm receives a garbled string of phonemes as input and based on a syntactically guided lexical access, reconstructs a syntactically correct sentence. This sentence can then be translated into a corresponding sequence of text editor commands. All this module can be expressed in the DCG formalism and we introduce an extension of it, the $DCTG$ formalism for the sake of readability and conciseness.

Keywords:
Logic Programming, grammars, speech understanding, pattern matching , ...

1 Introduction

The purpose of *speech understanding* is the transformation of an acoustic signal into a signal which can be understood by a machine. The acoustic level produces a continuous signal while the machine accepts discrete commands resulting from high level specialized programming languages. Speech understanding so requires the existence of a frontier up to which the classical techniques belonging to continuous signal theory go and from which the artificial intelligence techniques start. We have chosen to locate this frontier at the *phoneme level.*
The acoustic level produces phonemes by Dynamic Programming on Markov models (see [3,7]), due to signal distortion some of these phonemes may be wrong. These phonemes constitute the input entry (data) of a Prolog program which combines a *lexical investigation* with a *syntactic analysis* and a *semantic analysis.* The proposed algorithm first translates a sentence of (garbled) phonemes into a sentence of words and then associates with this sentence corresponding commands of the machine ([8]).
In order to illustrate the proposed methods we have realised a voice command (in French) of a text editor (which constitutes the machine to be driven). The Prolog program receives sentences of phonemes of the type:

[a,v,en,er,j,u,k,au,d,eu,z,er,m,k,a,r,a,E,r,d,u,m,o,s,ui,v,en].

A grammar first translates a sentence of phonemes into a sentence of (French) words understandable by the machine; simultaneously the grammar detects and corrects some errors which can occur at the phoneme level. The above sentence of phonemes is translated into the following sentence of words:

[avancer jusqu'au deuxieme caractère du mot suivant].

This sentence is in turn translated into a sequence of commands of a text editor; for the above sentence we have three successive commands:

[[one,word,forward],[beginning,word],[one,character,forward]].

2 Lexical investigation

The purpose of the first step of the algorithm will be the construction of words of the vocabulary (which are nothing but unit clauses, i.e. Prolog instructions) which have the following format:

word([list of phonemes], word of the (French) vocabulary,
translation of the word, semantic parameter)

A typical example of a verb is :

verbe([r,e,k,u,l,e,r], reculer, back, int)

It is a unit clause whose predicate "verbe" has four arguments; these arguments mean that the list of phonemes [r,e,k,u,l,e,r] represents the verb "reculer" whose translation is the command "back" and whose semantic character is "intransitive".
The technique for extracting words from a list of phonemes must be able to recognize words from garbled lists of phonemes. Our input data is a string of phonemes; the recognition of words will be obtained by comparing this string of phonemes with the correct phonetic transcription of the words of the dictionary (i.e. with the first argument of the unit clauses representing the vocabulary). This comparison will lead us either to extract (from the input string) the phonemes corresponding to the word under investigation, or to recognize that the string of phonemes cannot be identified with the phonemes of this word. In this last case the grammar will provide us with another candidate word for matching with the phoneme list.
A first version of the routine for extracting words (*extract* routine) has been implemented by simply making use of the pattern matching mechanism inherent to Prolog.
First of all, the Prolog pattern matching mechanism tries to match the received string of phonemes with the correct phonetic transcription of each word of an expected category. If,

e.g. the last word that has been recognized is a verb, the next expected syntactic category is an article; the pattern matching mechanism will try to match the phonetic transcription of each article of the dictionary with the beginning of the phoneme string. If the matching fails, we shall try to match the string of phonemes with some modified phonetic transcriptions of articles. Here is a list of the allowed modifications which can successively be tested:

- At the beginning of a word:

  1. Correct matching of the first phoneme (empty modification).
  2. Skip the first phoneme of the string.
  3. Skip the first phoneme of the word of the dictionary.
  4. Skip the two first phonemes of the string.
  5. Skip the two first phonemes of the string and the first phoneme of the word of the dictionary.

- Inside the word:

  1. Correct matching of the considered phoneme (empty modification).
  2. Typical confusion for example:
     $$\begin{aligned} er &\Longleftrightarrow iE\,, \\ I &\Longleftrightarrow i\,, \\ E &\Longleftrightarrow er\,, \\ z &\Longrightarrow s\,, ... \end{aligned}$$
  3. Insertion of a phoneme.
  4. Deletion of a phoneme.
  5. Substitution of a phoneme.

- At the end of the word:

  1. Correct matching of the last phoneme (empty modification).
  2. Deletion of the last phoneme of the dictionary word if the word has more than two phonemes and if there is no insertion, no deletion and no substitution just before.

The format of the Prolog routine "extract" is as follows: "extract(Syntact, S0,S,T0,T)" tries to extract a word of syntactic category "Syntact" from the beginning of the string S0 of phonemes. S represents the remaining string of phonemes while the list of words T is formed by the initial list of words T0 augmented with the extracted words.

For the matching algorithm of the received string of phonemes with the phonemes which represent the phonetic transcription of the words we shall assume that each of the syntactic categories has a maximum number of possible phonemes, for example:

Syntactic category	:	maximum number of phonemes
verbe	:	7
nom	:	8
...		

Let us finally mention that we plan to investigate a different version of the routine for extracting words. Instead of using the Prolog pattern matching algorithm for which we have to specify explicitly all the acceptable modifications (see the above list) we can also compute a global distance between the received string of phonemes and the expected list of phonemes. We can e.g. compute by means of a dynamic programming algorithm the Levenshtein distance [6] between the beginning of the string of phonemes and each of the (phonetic representations of) words of the expected syntactic category. The word with the lowest distance is then chosen provided that this distance does not exceed a given level.

3   Syntax

The usual way one attempts to make precise the definition of a language, whether a natural language or a programming language, is through a collection of grammar rules. The rules of a grammar define which strings of words are legal sentences of the language. As such, it can give useful information to the acoustic level. In addition, the grammar gives some kind of *syntactic analysis* of the sentence into a structure which makes its meaning more explicit: this structure is the *parse tree*. The parse tree provides us with the *syntactic categories* of the sentence which the semantics needs for understanding it. In the present case we shall consider syntactic categories which are words or groups of words (e.g.: verb, adjective-noun) with which a semantic meaning can be associated. The syntactic categories will be used during the semantic analysis for *understanding* the sentence: it is the syntax that tells the semantics what the action is and who is doing the action. Modelling the syntax and the semantics for an unrestricted language is a complex task but for a limited application, such as our text editor, this is possible via a DCG (Definite Clause Grammar) see ([5]).

A Prolog internal mechanism automatically translates the DCG rule:

$$phra \longrightarrow verbe(Tac, Mode), construct(Tac, Mode) \qquad (1)$$

into the Prolog clause:

$$phra(T0, T) : -verbe(Tac, Mode, T0, T1), construct(Tac, Mode, T1, T). \qquad (2)$$

which means that there is a *"phrase"* from $T0$ to T if there is a *"verb"* from $T0$ to $T1$ and a *"construction"* from $T1$ to T.

Since we are working on word strings *and* on phoneme strings, the instructions have to take into account two pairs of sequencing arguments: the first pair will manage the phoneme string while the second pair will manage the word string. In this respect, the instruction:

$$phra(S0, S, T0, T) \quad : - \quad verbe(Tac, Mode, S0, S1, T0, T1),$$
$$construct(Tac, Mode, S1, S, T1, T). \qquad (3)$$

has the following meaning:

"phra" extends from S0 to S in the phoneme string and from T0 to T1 in the word string if "verbe" extends from S0 to S1 in the phoneme string and from T0 to T1 in the word string and if "construct" extends from S1 to S in the phoneme string and from T1 to T in the word string. We introduce the Prolog notation "::-" which implicitly assigns to each predicate of the clause two pairs of sequencing arguments. This means that a Prolog internal mechanism automatically translates the instruction:

$$phra :: -verbe(Tac, Mode), construct(Tac, Mode). \qquad (4)$$

into the Prolog clause (3). The operator "::-" works with respect to two pairs of sequencing arguments in the same way as the operator "$\longrightarrow$" works with respect to one pair of sequencing arguments. Let us now introduce some additional Prolog operators connected to the use of the "extract" routine. We shall assume that the operator "::=" automatically applies the routine "extract" to each of the predicates of the right-hand side of the clause except to the predicates that are preceded by the symbol "$". This means that the instruction:

$$phra ::= verbe(Tac, Mode), \$construct(Tac, Mode). \qquad (5)$$

is translated by the operator "::=" into the Prolog Clause:

$$phra(S0, S, T0, T) \quad : - \quad extract(verbe, Tac, Mode, S0, S1, T0, T1),$$
$$construct(Tac, Mode, S1, S, T1, T) \qquad (6)$$

As quoted above, the Prolog clause (6) means that for finding the sentence composed of the list of words T0 from the garbled list of phonemes S0, we have to extract a "verbe" with the translation "Tac" and the semantic parameter "Mode" and to find a "construction" matching the remaining string of phonemes S1.

We introduce a last operator denoted "#"; this operator placed in front of a terminal or of a non terminal means that it can be omitted. E.g., the notation #(art(Art,2)) tells us that we have to extract from the string of phonemes one of the articles of the form "art(Art,2)" out of the vocabulary or to extract the word [ ] consuming no phoneme. The notation #(art(Art,2)" is thus equivalent to "art(Art,2) ∨ [ ]".

The terminals have two arguments corresponding to the translation and to the semantic parameter of the vocabulary. We give below a sample of grammar rules corresponding to the left branch of Figure 1 in the ATN formalism ([5,9]); these rules describe intransitive constructions. We can recognize the path leaving from the node "phra" with the arc "verbe" going to the node "construct". For the intransitive verbs (Mode=int) there are two branches corresponding to the two grammar rules for the non terminal "construct" respectively.

$$
\begin{array}{lll}
\text{phra} & ::= & \text{verbe(Tac,Mode),} \\
& & \$\text{construct(Tac,Mode).} \\
\text{construct(Tac,int)} & ::= & \{ \text{ Tac} = \text{go } \}, \\
& & \text{\# (preprel(Pr,Ii)),} \\
& & \text{chif(Quant,Im),} \\
& & \text{nom(N,In),} \\
& & \text{\#(\$orig ([])).} \\
\text{construct(Tac,Int)} & ::= & \text{\# prep(Pr,1),} \\
& & \$\text{posisuite.} \\
\text{posisuite} & ::= & \text{\# (art(A,1)),} \\
& & \$\text{gn(0,N).} \\
\text{posisuite} & ::= & \text{prep(Adv,0),} \\
& & \text{\# (art(A,2)),} \\
& & \$\text{gn(0,N)}
\end{array}
\qquad (7)
$$

4 Semantics

The semantics take into account the word and sentence meaning. The syntax gives us rules for building legal sentences but sentences can be syntactically correct but completely meaningless. With a simple test on the semantic parameter of the noun in the gn-rule we can prevent to accept sentences of the form: "erase the last word of the next word" or "erase the last word of the next character". The goal pursued by the semantics is twofold:

- It has to restrict the accepted language to meaningful expressions. This is mainly done by the semantic parameter in the lexicon.

- It has to understand the sentences.

By understanding the sentence, we mean here the translation of a natural language expression into a program giving the results expected by this expression. In our application, this program is expressed in terms of text editor *elementary commands*. For the cursor movement, the editor accepts elementary commands of the following forms:

- [end,X]
- [beginning,X]
- [Digit,X,forward]

- [Digit,X,backward]

where "X" is either "character" or "word" or "line" or "page" and "Digit" is a number. A list such as e.g.: [three,line,forward] constitutes an elementary command accepted by the editor for moving three lines forward. The elementary command [insert,mark] inserts a mark on the cursor position so that the commands [cut] or [cut,in,buff2] erase all the text between the mark and a new cursor position and save this text in a default or in the specified buffer "buff2" in the case of [cut,in,buff2].

In the vocabulary we associate a semantic translation to each word. The recursive noun group splits the sentence into embedded syntactic categories composed of a noun, a noun followed by an adjective or an adjective followed by a noun. Using these syntactic categories, we are able to build the elementary editor commands by assembling their semantic translation. For example, the association: "deuxième mot" (second word) with the semantic translation "one" for the adjective and "word" for the noun are assembled to get the corresponding command : [one,word,forward]. We can add to each grammar rule a parameter for building these editor commands. For example, to the recursive gn-rule :

gn(Inn,N)   ::=   adject(Ad,Iad),
                  nom(N,In), { Inn < In }
                  #(art(Ar,0)),
                  $gn(In,NN).

we add a third parameter:

gn(Inn,N,[Sf | [[**Ad, N, forward**]]])
              ::=   adject(**Ad**,Iad),
                    nom(N,In), { Inn < In }
                    #(art(Ar,0)),
                    $gn(In,NN,Sf)

With this third parameter, each embedded adjective-noun constituent is translated in a list structure with reverse order. The semantic translation of the adjective "Ad" and the noun "N" are assembled in the list [Ad,N,forward] building the corresponding elementary command. These embedded translations are assembled in reverse order with the Prolog list operator "|" creating a new list with the commands "Sf" of the embedded noun-group and the newly build elementary command. The expression "deuxième mot de la troisième ligne" (second word of the third line) is translated into the list: [[two,line,forward],[one,word,forward]]. The cursor movement is mostly based on the noun-group but for other actions, we need more complicated building rules.

For erasing a text, for example, we need a sequence of four actions

- going to the beginning of the text to be erased.

- inserting a mark.

- going to the end of the text to be erased.

- erasing all the text between the mark and the cursor.

This can also be done by the same list building mechanism so that the sentence: "Effacer tout le texte entre le deuxième mot de la troisième ligne et la fin de la page" (erase all the text between the second word of the third line and the end of the page) can be translated into the elementary command sequence: [[two,line,forward],[one,word,forward],[insert,mark],[end,page],[cut]] corresponding to the four actions mentioned for erasing. This is carried out by the augmented grammar rules:

```
construct(cut,trans,[COD | [[cut]]]   ::=   cod1(cut,0,COD)
cod1 (Tac,I,COD)                      ::=   #(adject1(Tout,0)),
                                            #(art(A,2)),
                                            nom(text,10),
                                            $testorig(Tac,COD).
testorig(Tac,[ORIG,[insert,mark] | [GOAL]]
                                      ::=   preporig(P,I),
                                            $orig2(I,ORIG),
                                            #($goal(P,GOAL)).
```

The object to be erased is determined by the COD argument of the "cod1" rule. This COD argument is composed within the "testorig" rule from the first three previously mentioned actions: going to the beginning (Orig), inserting a mark ([insert,mark]) and going to the end (GOAL).

For the replacement of an object by another one, we need to combine other actions. The grammar rule of this action contains the predicate "cod1" for the object to be replaced followed by the predicate "suite" for the object of replacement. The translation is obtained by the concatenation of several actions:

- saving the object of replacement in a buffer.

- erasing the object to be replaced.

- inserting the buffer contents.

The sentence : "Remplacer le mot suivant par tout le texte entre le deuxième mot de la troisième ligne et la fin de la page". (Replace the next word by all the text between the second word of the third line to the end of the page", is translated into:

```
[[two,line,forward], [one,word,forward],
    [insert,mark],
    [end,page],[cut,in,buff],[insert,buff],
    [here]
    [insert, mark]
    [one,word,forward],
    [cut], [insert buff]]
```

Using the following augmented grammar rules:

```
construct(replace,trans, [SUITE,[here],COD1,[cut],[insert buff]])
        ::=   $cod1(replace,0,COD1),
              # $suite(SUITE)).
suite([COD | [[cut,in,buff],[insert,buff]]])
        ::=   prep(Pr,5),
              $cod1([],0,COD)
```

This augmented grammar becomes more and more complex and unreadable with the increasing complexity of the actions to be performed. In addition, some syntactic constructions have different semantic translations depending on the semantics of their constituents and have thus to be repeated with different command building parameters. Therefore, for the sake of readability and conciseness, we are now studying a new formalism called the *Definite Clause Translation Grammar* [1,2] allowing a separate formulation of the syntactic rules and of the translation rules. Using this formalism, we reduce the syntactic-semantic part of the grammar used at the recognition level in an optimal way. The translation of the *gn-rule* shown before gives in DCTG formalism :

```
gn(Inn )   ::=   adject(Ia) ¨ Ad,
                 nom(In) ¨ NOM, { Inn < In }
                 #(art(Ar,0),
                 $gn(In) ¨ GN
<:>
(NOM,[Sf | [[Ad, NOM, forward]]])
            ::=   GN ¨ tradu(N,Sf)
```

The syntactical part (with some semantic tests e.g.: $\{Inn < In\}$) is separated from the translation part by the operator "<:>".

The translation rules constitute in fact a mini database associated to the node "*gn*" and the syntactical rule build a parse tree where each node is labelled with a variable name (e.g. Ad, NOM, GN, ...) containing the corresponding mini database. The operator "¨" labels a node with a variable name.

In the syntactical part, the variable names come after the operator ¨ showing which mini data base is called and in the translation part they appear before it. "GN ¨ tradu(N,Sf)" means that we have to look in the data base GN for a rule or a fact matching "tadu(N,Sf)". The whole process is thus carried out in two steps: first we build up a parse tree associating to each node the corresponding mini database and secondly, starting from the root we try to find a match looking in the children node mini databases. Each database acts as a Prolog program. This match gives us the corresponding translation. The DCTG can be viewed as an implementation of an attributed context free grammar.

The syntactical part is written as concisely as possible rejecting all ambiguity and redundance in the translation part.

For the some syntactical construction, we can have different translation. As an example, depending on the adjective, the noun group have different translation:

- "go to the first line of the next page" is translated into

  [[one,page,forward],[beginning,page]]

- "go the last line of the next page" is translated into

  [[one,page,forward],[end,page],[beginning, line]].

For the same *gn*-rule we have different translation rules:

```
gn(Inn )   ::=   adject(Ia) ¨ Ad,
                 nom(In) ¨ NOM, { Inn < In }
                 #(art(Ar,0),
                 $ gn(In) ¨ GN
<:>
(tradu(NOM,[Sf | [[end, Nfin],[beginning, NOM]]])
            ::=   Ad ¨ last,
                  GN ¨ tradu(Nfin,Sf)),
(tradu(NOM,[Sf | [[beginning, Nfin]]])
            ::=   Ad ¨ first,
                  GN ¨ tradu(Nfin,Sf)),
(tradu(NOM,[Sf | [[Ad, NOM,forward]]])
            ::=   GN ¨ tradu(N,Sf)).
```

In the same mini database we can also have clauses with different names. With the transitive construction for the verb "effacer" (erase) we have different translation rules depending on whether on individul item or a continuous part of text has to be erased.

- "erase all capitals in the next word" is translated into

  [[one,word,forward],[insert, mark],[one,word,forward]

  [cut,all,capitals]].

- "erase all the text from the beginning of the next line to the end of the next page" is translated into

  [[one line back],[beginning line],[insert mark],

  [here], [one, page, forward],[end,page]

  [cut]]

In the second case we use the command "cut" erasing all the text between a mark and the cursor and in the first case we use a more sophisticated command "cut" with arguments erasing items specified by the arguments.

Here follows the corresponding DCTG rule:

```
construct(cut,trans)   ::=   $cod1 (cut,0) ¨ COD,
                             #($cl(_)) ¨ CL
<:>
(tradu(cut,WP))        :=    COD ¨ traduone(N1) ,
                             CL ¨ tradu(P2),
                             (P2 = [in, NOM],
                             WP=[[beginning, NOM],[insert mark][end,NOM],[cut]]
                             ;
                             append(P2, [[cut | N1]], WP)
                             )),
(tradu(cut,WP)         ::=   COD ¨ tradu(N1,P1) ,
                             CL ¨ tradu(P2),
                             append(P2, P1, P) ,
                             append(P, [[cut]], WP)).
```

The first translation rule is used depending on whether "**traduone (N1)** can be matched in the database COD. This happens when the object to be erased is an individual item as in the first example. Otherwise we look for a "**tradu(N1, P1)**" in the database COD.

The DCTG formalism gives us an adequate and flexible framework in which the complexity of language understanding can be expressed.

It conserves at the same time a clear and concise formulation of syntactical constraints which has to be used in the speech recognition of well formed sentences.

5 Conclusion

We have seen how a syntax guided access to the lexicon can be implemented in Prolog and how the syntactical and semantic constraints can be adequately expressed in the DCG formalism. We have also explained how the language is "understood" by the translation of a spoken utterance into a sequence of commands that can be executed by an automata (a text editor in our case).

Finally, we have described an extension of DCG called the Definite Clause Translation Grammar which enables us to preserve the readability and the conciseness of syntax and semantics needed for the lexical access and at the same time gives us a great flexibility to express and modify the translation rules dedicated to our application.

Acknowledgement

This work was supported by the Belgian Ministry of Economic Affairs under IRSIA-IWONL Grant 4300.

References

[1] H. Abramson, Definite clause translation grammars, Proc, 1984 int. symp. on logic programming, pp. 233-241.

[2] H. Abramson, Definite clause translation grammars and the logical specification of data types as unambiguous context free grammars, Proc. 1984 int. conf. on fifth generation computer systems, pp. 678-685.

[3] H. Bourlard, Y. Kamp, C.J. Wellekens, " Speaker Dependent Connected Speech Recognition via Phonemic Markov Models" in Proc. 1985 ICASSP, Tampa, pp 31-5.1 - 31.5.4.

[4] A. Colmerauer, Metamorphosis grammars, in L. Bole (editor), Natural language communication with computers, pp, 139-169, Lecture notes in computer science, vol. 63, Springer-Verlag 1978.

[5] F. Pereira and D. Warren, Definite clause grammars for language analysis - A survey of the formalism and a comparison with augmented transition networks, Artificial intelligence vol. 13, pp. 231-278, 1980.

[6] D. Sankof and J. Kruskal, Theory and practice of sequence comparison: Time-warps, strings edits and macromolecules, Addison-Wesley, 1983.

[7] M.Schroeder (Editor), Speech and speaker recognition, Bibliotheca Phonetica, Karger, 1985.

[8] D. Snyers et A. Thayse, Réalisation d'un module de reconnaissance et de traduction de phrases en Prolog, 5ème congrès AFCET/INRIA sur la reconnaissance des formes et l'intelligence artificielle, pp.119-125, 1985.

[9] W. Woods, Transition network grammars for natural language analysis, Com. ACM, vol 13, October 1973.

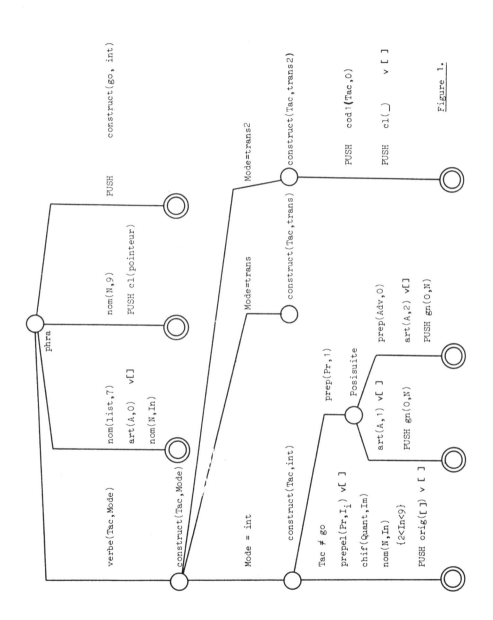

Figure 1.

A Knowledge Based System for Contextually Deformed Pattern Interpretation Applied to Chinese Tone Recognition

Y. Gong and J.P. Haton

CRIN, Vandœuvre (France)

ABSTRACT

Knowledge representation, uncertainty modeling and approximate reasoning in a knowledge based system for contextually deformed pattern recognition are discussed. The system performs production-rule based inference, domain independent pattern pre-classification and signal processing. Contextually parametrizable fuzzy predicate is used for representing the meaning of inherently imprecise linguistic description in the rule set. Uncertainty of data and of deduction is modeled by certainty coefficients and by fuzzy reasoning. Interaction between the symbolic manipulation level and the signal processing level reduces computations and provides a refined pattern segmentation. The system is applied to Chinese tone recognition, a previouslly unresolved problem of the recognition of contextually deformed patterns. Very low recognition error rate is obtained. The system can be adapted to solve other signal interpretation problems.

Keywords: signal interpretation, speech recognition, knowledge based pattern recognition, fuzzy predicate, approximate inference

1. INTRODUCTION

Signal interpretation, such as speech recognition and understanding, involves a hierarchy of several abstract level processing [Hat85]. The first step of an artificial intelligence based signal interpretation consists identifying and specifying real world phenomena into a set of primitive objects known to the system, called patterns. This step realizes a conversion of signals into a finite set of symbols and has important influence on the system performance. In general patterns have the following properties: they have been altered by various noises including errors in parameter detection; it is not easy to formulate a general grammar to describe relations between the patterns; high level constraints are not very restrictive to the patterns and thier utilization is unefficient; more importantly, there exist contextual deformations that can not be readily modeled mathematically and the interpretation of these patterns involves knowledge that is not carried by the signal. We discuss in this paper the design considerations and the implementation of a knowledge based pattern interpretation system capable of performing fuzzy reasoning. The objective of the work is to provide a tool for solving this kind of problems and to formulate and evaluate rules for the specific application of tone interpretation in the Chinese language. In this application knowledge is used to recognize contextually dependent patterns corresponding to the five categories of perceptually significant variations of the fundamental frequency of speech, i.e: $-$; $\nearrow$; $\smile$; $\searrow$; etc.

2. CONTEXTUALLY DEFORMED PATTERN RECOGNITION

Let's consider a sequence of conceptual symbols $\{S_i\}$ carried in the real world by a sequence of patterns $\{p_j\}$ when no mutual influence between S_i's exists. The relations between symbols and patterns are in this case one-to-one correspondence. As a consequence of the presence of the mutual influence of symbols, while the order of patterns is unchanged, the p_i's are, however, deformed and the mapping is no longer one-to-one. The problem of recognition of contextually deformed pattern is to recover the original sequence $\{S_i\}$ form the deformed patterns observed. It should be noted that the margins between the deformed patterns may be perturbed and in general, the closer the indexes of two symbols, the greater the mutual influences. We conclude that the association of an observed pattern to a symbol depends on the neighboring patterns. Phoneme recognition is a typical contextually deformed pattern recognition [Car86], where phonemes and measured speech signal are respectively the symbols and the pattern sequences. In this case the contextual deformation is mainly produced by coarticulation and phonological phenomena.

Two conventional approaches [Nan85]: statistical and syntactical, have been used in pattern recognition. The statistical pattern recognition assigns the signal to one of a finite number of classes using a classification function based on various criteria as local minimization of error probability or of distance between the signal and a reference in a parameter space. The key problem of this approach is to represent the signal in a suitable parameter space. However, whatever the feature space and the decision function used, errors caused by context influence cannot be eliminated since this approach is local and no contextual information is incorporated.

Syntactical pattern recognition takes into account the internal structural relation of patterns. A pattern is described by a sentence, a string of pattern primitives, which is generated by a pattern grammar which gives all allowable primitive combinations. A syntax analyzer is used as recognition procedure. To deal
with pattern distortion and erroneous primitive measurement that would make the
analyzer reject a noisy sentence, stochastic language and error-correcting syntax
analyzer have been proposed [Fu77]. However, the contextual dependency
phenomenon is an intrinsic property of the signal and not a kind of noise and is
produced by several interactively coupled sources, so it is difficult to construct the corresponding grammar.

We consider the contextually deformed pattern recognition problem as an interpretation problem in A.I. where the meaning of an event depends on the neighboring
events as well as on the event itself. Here we know by observation some properties of a sequence of symbols and empirically we know *a priori* the correspondence
between properties and symbols and the relations between the properties. The purpose is to deduce the presence of a symbol sequence to make the knowledge as consistent as possible. The problem is characterized by, firstly, the fact that the
appearance of patterns is almost random because of the weak restrictions from
high level constraints such as syntax and, secondly, the contextual dependency
obeys a set of relations which generally have not yet been entirely and formally
formulated. Therefore the interpretation requires reasoning about the event
sequence. Our system consists of two interacting parts: the knowledge based
interpretation (symbolic manipulation) which gives the recognized pattern
sequence and the pre-classification (signal processing) which segments signal and
provides the required pre-classified patterns. We present the system in the
following sections.

3. KNOWLEDGE REPRESENTATION

The first problem to solve in the design of a knowledge based system consists of
selecting an adequate knowledge representation scheme. We will briefly review
some classical schemes and discuss thier adequation to the problem of signal
interpretation.

Semantic networks model the real world entities as nodes and the relationship
between such entities as labeled arcs. While this representation provides the
possibility to construct complex knowledge bases, the deletion and addition of
knowledge during the development of the system require, however, the examination
and redefinition of the entire base since the entities are interconnected.
Semantic networks are used in complex knowledge prepresentation as in natural
language processing and in speech understanding [Pie82].

Frame and object-oriented representations are very suitable for representing
knowledge having high degree of structure or of hierarchical dependence between
objects. While these representations facilitate the objects to inherit properties from conceptually more abstract object classes, they are not efficient to
represent inferential knowledge but they can be associated with other representation modes such as production rules. This kind of representation has been successfully used in domain where knowledge is well structured as in image recognition and computer vision [Kim84]. Frame and object-oriented representations

require a detailed consideration (coherence verification for example) about relations between objects and procedures. In the development stage, the knowledge
base is frequently modified and updated and the verification of the entire
knowledge base is not desired at each time.

In the problem of interpreting contextually deformed pattern, the well structured knowledge and the inheritance property can hardly be exploited. We have
therefore not adopted semantic networks nor frame or object-oriented representations in which the manipulation of knowledge base requires a great complexity
of implementation and in which a complete knowledge of the problem is desired
for starting the construction.

Production rules are currently the most common knowledge representation technique
employed in expert systems. Each rule in the knowledge base is an independent
fragment of knowledge and does not rely on the correction of other rules. This
representation has the property that if all rules are locally correct then the
knowledge base is globally correct. This facilitates successive updatings since
rules are independent of each other and the order of declaration of rules is not
important. The conversion of the real world knowledge into a machine exploitable
formalism is easy. For most A.I. application domains the production rule offers a
natural way of encoding knowledge not yet systematically formulated. Besides,
production rules provide an easy way to partially explain the behavior of the
system. We use production rules to represent domain knowledge about pattern
dependency and deformation.

The most severe criticism of production rules is the lack of visibility of the
static structure of (or the relations between) objects described by the rule set.
This can cause difficulty when investigating the dependency of the rules and performing efficient inference. Fortunately, in our system where the objective is
to interpret low level objects highly hierarchical relations are not frequently
involved. Consequently, another related criticism that the rule structure is
"plate" and not suitable for expressing the global and internal relations of the
system, as has been noted [Aik83], does not have considerable influence in our
case.

4. FUZZY REASONING MECHANISM

In solving real world problems as pattern interpretation by A.I. approach, we
have to represent two types of knowledge respectively related to the definition
and the observation of patterns. The first type describes abstract objects and
restrictions or relations between them with complete certainty. Example of this
kind of knowledge are language grammar rules. The second type of knowledge
describes real world objects and observed relations between these objects. These
relations are only possible but not necessarily always true and the the observations are limited by experience. The determination of real world objects
involves a supplementary decision making when performing logical deduction. In
pattern interpretation, the measured signal may be corrupted by noise, the pre-
classification of the signal into patterns may produce erroneous results, the
description of rules used for interpretation may contain vague statements and in
general, the knowledge base of a system is an incomplete description of the world
it is intended to model. These points have important consequences for the operations defined over a knowledge base [Myl83].

4.1. Uncertainty and Approximate Inference

The inference quality may be influenced by two factors related to the uncertainty: (1) The signal is perturbed by noise and therefore symbols to reason with and conclusions obtained can never be absolutely reliable; (2) The knowledge used for inference is not absolutely certain. We are not always sure of each condition-conclusion pair. So conclusions, even deduced from perfectly certain facts, are uncertain. We need therefore weighting the rules in order to take into account this uncertainty.

Bayes's theorem and belief function has been used in reasoning [Dud76,Sho76]. However, in real inference context the basic assumption of an exhaustive and mutually exclusive hypothesis space is difficult to maintain. Together with the lack of prior evidence, this makes it highly problematic to estimate the *a priori* probabilities for the events described by the knowledge base which is required by Bayes's theorem [For85].

Certainty factors have been successfully used in uncertain knowledge representation [Liu85]. The basic requirements for computing the certainty of a fact are that, firstly, the certainty must be enforced when several rules conclude the same fact and, secondly, the order of applying rules should not affect the resulting certainty. In our system rules are associated with certainty factors to model the fact that we are not always sure of the correlation between the premises and the conclusion (for example: A tends to be B). We have used, as most approximate reasoning systems based on the certainty factor, the following *ad hoc* rules:

$$CF = CF_{rn} \times \min_{i} \{CF_i\} \text{ for AND-graph} \qquad (Eq.4.1.1)$$

$$CF = 1 - \prod_{i=1} (1-CF_i) \text{ for OR-graph} \qquad (Eq.4.1.2)$$

Where CF is the resulted certainty; CF_i the certainty of the i-th fact to be combined; CF_r the certainty of the rule.

In our system, inferences are based on two kinds of observed objects: the independent parameters that describe the different aspects of a pattern (local objects) and the pre-classified patterns in different positions in the input sequence (contextual objects). Because the relations between objects are simple, an inference engine without variable is used. For interpreting the pre-classified patterns, the inference engine performs depth-first backward-chaining search. In the inference graph, AND-graph is searched until the first branch is rejected or all branches are established. Each branch of an OR-graph is exploited for combining the certainty given in (Eq.4.1.2). In general, the premisses of a rule describe the currently interpreted pattern segment and the context of the segment: left (previous) and/or right (next) segments. Globally, the interpretation works from left to right but the interpreter is capable of stacking the sub-problems created when deducing the current segment in order to interpret the left or right context if necessary.

4.2. Imprecision and Fuzzy Predicate

Part of the knowledge acquired during observation of the phenomenon is not
numeric but linguistic. For example properties of an object may be described in
terms of "great", "small", "about", etc. That requires a conversion of the
natural language terms into a numerical representation. The use of probabilistic
models in this case is rather limited. The descriptions of objects have three
basic properties. First, the range in which the description of a given object is
correct is not precise. Second, this fuzzy range is relative and varies according
to object types and to the context of description. For instance, the tolerated
ranges for the linguistic value "great" in the description "the interval between
two speech segments is great" could hardly be the same as that in "the slope of
the fundamental frequency of the segment is great". Lastly the descriptions
involve imprecision rather than randomness. We model this knowledge by fuzzy
predicate in our rule based system. A fuzzy predicate is a membership function
[Zad65] from the object set U to the unity interval $[0,1]$ subjected to the restriction R, giving the membership degree of an element $e \in U$ in the fuzzy set F:
P_F: $U \times R \rightarrow [0,1]$. A value of 1 of a fuzzy predicate means a full membership
and indicates the complete truth of the predicate. 0 means the exclusion of the
set and a complete untruth of the predicate. The intermediate values represent a
truth certainty. The range of fuzzy membership varying with context is specified by R that parametrizes the predicate. For example, we can express the interval between two pattern segments as an object set of all positive real values. A
value of 0 (INTERVAL<a) of the fuzzy predicate "is-great(INTERVAL,a,b)"
corresponds to the judgement "INTERVAL is not great at all", 1 (INTERVAL>b)
"INTERVAL is absolutely great". A value between 0 and 1, obtained by a prespeci-
fied monotone interpolation of a and b, gives the degree of certainty of the
judgement "INTERVAL is great".

Fuzzy predicates clarify the imprecision and contain more significant description
for an observation than the precise predicates. They help the user specify the
imprecise part of a description and provide a tool for converting the imprecise
linguistic variable into precise numeric description. Fuzzy models have been successfully applied to phoneme recognition, a kind of contextually deformed pattern recognition [Mor80,Gub86], as well as to other domains.

4.3. Incompleteness and Counter Fact

In working with real world objects, we cannot know all about the whole universe
of the problem, a complete modeling is therefore impossible. The rule base is
incomplete in the sense that not all facts or conditions resulting in a conclusion are in the knowledge base. So it is generally incorrect to conclude that a
fact is false if it is impossible to prove that it is true. The decision is particularly difficult to take when the certainty is neither near zero nor near one.
However, to decide whether to accept, refuse or not conclude is inevitable in
approximate inference process. Human experts would try to prove the counter fact
(or to eliminate the fact) to get rid of this situation. Instead of proving the
fact F, he would prove "not(F)" using the related rules. This strategy will provide more evidence on F and therefore aid the decision. To prove the counter
fact prevents also the inference from exhaustive searching in proving the fact
that is not described confirmatively by the rule set. We have used two
exclusive fact sets: the PAS (proven and accepted set) and PRS (proven and

rejected set). A simplified procedure for inferencing a fact "F" is as: If F is in PAS then F accepted else if F is in PRS then F rejected else prove F, prove not(F) and combine the certainties to decide whether accept or reject F.

5. SIGNAL-SYMBOL INTERACTION

In most A.I. systems for interpretation, the signal processing level is activated only once at the beginning of the interpretation, transforming the digitized signal into a string of hypothesized symbols by segmentation and classification. In the recognition of contextually deformed patterns, combination of sophisticated classification techniques must be used, and even so the result is still erroneous in tricky situations. While it is almost impossible to have an error-free result at the signal processing level, symbolic processing using knowledge about the pattern deformation mechanisms may readily remove some of these errors. In fact, in some cases it is obvious to assign a segment of signal to a pattern class on the observation of some easily extracted parameters instead of using all set of parameters. In our system, errors at the segmentation and classification stages are tolerated and then corrected by rule based interpretation. Because the uncertainty exists in the output of the pattern pre-classification, certainty coefficients are associated with the patterns to be interpreted in order to be exploited during interpretation if necessary. In the tone recognition application, we keep the information on fundamental frequency contours at the symbolic level by a polynomial approximation. These coefficients are exploited only when more detailed description requiring a fine signal processing is needed, thus reducing the computational effort. The errors in classification and in segmentation are decreased thanks to the interaction between the signal processing and symbol processing levels. This kind of interaction is especially useful to correct over-segmentation or under-segmentation errors where contextual information is desired. This interaction permits (1) the usage at the low level of the knowledge of statistical nature by signal-reference comparison and efficient data reduction and (2) the application of inference only on signal segments where a high level interpretation is necessary.

6. CHINESE TONE RECOGNITION

Spoken Chinese is a lexical tone based, monosyllabic language. We define tones as the variations of fundamental frequency (F_0) of speech. There are five tones in Chinese (T_1, T_2, T_3, T_4 and T_0) that class the words into five categories. The same vocal tract configuration with different F_0 implies different meanings. It is therefore mandatory to be able to recognize these tones for the spoken Chinese understanding. Furthermore, statistics over 200 Chinese sentences shows that the tone combinations of these sentences are all different. In consequence, it is possible to design a Chinese speech understanding system based on tone recognition and assisted by phoneme recognition.

However, just as other set of speech parameters, these tones are only defined at a linguistic level. In real speech, because of the inertia of the speech production system and of the speaker's trend to relax pronounciation, the realization of tones is context dependent. This dependency involves changes both in tone variations and in intensity contours (the maximum value within one period of speech signal estimated over about 40ms). We have for example the following observations: $\{T_3\}_n \rightarrow \{T_2\}_{n-1} + T_2$, $T_1 + T_3 \rightarrow T_4 + T_4$ and $T_3 + T_4 \rightarrow T_2$. We use the notation "→" to note that the phenomena are possible but not always reproducible. The context influence is so important that the Chinese listeners cannot recognize isolated tone of speech segments extracted from real speech and randomly arranged (51% error) [Lee86]. Statistical methods have been tried for tone recognition. However, since they are based on the local distance measures results are not sufficiently reliable to be really used by higher level (error rate 30-40% [Hal85]). We conclude that the use of contextual information is mandatory. Our system interprets the pre-classified patterns to determine the linguistic tone sequence of an utterance. As discussed in section 5, the segmentation and recognition are achieved in two steps: Pre-processing using unsophisticated techniques where errors are tolerated and knowledge based interpretation of the results in which contextual information is used.

In the pre-processing part, the pitch contour is first estimated in terms of variation of the fundamental frequency and of voice-unvoiced or silence decision. The speech intensity contour is estimated at the same time, for segmentation purposes. The segmentation is based on the morphological analysis [Ser82] (dilation followed by erosion) of the intensity contour. Finally, according to the tone variation, we classify each segment into a candidate patterns. That results in a list of: {pre-classified patterns and probabilities (P_i pr_i) i:[1,3], index of first sample and length of the segment (DS, LS), N-th polynomial coefficients (A_j) j:[0,N]}. Detailed description of the signal processing and the classification part of the tone recognition system can be found in a previous paper [Gon86].

The inference part of the system is implemented in LISP while the signal processing part is in C language. In the following example of rule, the current speech segment C and the previous speech segment P have already been pre-classified. The purpose of this rule is to detect and cancel an over-segmentation in which T_3 is over-segmented and classified as $T_3 + T_2$. This rule has an *a priori* certainty of 0.9. It states that if the current segment is pre-classified as T_2, and the previous segment is pre-classified as T_3, and the duration of the current segment, the interval between the previous and the current segments and the sum of durations of the two segments are all small, then the tone of the current segment is T_3. An action is performed to merge the two segments and to decrease the current segment counter. The numbers in the predicate "is-small" specify the boundaries of fuzzy membership function.

```
        RULE-011:
        (IF    ((in-class C "T2")
                (in-class P "T3")
                (is-small (duration C) 10 20)
                (is-small (interval P C) 8 15)
                (is-small (+ (duration C)(duration P)) 50 60))
        THEN   ((is-a C "T3"))
        ACTION ((merge P C)
                (decrease POINTER))
        RULE-CERT 0.9 )
```

We have carried out a preliminary experiment with a set of 156 digits pronounced by one Chinese speaker. The classification algorithm gave about 93% of correct recognition for the 4 categories (whithout T_0 in these digits). The 7% of errors were all recovered by the expert system [Gon86].

7. CONCLUSIONS

The problem of recognizing contextually deformed patterns cannot be solved by using only local information based classification techniques. On the contrary an A.I. system based on specific knowledge is required. It is necessary to represent and exploit the domain knowledge, to perform signal processing, randomness and fuzziness treatment, and approximate inference. Production rules are suitable for encoding the empirical knowledge in the system development stage. Fuzzy predicate is a natural way for imprecise knowledge acquisition and representation. Certainty factors modeling the fact and rule uncertainties prevent the inference process from being too "binary". The interaction between the signal and symbol levels allows an efficient use of both non-declarative and declarative knowledge in one system. The system provides a good tool for approximate reasoning as shown by its application to the problem of tone recognition in spoken Chinese. The knowledge base in the system should be further enlarged and tested over a more important speech data base.

References

Aik83.J. S. Aikins, "Prototypical Knowledge for Expert System," Artificial Intelligence, vol. 20, pp. 163-210, 1983.

Car86.N. Carbonell, J. P. Haton, D. Fohr, F. Lonchamp, and J. M. Pierrel, "APHODEX, Design and Implementation of an Acoustic-Phonetic Decoding Expert System," Proc. IEEE Int. Conf. Acoust., Speech, Signal Processing, Tokyo, 1986.

Dud76.R. Duda, P. Hart, and N. Nilsson, "Subjective bayesian methods for rule-based inference systems," Tech. Note, no. 124, SRI International, Menlo Park, 1976.

For85. Richard Forsyth, "Fuzzy Reasoning Systems," in Expert Systems - Principles and case studies, ed. Rechard Forsyth, pp. 51-62, 1985.

Fu77.K. S. Fu, "Error-Correcting Parsing For Syntactic Pattern Recognition," in Data Structures, Computer Graphics, and Pattern Recognition, ed. T. L. Kunii, pp. 449-492, Academic Press, inc., 1977.

Gon86.Y. Gong and J. P. Haton, "Un Système à Base de Connaissances pour la Reconnaissance Automatique des Tons du Chinois," Actes des 15-ième Journées d'Etudes sur la Parole, Aix en Provence, 1986.

Gub86.R. Gubrynowicz, K. Marasek, and W. W. Wiezlak, "Reconnaissance de mots isolés par la méthode descriptive de traits phonétiques," Actes des 15-ième Journées d'Etudes sur la Parole, pp. 235-238, Aix en Provence, 1986.

Hal85.P. Hallé, "Les Tons du Chinois de Pékin, Leur Comportement en Parole Continue," Actes des 14-ième Journées d'Etudes sur la Parole, GALF, PARIS, 1985.

Hat85.J. P. Haton, "Intelligence artificielle en compréhension de la parole: Etat des recherches et comparaison avec la vision par ordinateur," TSI, vol. 4, no. 3, pp. 265-287, 1985.

Kim84.J. H. Kim, D. W. Payton, and K. E. Olin, "An Expert System for Object Recognition in Natural Scenes," Proc. 1st Conf. on Application of A.I., Denver, U.S.A., 1984.

Lee86.P. W. Chi Lee and M. H. Peron, "La Perception des Tons du Chinois par des Francophones et par des Chinois," Actes des 15-ième Journées d'Etudes sur la Parole, pp. 143-145, Aix en Provence, 1986.

Liu85. Hsi-Ho Liu, "A Rule-Based System for Automatic Seismic Discrimination," Pattern Recognition, vol. 8, no. 6, pp. 459-463, 1985.

Mor80.R. De Mori and P. Laface, "Use of Fuzzy Algorithms for Phonetic and Phonemic Labelling of Continous Speech," IEEE Trans. PAMI., vol. PAAMI-2, pp. 136-148, 1980.

Myl83. John Mylopoulos and Hector Levesque, "An Overview of Knowledge Representation," in On Concepual Modelling: Perspectives from Artificial Intelligence, Databases, and Programming Languages, ed. J. V. Schmidt, Springer-Verlag, 1983.

Nan85.N. Nandahakumar and J. K. Aggarwal, "The Artificial Intelligence Approach to Pattern Recognition - A Perspective and An Overview," Pattern Recognition, vol. 18, no. 6, pp. 383-389, 1985.

Pie82.J. M. Pierrel, "Utilisation des contraintes linguistiques en compréhension de la parole continue: le système Myrtille II," TSI, vol. 1, no. 5, pp. 403-421, 1982.

Ser82.J. Serra, Image Analysis and Mathematical Morphology, Academic Press, 1982.

Sho76.E. H. Shortliffe, Computer-based Medical consulation: MYCIN, American Elsevier, New York, 1976.

Zad65. Lotfi A. Zadeh, "Fuzzy Set," Information and Control, vol. 8, pp. 338-353, 1965.

Applications to Technical Domains: General Tools

Another Use of Inference Engines: Interactive User's Guide for Large Numerical Software (Aiglon)

D. Guérillot

Institut Français du Pétrole, Rueil-Malmaison (France)

E. Petiot

Laboratoire d'Informatique Fondamentale,
Université Pierre et Marie Curie, Paris (France)

Abstract: Large numerical simulation software often calls for a large amount of input data. This article describes an interactive software that helps build the input data file needed by oil reservoir simulators. A professional inference engine was used to build this interface. This approach offers many advantages concerning the quality of the software produced such as reability, extensibility, user friendliness, etc

Keywords: Artificial Intelligence, Expert Systems, Inference Engine, Software Engineering, Interface, Numerical Simulation, Reservoir Modelling.

Résumé: Les gros codes de simulation numérique nécessitent souvent l'entrée de nombreuses données. On présente un programme interactif d'aide à la constitution d'un jeux de données pour un modèle de gisements d'hydrocarbures. On a utilisé un moteur d'inférences professionnel pour écrire cette interface. Cette approche comporte de nombreux avantages concernant la qualité du logiciel produit: fiabilité, extensibilité, facilité d'utilisation...

Mots clés: Intelligence artificielle, Système expert, Moteur d'inférences, Génie logiciel, Interface, Simulation numérique, Modèle de gisements.

1   INTRODUCTION

Many software products for simulating complex physical phenomena
are available today in various fields.   They compute approximate solutions to problems stemming from the modeling of fluid
mechanics, elasticity, electromagnetism, neutron physics,
etc.   They generally manipulate a considerable body of data.
An interactive system helps build the input data file in a
"pleasant" manner for the user.   The authors propose using
an inference engine to build such a system.   After describing
the different data categories specific to these simulation
models (Article 2), they present the AIGLON system (Article
3), explaining the choice of an inference engine, and emphasizing its many advantages over a procedural system (Article
4).   The final part (Article 5) is devoted to an operational
application for a simulation model of the behavior of a hydrocarbon reservoir.

2   DESCRIPTION OF DATA

Many physical phenomena are modeled in the form of one or
more equations with partial derivatives, supplemented by the
boundary conditions and, if the problem is an evolving one,
by the initial conditions.   Solutions to boundary problems
are often approximated by using a finite-difference or finite-
element model.   The often bulky codes resulting from these
methods call for vast input data.   Despite the wide variety
of fields of application of these problems of equations with
partial derivatives, it has been observed that the data required for the use of these data processing programs can be
classed in different families independent of the problem dealt
with.   An idea is provided by using a model problem ((1),
for example) to describe these different data categories.

If D is a domain of the plane (a rectangle, for example),
thermal conduction inside D causes a change in temperature
T(t,x,y) (t denotes the time variable and x,y the space
variables) in the presence of a heat source f(x,y), by the
following equation with partial derivatives:

$$r.c.\frac{\partial T}{\partial t} - \frac{\partial}{\partial x}(k.\frac{\partial T}{\partial x}) - \frac{\partial}{\partial y}(k.\frac{\partial T}{\partial y}) = f$$

where k, r and c are respectively the thermal conductivity,
density and specific heat of the solid making up domain D.
These parameters may vary with the space variables.

Let F be the boundary of the domain, and let us assume that
the temperature is fixed at any time at a given temperature
on this boundary. The following boundary condition is obtained:

    T(t,x,y) = u(t,x,y) ; (x,y) belongs to F.

Finally, let us assume that at the initial time (t=to), the
temperature To is known in domain D. This gives the initial
condition:

    $T(t_0,x,y) = T_0(x,y)$; (x,y) belongs to D.

The data concerning the following are distinguished in the
codes corresponding to these numerically resolved problems:

1.   **Geometric description of the integration domain.**   These
     geometries may have 1, 2 or 3 dimensions, and simple
     or complex forms. (e.g. domain D has 2 dimensions in
     space and can be characterized by its length and width).
     It is necessary not only to describe the boundaries of

this domain, but also its breakdown into meshes or discrete
elements.   Many automatic mesh software products exist
in finite elements.   An expert system, called SYMATRAU,
was developed (2) to automate this part of the construction of the data file, taking account of the boundary
conditions.

2.   **Boundary conditions.**   As a rule, the value of the unknown
is imposed (as in the model problem) or the value of
its derivative on the edge of the domain, but many other
conditions are possible.

3.   **Equation coefficients and the second member.**   These
data are generally associated with each element of the
mesh.   However, it is often important to supply a single
value for a group of elements (e.g. if a solid consists
of two different materials, coefficients k, r and c are
different in the two regions of domain D).   If these
data vary as a function of the unknowns, tables of values
are given.

4.   **Numerical instructions.**   The codes often propose
different resolution-time schemes of the differential
system (explicit scheme, implicit scheme, with one or
more steps), and different methods for resolving linear
systems (direct, iterative).   Many control parameters
are also available for numerical resolution (convergence
tests, bounds of variations in unknowns, of the time
step etc).

3   SPECIFICATIONS OF THE AIGLON SYSTEM

3.1   Objectives of the system

Most powerful numerical software products calling for considerable data acquisition, some of which are conditioned
by the presence or absence of other data, may appear difficult
to employ for a user not thoroughly familiar with the field.
It therefore seems important to develop an interactive system,
whose chief role is data **acquisition**, but which can also **guide**
and **inform** the user.

Data is acquired by a series of questions directed at the
user. The information is closer to the field of application
than to the internal representation of the data, specific
to the simulation model.   By asking for help (by typing
"?", for example), the user obtains a series of data on the
different technical terms used, the units employed, etc.
This aid is not imposed on the appearance of a question, to
ensure that the system will not be too talkative, because
these data become useless and even disturbing for a user
familiar with the field.

3.2   Why an inference engine?

An inference engine manipulates production rules.   A production rule is an expression of the form:

If condition(s) then consequence(s)

The **conditions** (or "premisses" of the rule) specify a set
of facts.   The **consequences** (or "conclusions" of the rule)
constitute the operations to be performed if the conditions
are satisfied.

In a user's manual, in fact, we can find for a data item A:

"Item A is prohibited if item B = x;
prohibited in the presence of item C or of item D;
if not, mandatory."

or, for example:

"Item A is mandatory if item B = x
and item C = y and absence of item D;
prohibited if item C greater than y
and presence of item D."

Note that the data B, C and D may also be subjected to rules
of the same type. Thus, the level of interleaving of the
rules is sometimes high. The presence of a data item and
the conditions associated with it can be modeled in the form
of production rules. This is one justification for using
an inference engine. We shall specify the other advantages
of this approach in the next section.

4   ADVANTAGES OF THE SYSTEM PROPOSED OVER A PROCEDURAL SYSTEM

The use of an inference engine is generally associated with
the design of an expert system. However, the system described here is not an expert system, in the sense that it
does not simulate the reasoning of a specialist. Its field
of application does not require the use of knowledge associated
with the appearance of an expert, because the data it needs
are rigorously known, and are conditioned by the read orders
of the simulation software and shown explicitly in the software
user's manual. We shall list the advantages of this approach
in the following sections.

4.1 Reliability

Definition (3): The ability of a software product to operate in abnormal conditions.

The use of a professional inference engine, employed for many applications, is a guarantee of reliability. This represents a similar situation to that of the use of a compiler. Moreover, many inference engines perform complete control concerning the type of input data and their field of definition.

4.2 Extensibility

Definition (3): the ease with which a software product lends itself to modification or an extension of the functions required of it.

Declarative programming allows for easy extensibility. In fact, the order in which the rules are introduced into the system has no effect on the result. The operation of the engine is totally independent of the architecture of the knowledge base. This feature is important for our application, because a simulation software is not fixed, and its evolution entails a constant update of the data to be supplied. An order is only imposed between the different data families (Article 2) by a control structure. This may, for instance, be one set of rules for the boundary conditions, another for the numerical parameters, etc. But within a given set of data, the order of the rules is random.

4.3 Portability

Definition (3): **the ease with which a product can be transferred among different hardware and software environments.**
The suppliers of inference engines adapt their programs to
the maximum of computers for obvious commercial reasons.
This guarantees good portability of the application developed
with a professional inference engine, because the knowledge
base is written in a language specific to it.   The only
difficulty may arise from connections with computer programs
external to the engine, or with databases.

4.4 Ease of use

Definition (3): **ease of learning, of use, of data preparation,
of interpretation of results, and of correction in case of
user error.**

Ease of use is inherent in the interactive system.   The user
is guided by the system, which poses the questions according
to the answers given.   This ease of use is backed by an intrinsic property of the intrinsic property of the inference engine,
its capacity to explain: explain why a particular query
is asked, show the rules used during the reasoning.   At any
time of the session, the user can also check the values of
the entered or inferred data.   This feature is useful if
the user wants to consult the value of a parameter to clarify
the value of another data item.

Furthermore, inference engines often have an interface in
virtually natural language, which considerably increases the
friendliness of the dialog.

4.5 Speed of development

The building of a knowledge base is rapid because there is
no concern for the overall organization of the system, nor
in particular, for the interface with the user.   These tasks
are handled by the inference engine.   Moreover, from the
start of development, an application can "run" even if it
is incomplete, thus facilitating checking out.

4.6 Reusability

Definition (3):   **the ability of a software product to be re-
used, fully or partly, in new applications.**

We have demonstrated the possibility of classing the data
acquired for the numerical resolution of problems of equations with partial derivatives.   This classification is
refined as the field of application is clarified (structural
computations, fluid flows in aeronautics, in porous media).
As a rule, many codes exist dealing with related physical
phenomena.   This applies in particular to reservoir models
(Article 5.2).   The encoding of these families of data in
object structures, as is often possible in sophisticated inference engines, considerably improves the reusability of
many parts of the knowledge base.   For example, there is
only a limited number of ways to re-enter the coefficients
of an equation or to describe the boundary conditions.
The objects and rules associated with these methods can therefore be retained for various applications.

**If the use of an inference engine is considered as a programming
method, it becomes clear that for this type of application,
it successfully meets the quality criteria set in software
engineering.**

5   APPLICATION FOR A PROGRAM TO SIMULATE THE BEHAVIOR OF
A HYDROCARBON RESERVOIR

This section gives a detailed description of the use of an
inference engine (Article 5.1) to develop a system for aid
in building the input data file (Article 5.3) for a reservoir
model (Article 5.2).

5.1 Engine used

System S.1 was selected for its performance, particularly
for its organization of the objects into a set of "frames",
a user interface in virtually natural language and its portability, since the version employed is written in language
C.   Refer to (4), (5) for the technical specifications of
S.1.

5.2 Field of application

Interest in the numerical modeling of fluid flows in porous
media has grown sharply in recent years (6, 7).   This modeling
is particularly important for optimizing the production of
a hydrocarbon reservoir.   The physical and chemical processes
involved in these problems are complex, and reservoir simulation codes are generally very bulky.   They may have as
many as 100,000 FORTRAN instructions and demand over 10 engineer-
years for their development.   For the time being, AIGLON
is applied to a model for simulating steam injection in a
hydrocarbon reservoir (8).   Its use requires the input of
several data that are classed by keywords.   Its manual contains about 150, but fifty keywords are sufficient to build
a data file (about 1000 lines). AIGLON can be extended to other
software products of the same type.

5.3 The AIGLON system

The data are grouped into several classes: geometry, petrophysics, relative permeabilities, capillary pressures, thermodynamics, initializations, periods, wells, etc.   Each class
has a number of attributes.   For the geometry, for example,
the attribute **grille** defines the type of grid, the attribute
nz the number of meshes in the z direction, the attribute
rmaxi the outer radius for a cartesian grid.   Different items
(or "slots") define an attribute.   An extract of the knowledge base concerning the attribute **grille** is shown below:

```
DEFINE ATTRIBUTE          grille
::DEFINED.ON              geometrie
::TYPE                    text
::LEGAL.VALUES            {xyz, rtz, rtzc}
::LEGAL.MEANS             {query.user}
::DETERMINATION.MEANS     {query.user}
::PROMPT                  "What is the type of grid ?"
::REPROMPT                "XYZ: determines a (x,y,z) cartesian grid."
            ! new.line() ! "RTZ: determines a (r,theta,z) grid."
            ! new.line() ! "RTZC: determines a radial (r,theta,z) grid
closed in theta (complete)."
::TRANSLATION        "Type of grid"
END.DEFINE
```

Let us now summarize the significance of the different "slots".
The attribute **grille** is defined on the geometry class.   It
is of the **text** type.   The value of this attribute is included
in the set {xyz,rtz,rtzc} .   The method to determine this
value is to query the user by the question defined in the
"slot" **PROMPT**.   In case of a wrong answer (not included in
the set mentioned above) or of a request for help by "?",
the data given in the "slot" REPROMPT are supplied.   The
item **TRANSLATION** serves to give a definition of the attribute
in clear language.   This definition is used for a "translation"

into English of the rules which use the attribute `grille`.

Another example of an attribute containing other items:

```
DEFINE ATTRIBUTE        rmini.value
::DEFINED.ON            g:geometrie
::TYPE                  real
::LEGAL.MEANS           {query.user}
::DETERMINATION.MEANS   {query.user}
::PROMPT      "What is the grid blocks inner radius in " ! lmail.unit°g§ !
"?"
::CHECKING.FUNCTION        check.real
::TRANSLATION           "the grid blocks inner radius"
END.DEFINE
```

For this attribute, the question asked of the user contains
the value of an attribute, here the appropriate unit `lmail.`
`unit` which depends on the system of units employed.   The
function **check.real** checks that the value supplied is definitely positive, and if not, the user is queried again.

Here is an example of a rule extracted from the knowledge
base:

```
DEFINE RULE         geol
::APPLIED.TO        g:geometrie
::PREMISE      grille[g] known and nx[g] known and ny[g] known and nz[g]
known
::CONCLUSION      grid.blocks[g] = written("Grid description","GRILLE =
",upper.case(grille[g]),nx[g],ny[g],nz[g])
END.DEFINE
```

The rule **geol** applies to any object **g** of the type **geometry.**
The "slot" PREMISSE expresses the conditions relative to the

writing of the keyword **GRILLE**.   The function **written** is a
file write function.

AIGLON writes on a file all the keywords necessary for a
simulation.   Only the scalar data are demanded of the user.
For the tables of values, it can include them directly in
the keyword file generated.

The reasoning of AIGLON is planned.   The geometry is first
described, then the petrophysics, then the relative permeabilities, capillary pressures, etc, to avoid confusing the
user by questions pertaining to sets of data relative to
different classes.   The strategy is specified in a control
structure, called **control.block**, which specifies the order
in which the attributes are determined.

The system is **operational** for the time being.   It has 12
classes, 224 attributes, 11 control blocks and 123 rules.

5.4   Example of a session

The following is an extract of dialog concerning part of the
description of a petroleum reservoir:

                    Welcome to AIGLON
                    ==================

    . . .
    . . .

GEOMETRY

```
6:  What is the type of grid ?
6> ?
Enter one of the following: xyz, rtz, rtzc
6:  XYZ:  determines a (x,y,z) cartesian grid.
    RTZ:  determines a (r,theta,z) grid.
    RTZC: determines a radial (r,theta,z) grid closed in theta (complete).
6> xyz
7:  What is the number of grid blocks in x direction?
7> 15
8:  What is the number of grid blocks in y direction?
8> 15
9:  What is the number of grid blocks in z direction?
9> 4
10: Do you want to define grid blocks net thicknesses in their relation to
    gross thicknesses ?
10> why
I asked whether you want to define grid blocks net thicknesses in order to
apply geo10.  Geo10 is used to determine Grid blocks net heights.

    geo10:
      If
         you want to define grid blocks net thicknesses,
      then
         Grid blocks net heights is written.


10> what nz
Nz is 4.

10> no
I1: How do you want to define the top of the reservoir?

    a - with reservoir top dip.

    b - with reservoir top elevation.

    c - with grid blocks tops elevations.

    d - with grid blocks nodes elevations.
```

```
        Type the letter corresponding:
11> a
12:  What is the top angle with Ox in RAD?
12> 0
13:  What is the top angle with Oy in RAD?
13> 0
14:  What is the top first elevation in M?
14> 10

...
...
...
```

This dialog served to generate part of the data file given
in the extract below:

```
        <Grid description>
        GRILLE =  XYZ 15 15 4

        <Grid blocks lenghts>
        DX

        <Grid blocks width>
        DY

        <Grid blocks gross thicknesses>
        DZ

        <Reservoir top dip>
        PENDAGE = 0.000000 0.000000 10.000000
```

The strings of characters in brackets are considered as comments
by the computer program.

6   CONCLUSIONS

The AIGLON system can be extended to a family of simulation
models of the behavior of a hydrocarbon reservoir.   The data
syntax is different for each code, but the data themselves
may be common to several of them.   In all the models, for
example, the description of the geometry and the definitions
of the relative permeabilities are mandatory.   Thus the same
rules and objects attached to these readings can be used by
the different models.   These common parts hence make it
easy to construct a **complete system** which, according to the
model selected by the user, will help to generate a data file
in the corresponding syntax.   For the user, the specific
syntax of the model selected is completely transparent.
Programming with an inference engine thus offers real flexibility for the extensibility of this type of system.

It is estimated that this **programming technique** could be extended
to the very core of simulation programs.   In fact they consist
of purely calculating parts which would remain algorithmic,
but also of parts formalizable in the form of production rules
(all the parts having many conditional tests: inputs/outputs,
time step management, etc).   This type of extension can only
be considered when these two programming paradigms can be
mixed without harming program performance.

REFERENCES

(1) M. Sibony and J.C. Mardon, "Approximation et equations differentielles", Analyse numerique, Volume 2, Chapter 6, Hermann, Editeurs des Sciences et des Arts.

(2) P. Trau, "SYMATRAU: Systeme expert de maillage tri-dimensionnel automatique", Fifth International Conference on experts systems, (May 1985), Volume 2, pages 1165-1176.

(3) B. Meyer, "Introduction au Genie Logiciel", in publication in the Encyclopedia **Techniques de l'Ingenieur,** (November 1985).

(4) "S.1 Version 2, Reference Manual for Knowledge Engineers"; FRAMENTEC (1985).

(5) "S.1 User's Guide." FRAMENTEC (1985).

(6) K. Aziz and A. Settari, "Petroleum Reservoir Simulation", Applied Science Publishers Ltd, (1979).

(7) Richard E. Ewing editor, "The mathematics of reservoir simulation", SIAM, Philadelphia, (1983).

(8) P. Lemonnier, "Projet de modele numérique thermique compositionnel", IFP report No. 29 877, (January 1982).

Applications to Technical Domains: Process Control

Knowledge and Vision-Based Control of Burning Process

H. Ahonen, S. Jakobson and R. Ylinen

Technical Research Centre of Finland, Espoo (Finland)

ABSTRACT

Major problems in burning process control of a grate-fired boiler is the great number of process variables and inefficiencies in the computer implementation of the control. This work presents an application of knowledge-based methods to solving these problems. An experimental system with two subsystems, the scene analysis subsystem and the control subsystem, is described. The knowledge-based components of the both subsystems are written in Prolog.

KEYWORDS: grate-fired boiler, qualitative process model, scene analysis, scene understanding, inference explanation

1 INTRODUCTION

The problem of building a control system for the burning process in a grate-fired boiler is difficult because the process model tends to be very complicated. It contains a great number of variables, many of which cannot be expressed in a quantitative form. The efforts to build computer implementations for the control lead easily to inefficient solutions.

The supervision of the burning process is normally done manually through inspection holes or with the help of video cameras. No computer intervention is normally present. Thus the automating of the process control requires development of suitable methods for digital image processing in order to provide the control system with the information necessary for its decisions.

The work to be presented here focuses on the problems of producing the image information sufficient for the control system and on the problems of building a system to give control recommendations. The application of knowledge-based methods seems to be very useful for solving these problems. Further motivation to use this methodology comes from the need for experience of its applicability in the process control environment in general. The exploitation of domain knowledge also in the scene interpretation brings the use of visual information closer to the real situation in which the operator makes his decisions on the basis of his (often inconscious) scene analysis.

To verify the feasibility of the approach, a small experimental system has been built. It has been divided into two subsystems, the scene analysis subsystem and the control subsystem. The computer programs of the knowledge-based part of the system have been written in Prolog (MPROLOG 1986) and run in VAX 11/750.

2 GRATE-FIRED BOILER

Grate furnaces are used to burn solid fuels like bark, wood waste and peat. They generate steam or hot water for the purpose of heating or power generation. The grate burning process is schematically depicted in Fig.1. The fuel is fed onto the grate mechanically and it moves down because of the gravity. In large modern furnaces the fuel can be pushed down by means of mechanical (hydraulic) pistons. Four grate zones can be identified, the zones of drying, gasification and burning and the zone of ash.

The process is controlled by the fuel feed and the movements of the pistons, by the primary air flow through the grate and the fuel bed and by the secondary air flow to the upper side of the grate. It is important for the efficient burning that the ash line, i.e., the border between the burning and ash zones, keeps close to the lower edge of the grate. In this case, there is fire on a large grate area so that no burning material will exit unused. Burning of heterogeneous fuels like bark and wood wastes is difficult due to the great variations in the fuel quality and to the lack of reliable means to measure both the actual fuel flow and the conditions on the fuel bed over the length of the grate.

In many plants the process is supervised manually through inspection holes. In large boilers video cameras are used. Other means to estimate the fuel bed conditions are pyrometers for bed temperature measurement, pressure difference transmitters for air penetration measurement and gamma-detectors for measurement of the fuel layer thickness. The sensors cannot cover the whole area of the grate.

A fire-room camera allows the operator a wide view over the burning zone and over the fuel bed. Thus the operator can control the size, location and shape of the burning zone and, in particular, the location of the ash line. He can also identify local burning areas ("craters") on the drying and gasification zones. This is important, because craters decrease the efficiency of the boiler and have therefore to be eliminated.

The quality of the monitored black and white image is usually poor due to disturbances like smoke, flying ash, soot, flue gas and spatial illumination variations. Furthermore, the process is so slow that it is very difficult to estimate trends in the process with the help of the image. Therefore, the instantaneous camera image is usually used only for checking that the burning is going on and for detection of very great disturbances. On the other hand, the camera gives the most immediate information about the burning process so that a proper image together with suitable trend estimations will assist the operator to improve the manual control of the process (cf. Lilja, et al.,1986 and Dahl et al.,1986). The interpretation of the image and the trends, as well as the determination of the corresponding control actions are the most important problems to be solved in the automating of the process control. One solution to these can be an expert system like the one presented in this paper.

The expert system to be presented here gives recommendations for control operations. It is based on a model of the process, and it employs process measurements, the most important of which is the image. The knowledge in it consists of instructions, rules, goals and criteria for good control.

3 QUALITATIVE PROCESS MODEL

The length coordinate of the grate is quantized into three values,"low", "medium" and "high", while the possible breadth coordinate values are "left", "medium" and "right". For the lenght coordinate there is also the value "very low". The distribution of the variables in the height direction is neglected. The measurement and control system is included in the process model.

The following variables are used in the model.

    Manipulated variables:
        fuel feed rate (3 by 3 variables)
        air flow (3 by 3 variables)
        fuel thickness (3 variables)
    Measurable inputs:
        load
    Nonmeasurable inputs:
        fuel quality
    Measurable outputs:
        burning zone location
    Nonmeasurable outputs (state variables):
        burning zone velocity
        burning power
        efficiency of burning

The values of these variables are quantized very coarsely,too, except the values of the variable "load", which can be measured accurately. Some cause-effect relationships between the variables are obvious but most of them have to be constructed by means of experimental rules. The rules can be divided into the steady state relationships and the transient relationships. The rules

- if the load is high then the burning power is high
- if the burning power is high then the ash line (the lower edge of the burning zone) location is low
- if the fuel quality is good then the burning zone is long
- if the air flow is too high then the efficiency is low
- if the air flow is too low then the flames are flickering

are typical examples of the steady state rules. The rules

- if the load is increasing (decreasing) then the fuel feed rate and the air flow are increasing (decreasing)
- if the fuel feed is increasing (decreasing) then the burning zone is going down (up)
- if the air flow is increasing (decreasing) then the burning power is increasing (decreasing)

are examples of the basic transient rules. In these rules, the other input variables are assumed constant. There are also some rules concerning the joint effect of two input variables. An example of the rules of this kind is

- if a separate burning region is located up and the flames there are not flickering then it is a crater.

4 SCENE ANALYSIS SUBSYSTEM

A knowledge-based approach

Although the burning process as such tends to be very slowly changing, sequential images in video recordings of the burning scene can vary substantially. This variation is due to disturbances in the scene as described in section 2 and sometimes also to disturbances in the imagery equipment. In contrast to the systems in which image information is employed by computation of time averages of certain quantitative image parameters (as e.g. in Lilja et al.,1986 and Dahl et al.,1986), this work is based on a qualitative approach. In it, image processing and image parameter extraction is kept as minimal as possible and emphasis is laid on qualitative reasoning on the basis of certain basic features extracted from relatively few images. The term "qualitative reasoning" here refers to an expert system-like reasoning, where hypotheses about the existence of relevant scene objects are generated and tested with the help of general knowledge about grate-fired boiler scenes.

Another distinction from the "quantitative" scene analysis can be seen in the way how the results of the analysis are expressed as qualitative scene descriptions, not as numerical values of the scene parameters. Typical examples of the expressions of this kind are the characterizations of burning zones by their lengths and by the locations of their upper and lower edges.

Scene analysis steps

The visual analysis of an instantaneous state of the process is divided into the following three steps:

Step 1: Image formation and image transfer
Step 2: Image preprocessing
Step 3: Scene understanding

The first step consists of making images of the burning scene with video camera attached in a suitable position above the grate (see Fig. 1). The images are digitized and transferred into computer memory for further processing. In the experimental version the camera has been replaced by video tape. Four separate images with time intervals of about five seconds have been considered to form a sample of the grate scene at the given time. Thus the final analysis consists of building a scene description by comparisons between these four images.

In the second step, the necessary image preprocessing operations are applied to the raw images. These include reducing the number of the brightness values by means of a simple thresholding algorithm, smoothening the variation of these values, and finding the separate

connected regions in each of the images. Two series of images after thresholding and smooth-
ing can be seen in Figs. 2 and 3. The four images in Fig. 2 represent a normal burning
situation while the images in Fig. 3 show how the whole scene can sometimes be covered
by smoke. The algorithms employed in the preprocessing of the images are all very simple,
and no extensive computation of image parameters has been carried out. The results of this
second step contain, for each of the four images, the number of regions found, the brightness
value limits of the pixels in each region, and the pixel distribution of each region over the 3 x
3 grid placed regularly on the whole image area. The description of the regions in one image
can be written as Prolog facts in the following form:

```
n_rgns(1,6).     ; number of regions in image 1 is 6
rgn(1,1,[0,1]).    ; region 1 in image 1 consists of
rgn(1,2,[2,4]).    ; pixels with brightness values 0 or 1
rgn(1,3,[5,6]).
rgn(1,4,[2,4]).
rgn(1,5,[0,1]).
rgn(1,6,[7,9]).
rgn_distr(1,1,[59,0,0,0,0,0,0,0,0]).
rgn_distr(1,2,[277,60,0,119,0,0,23,0,0]).
rgn_distr(1,3,[105,402,126,256,324,282,94,66,239]).
rgn_distr(1,4,[0,0,264,0,0,180,0,0,138]).
rgn_distr(1,5,[0,0,51,0,0,0,0,0,0]).
rgn_distr(1,6,[0,0,0,87,160,0,324,396,64]).
```

(The numbers inside the brackets give the pixel values in the blocks of the 3 x 3 grid. The
first three are the values in the upmost, the next three in the middle and the last three in
the lowest part of the image (from left to right).)

This description shows that there are dark regions on the upper left and upper right, a bright
region almost on the lower left, and a large and medium bright region almost overall in the
image. An image like this can be seen in Fig. 3.

The process knowledge comes to use in the step three. The understanding of the scene means
determining the existence of those scene objects which are relevant to the burning process.
For this, it is necessary to know, which are the possible attributes for a region to represent
such an object. In addition, criteria for making comparisons between the four sample images
are needed. The next section is devoted to the details of the step three.

Scene understanding

The features of the scene which are relevant to the control of the burning process are divided
into three scene categories. Each category consists of various scene objects. The categories
and the corresponding objects are listed in Table 1.

Category	Objects
burning	burning zone
	separate burning regions
	craters
smokyness	smoky scene
	smoke zone
	smoke regions
not-burning	dark and stable regions
	no burning

Table 1. Categories and scene objects to be analyzed.

The analysis is based on the investigation of the attributes which a region in an image can have. The possible attribute types are the position of the region ("down", "up" or "vertically in the middle"), the brightness of the region ("dark", "bright" or "medium bright") and the size of the region ("small", "large" or "medium size").

Each scene object is characterized by legal combinations of attributes. For example, a burning zone is an object which consists of only one region with brightness "bright", with size "large" or "medium size", and with position "any position". Regions with given attribute combinations are looked for in each of the four images. The decision whether the existence of a scene object can be inferred or not is based on decision criteria stated separately to each object. For example, to infer the existence of a burning zone it is required that a region with the given attribute combination exists at least in three images of the four.

The attribute system demands descriptions of the meaning for each attribute, i.e., it has been necessary to build a small system of attribute semantics. The descriptions are based either on the pixel distributions of the regions or on the brightness values of the regions. Thus, for example, the description of the attribute "up" says that only ten per cent of the pixels of the region with this attribute may lie outside the upmost part of the image.

The analysis is carried out category by category. It starts by the choice of the object to be looked for. The first attribute combination in its characterization is chosen to be either the same as the one used in the analysis of the previous scene (at the previous time instant) or the given default combination. If the object with the chosen attribute combination is found, a new combination with stricter attributes is generated and the search of regions is repeated. This makes it possible to detect changes in the scene. If, on the other hand, the object is not found, a weaker attribute combination is generated for the search. The generation of possible attribute combinations is determined by restrictions written separately for each object.

The presentation of the results after the search of scene objects requires in some cases further analysis of the regions establishing the existence of the object. For instance, the position of edges is in the case of a burning zone determined by the pixel distributions of the regions found. The building of the final predicates for the control subsystem as well as the update of history predicates belong to the tasks to be carried out in the step three, too.

Discussion

The need for employing domain knowledge in scene analysis has been emphasized in the literature (see e.g. Tsotsos 1984). In this work, the use of domain knowledge enters in the analysis only in the final step. Thus the preprocessing step, i.e., the low level image processing, is seen only as a mechanical device producing input data for the later high level processing step. There are, however, difficulties in the low level processing, especially in choosing the threshold values so that the subsequent region segmentation would give the optimal result. These difficulties are due to variations in the scene brightness and cause inaccuracies in the distinction between burning zone and smoke regions. As a continuation of the present work, it will be tried to find out whether these problems can be solved by applying expert system methodology in low level image processing like in (Nazif et al., 1984). Another approach could be to apply the results of the analysis on the previous time step in the low level processing,too. This relies heavily on the assumption about the slowness of the underlying burning process.

In the first phases of the present work, an attempt was made to build the subsystem for scene understanding to consist of a set of declarative rules and of a separate inference engine. The idea was thus to follow the well-known principle of separating logic from control (cf. Kowalski 1979). Although criteria for a region to represent a burning zone, for example, were easy to write in a rule form, their implementation turned out to be difficult. The main difficulty seems to be due to the need for comparisons between the four images. Also the need for inferring the positions of the scene objects caused difficulties to the rule implementation. Both the comparisons and the position determination required computations in the procedural form.

The idea to separate the knowledge and the control of inference was not abandonded, however. The domain knowledge is now embedded in three parts of the system, in the attribute semantics, in the constraints for scene object attributes, and in the final decision criteria for comparisons between the four images. The part of knowledge that remains intermingled with the control consists of the rules which determine the objects to be searched for in the scene.

The experiments with video tape material collected from a real burning process showed that our choice to keep the basic image processing very simple was quite adequate for this kind of process. The scene description was, of course, very elementary, but in good relation to the needs of the control subsystem. The main inaccuracies turned out to be in the position decisions of the burning zone edges, since no geometrical edge information was computed. The inaccuracies of the decisions based only on the pixel distributions over the chosen grid can, however, be interpreted as a question of resolution: the choice of a finer grid would lead to better estimates of the edge positions. This solution would, however, need changes either in the attribute system expressing the positions or in the inference mechanism of positions so that an extensive growth of different test alternatives could be avoided.

5 CONTROL SUBSYSTEM

Knowledge-based control

The qualitative model and the measurements with their interpretation discussed above can be used in the process control in principle in the same manner as the quantitative models are usually used in the modern state control of processes. In practice, the existence of qualitative variables makes it impossible to apply the efficient numerical methods of the control theory. The tools and programming languages developed for dealing with symbol-valued variables (like logic programming, Lisp, Prolog, and expert system development tools) offer means to develop methods for the qualitative control. So far, such methods have been applied to the process control only in the form of some simple simulation and laboratory experiments.

The process control is usually divided into the state estimation and the state control. In addition, it can include the estimation of some parameters, disturbances and other nonmeasurable input signals. If a process model describing the cause-effect relationships is available then the state and the unknown inputs can be computed from the known input and output sequences with the help of backtracking. This kind of computation can be carried out also in connection of qualitative process models.

The realization of the state control in the qualitative case is a more complicated task than it is in the case of quantitative models. The methods which can be used for constructing a control are now based on the given reference values for the outputs and on the available process knowledge represented as a collection of instructions, rules, goals and criteria. The reference values for the state can first be determined with the help of the process model, reference values and backtracking as it was noted above. After this, the control operations bringing the process to the reference state can be constructed by means of the additional process knowledge.

The following instructions, for example, are derived from the burning process knowledge and they are applied to bringing the process to its reference state.

- keep the efficiency high
- increase the fuel feed rate above a crater, and decrease the air flow in the location of the crater.

The recommendations produced by the experimental system of this work are expressed as instructions of this type.

Implementation

The knowledge of the control subsystem is mainly organized in rule-like entities according to the standard syntax of MPROLOG. Descriptions of what is going on on the grate as well as recommendations concerning what control actions to take are produced by means of this knowledge. (N.B. the control loop is not closed). The rules are calling each other in a structured manner and the last of all the conditions are based on the facts produced by the scene analysis subsystem.

The rules are making use of qualitative values for the variables, typically "low", "medium", or "high". The values of the variable "load", however, are initially expressed numerically, but later on transformed to qualitative values (e.g., "increasing", "decreasing").

General descriptions of the process state are produced simply by sequentially working through all possible characteristics of the grate. The characteristics can either be directly obtained from the descriptions generated by the scene analysis subsystem or deduced on the basis of these and the measurement results. In case that a certain relation is found to be true (or in Prolog terms: can be proved) a corresponding message is sent to the operator of the system. The number of descriptions and recommendations varies according to the type of the facts produced by the scene analysis subsystem.

An explanation facility, which if required can trace the chain of reasoning, is provided. The explanations are produced and saved as a compound list of lists at the same time as the deduction is made. The head of the rule and the conditions in the body of the Prolog-rule are all expressed by means of an infix operator "since". On the left hand side of the operator a Prolog-term to be proved is given, e.g. burning_power(high,T), and on the right hand side there is the explanation. T denotes the current time. An example of this is the rule

    air_flow(very high, T) since ["air flow is very high", [E1,E2]]:-
        lower_edge2(high,T) since E1,
        fuel_feed(low,T) since E2.

Here the two conditions trigger other rules of the knowledge base. The chain of reasoning is relatively short. More than four levels of rules are generally not involved. The explanations in the list are printed to the terminal in a readable way when requested. The explanation facility is very simple and can answer just the questions of the type "how did you draw this conclusion".

The video tape material employed in the experiments contained images, in which the scene analysis subsystem could only find a smoky scene. These were interpreted to represent situations in which sufficient scene information was not available and they were managed by the recommendation "keep the control steady". Thus it was assumed that there will soon again be sufficiently information for deciding what to do.

The computing time of few seconds consumed by the control subsystem was only a fraction of the time needed by the scene analysis subsystem.

A schematic presentation of the experimental system of this work is given in Fig. 4.

6 CONCLUSION

The experimental system built for the control of a grate-fired boiler shows the feasibility of the knowledge based approach in process control. There is, of course, a long way to go from the system built to a realistically working control system. The main problems to be solved are in guaranteeing the security of the system, in speeding up the scene analysis if process monitoring with shorter time intervals is desired, and in keeping track of trends in the process state during long time periods.

The work shows how by a relatively simple image processing a sufficient amount of information for the needs of the process control can be obtained. The computations of additional image parameters are necessary, if more accurate descriptions of the locations of the scene objects are needed.

The slowness of the scene analysis subsystem can be a decisive factor in enhanced real time process control. The improvement of the speed requires a very careful analysis of the inference system and including of additional control structures in it. The questions of the efficiency of the Prolog programming language come only after these steps have been taken.

REFERENCES

Dahl, O. and Nielsen, L. (1986), Ash line control. 1st IFAC Workshop on Digital Image Processing in Industrial Applications (Vision Control), June 1986, Espoo, Finland.

Kowalski, R. (1979), Logic for problem solving. North–Holland.

Lilja, R., Ollus, M. and Sutinen, R. (1986), Image processing for control of burning process. 1st IFAC Workshop on Digital Image Processing in Industrial Applications (Vision Control), June 1986, Espoo, Finland.

MPROLOG language reference manual, (1985). Logicware Inc., Toronto, Canada.

Nazif, A.M. and Levine, M.D. (1984), Low Level Image segmentation: an expert system. IEEE Trans. Pattern Anal. Machine Intell., PAMI-6, pp. 555–577.

Tsotsos, J.K. (1984), Knowledge and the visual process: content, form and use. Pattern Recognition 17, pp. 13–27.

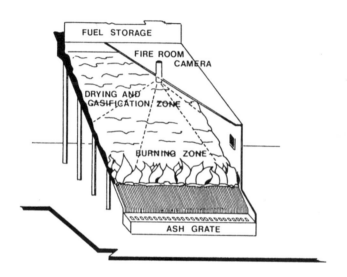

Fig. 1. Principle of grate burning process

Fig. 2. Four grate images after thresholding and smoothening. The bright areas represent burning. A burning zone can be found.

Fig. 3. Four grate images after thresholding smoothening. The bright areas represent burning. The two upmost images represent a totally smoky scene. It is unreliable to infer the existence of a burning zone.

INPUT

| Four raw images | Measurements |

SYSTEM

| Scene analysis subsystem   Control subsystem |

OUTPUT

| Image output | Recommendations, e.g. |
| Four preprocessed images on the video display | Increase thickness
Increase air flow |

Scene descriptions, e.g.	Explanations, e.g.
upper_edge very low, very low, low lower_edge very low, very low, very low burning_zone_length low, low, low flickering_flames	Increase thickness since fuel quality is low -burning zone length is low in 2 parts –burning_zone_length(low,low,low,13) given
	Increase air flow since load is increasing - load change is 7 – numerical_load(50,13) is given – numerical_load(43,12) is given

Fig. 4. A schematic presentation of the experimental system.

Man-Machine Communication

A Rule-Based Gracefully Interacting Dialoguing System

F. Fusconi and B. Ortolani

ELSAG, S.p.A., Genoa (Italy)

ABSTRACT

This project, named DIAVOLO, concerns the development and implementation of a system for dialogue management, the scope of which is to execute commands and answer questions given by voice. The ultimate task of the system is to furnish a room (simulated on a display) by drawing and moving around pieces of furniture. The vocabulary of 120 words and the defined syntax enable the system to accept over 100000 different sentences in natural language, including ellipses, fragments and answers. The main objectives pursued in this field of research are to investigate the rules underlying the dialogue conduction, according to the precepts of graceful interaction, and the possibility of explicitating them in a production system.

KEY WORDS: man-machine dialogue, graceful interaction, syntax, semantics, production system, rule-based system.

1 THE PROBLEMS OF DIALOGUE

In the development of the system we had to face several
problems mostly due to the speech recognition process and to the
graceful management of the dialogue. The first and most important
of these problems comes from the uncertainty about the actual
words pronounced by the speaker. For each word a vocal recognizer
[Vic '82] produces a list of alternatives which are then processed by an "island" parser [Bor '82].
This is able to connect isolated words into syntactic substructures and finally produces different sentence hypotheses. Even
for very simple sentences, the result of this process consists in
multiple alternatives, which are syntactically and/or semantically different and make it very complex to derive a unique meaning.

Moreover we have to deal with natural language ambiguity at
various levels: lexical, structural and semantical. To solve all
these ambiguities it is necessary to exploit information from the
extra-linguistic context, and eventually activate clarifying
dialogues, which are the main subjects of this work.

To allow an effective conversation, it is important for the
system to interact gracefully. This is necessary not only to make
the interaction between man and machine more pleasant but, most
of all, to guarantee the reciprocal comprehension.

"Graceful Interaction" actually means to guarantee the correct information exchange and to prevent the conversation from
being scrubby or from leading to a dead end.

This requires the application of a series of not codified
rules, which are used implicitely, and which represent an essential component of our linguistic knowledge.

The identification and formalization of these conventions as
explicit knowledge has been the most stimulating and challenging
aspect of this project [Ort '85].

2 SYSTEM DESCRIPTION

A number of works in NLU give hints about the kind of
information necessary to solve specific problems such as, for
example, focus [Gro '77] and anaphoric reference [Hay '81]. There
is, however, no comprehensive description of the problem and,
most of all, no indication on how to integrate heterogeneous
sources of information into a unique understanding mechanism.

We have identyfied several sources of information which, all
together, allow our system to deal successfully with most of the
problems we have discussed so far. Such information sources have
been classified into the following knowledge domains:

SENTENCE –   a series of facts which represent the alter-
              native sentences obtained by the parser

WORLD   –   all information regarding the environment
              where the system operates

DIALOGUE –   information about the last executed command,
              the structure of active subdialogue and
              various other information collected during
              the conversation. As a whole they define the
              current focus and the preceeding conversation

USER   –   statistical data concerning the degree of
              intelligibility of that paricular user (from
              the point of view of both speech recognition
              and familiarity with the system)

APPLICATION – information concerning the relationship
              between the actions executable by the system
              and the surrounding world. They refer to
              temporal constraints and possible
              inconsistencies

These pieces of information are represented homogenously by facts with this structure: "concept1(.concept2(.concept3)) relation concept4". Syntactic and semantic relations are also represented according to this formalism. For instance:

chair.5.shape is square

chair.5.dimension_x is 3

chair.5.dimension_y needs_specification of_type_question.

When the essential knowledge sources have been recognized we still had to face the problem of how and when utilize them. Hayes and Reddy [Hay '79] propose to subdivide the "ability to interact gracefully" into a set of primary capabilities which solve specific subproblems. These capacities are implemented as dedicated modules.

Since we adopted this approach, it was necessary to organize the communication among the various modules and to find out a precise separation line among the expertises required.

The implementation of the modules as independent sets of Production Rules has made it possible to overcome these problems. The architecture of the whole system, including the knowledge domains and the most important sets of rules, is sketched in Fig.1.

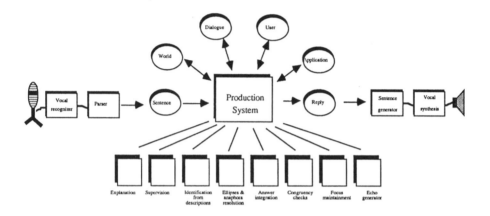

Figure 1
General Layout of the Dialoguing System

The rules of the Production System are based on Predicate Logic [Kow '84] and are applied in a forward direction; they are written according to the following syntax: IF <CONDITIONS> <CONCLUSIONS>, where <CONDITIONS> stands for a conjunction of "facts" containing variables each one preceeded by an identifier of the domain which it belongs to and, eventually, by a negation; while <CONCLUSIONS> stands for a conjunction of "facts" each preceeded by one of these three key-words: ADD, DELETE, EXECUTE. The following is an example of rule:

```
if (in SENTENCE) action is building
and (in SENTENCE) furniture.quantity is X
and (in WORLD) available_working_areas is Y
and X > Y

add (in SENTENCE) furniture.quantity is Y
and execute print_warning_no_areas
```

(if pieces of furniture to be built are more than the available working areas, then give user a warning and build as many as you can).

The EXECUTE keyword has been introduced to formalize procedural attachment.

Some predefined procedures, in particular, make it possible to treat the data-base as a push-down stack and permit to activate sets of rules as if they were subroutines of a programming language. For example :

```
if not (in SENTENCE) action is complete_failure
and not congruency_check.X has_produced error
and not (in SENTENCE) X needs_specification Y

add file_to_load is execute_action
and execute load_file
```

(if everything o.k., then load rules for execution).

The knowledge-base has been gradually implemented by developing separately the different groups of rules. During this process many solutions to each specific problem have been tested. For example, a solution to the problem of keeping track of focus in the course of dialogue has been obtained by equating the focus with the last action carried out by the system, together with the current information on the new command being defined. This has been accomplished by rules which identify and memorize parameters in the DIALOGUE domain in order to exploit this information later to integrate incomplete SENTENCES and solve anaphoric references (these rules correspond to the modules indicated as "ellipses and anaphora resolution" and "answer integration" in the preceeding figure).

The ambiguity due to the speech recognition, or intrinsic in the sentence pronounced, is solved in several steps. First the system tries to reduce the alternatives verifying the internal correctness of the SENTENCE; then it tests its congruency with the current state of the WORLD and DIALOGUE, and finally applies pragmatic information about the APPLICATION domain. These tasks are accomplished by the rules we have synthetically indicated as "Identification from Descriptions" and "Congruency Checks".

The task of controlling and co-ordinating the entire knowledge-base is left to another special set of rules. They make up a finite states automaton, whose main states are the INITIAL, ANSWER, CONFIRMATION and ERROR states. The last two deal with misunderstandings and communication difficulties and represent the means to ensure "robust communication". Transitions between states occur in relation to each utterance of the user and constrain the activation of the appropriate sets of rules.

To give the flavour of how the system works, we report here some excerpts of an actual dialogue, translated into English.

DIALOGUE	COMMENT

SYSTEM:	Hello, here is DIAVOLO at your disposal, what shall I do for you ?	
USER:	Set the value three as scale factor for furniture	
SYSTEM:	Ok!	A FULLY UNDERSTOOD COMMAND

USER:	and also for the room	A FRAGMENT REFERRING TO THE PRECEEDING UTTERANCE
SYSTEM:	Very well.	
	...	
USER:	Build table number one	INCOMPLETE COMMAND
SYSTEM:	You should give me size and shape	
USER:	rectangular five per seven	ELLIPTICAL ANSWER
SYSTEM:	I have a doubt about the second dimension: is it 6 or 7 ?	AMBIGUITY DUE TO VOICE RECOGNITION
USER:	seven	
SYSTEM:	Ok. I am building table 1 measure 5 * 7.	EXPLICIT CONFIRMATION ECHO
USER:	Draw four chairs measure two	
SYSTEM:	I haven't enough working areas, I'm drawing 3 chairs only (I set default values for labels)	SYSTEM DETECTS A PRAGMATIC ERROR; SHAPE IS INFERRED; DEFAULT VALUES ARE USED.
USER:	then move the table to the center of the room	
SYSTEM:	Done.	
USER:	now build the fourth stool	THREE UNKNOWN WORDS: TOTAL INCOMPREHENSION.
SYSTEM:	I haven' t understood; could you repeat, please	
USER:	Build a stool	STILL TOTAL INCOMPREHENSION
SYSTEM:	I still don' t understand. I can just SET values, BUILD, ROTATE, DELETE chairs, tables, sofas, armchairs and carpets, and answer questions like: "how far is ... from ... ? ". Make sure to use correct words and grammar.	AFTER TWO COMPLETE FAILURES SYSTEM PROMPTS THE USER WITH A FIRST SET OF INFORMATION REGARDING THE MOST COMMON WORDS AND SENTENCES.

USER: Build a square chair   AT LAST A CORRECT COMMAND
           measure two

SYSTEM: Perfect. I'm executing   AN ECHO IS GIVEN DUE TO THE
           a building action.   NUMBER OF PRECEEDING FAULTS

USER: Delete everything

SYSTEM: What ? I have just   SYSTEM DETECTS A PRAGMATIC
           finished building and   INCOHERENCE
           you command me to
           delete everything.
           Anyway I execute your
           command.

USER: Stop

SYSTEM: Ok, bye bye.   END OF SESSION.

3 IMPLEMENTATION

The system described has been almost fully implemented and tested, the only part not yet developed being the interface between the voice synthesis module and the rest of the system (at present replies appear on the screen).

The experimental hardware configuration relies on a multi-processor machine, EMMA, developed in ELSAG laboratories to solve real time recognition problems, and on a PDP/11/23, that acts as an interface to communicate with EMMA. The speech recognition and speech synthesis modules are implemented on the multiprocessor, while the rest of the system is running on the PDP.

The implementation of the system was mainly aimed to test the correctness of the dialogue model. Therefore we did't pay much attention to time considerations, also due to the constraints imposed by the machine (most of the time is spent in disk swapping operations).

Actually, the response time is of the order of one minute, strongly dependent on the quantity of rules evaluated. Complete and full understood sentences (like the first command in the given example) mainly require the activation of "congruency checks" rules, while fragments or elliptical answers (see the second and fourth user utterances) activate a larger number of rules, about a hundred more.

4 CONCLUSIONS

The initial intent of modelling the dialogue process and applying the graceful interaction precepts has been satisfied.

The rule formalism has allowed, in the development stage, to extend and modify in an incremental manner the skills of the system by dealing with the different aspects of the interaction one at a time. That made it possible to investigate individually the problems involved, verifying step by step the solutions suggested and delegating the task to co-ordinate every feature to a following stage when the results already obtained could be applied.

Besides, the homogeneous representation formalism and the unique structure of the data-base provided by the Rule-Based system have guaranteed an easy communication between different components, allowing each of them to access the whole of available information.

The main advantage of our approach consists in tackling a big problem by gradually solving easier subproblems by means of rules, and it is perhaps the most direct way to achieve practical results in Natural Language Understanding and similar subfields of Artificial Intelligence.

References

[Bor '82] L. Borghesi, C. Favareto, "Flexible Parsing of discretely uttered sentences", Proc. of the Ninth Int. Conf. on Computational Linguistics, Prague 1982

[Gro '77] B. J. Grosz, "The Representation and Use of Focus in a System for Understanding Dialogues", Proc. of the V Conference on Artificial Intelligence, M.I.T. 1977

[Hay '79] P. Hayes, R. Reddy, "An Anatomy of Graceful Interaction in Spoken and Written Man-Machine Communication", Tech. Report, Computer Science Department, Carnegie Mellon University, Pittsburgh 1979

[Hay '81] P. J. Hayes, "Anaphora for Limited Domain Systems", Proc. of the VII Int. Jt. Conf. on Artificial Intelligence, Vancouver 1981

[Kow '84] R. Kowalsky, "Logic for Problem Solving", North Holland, Amsterdam 1984

[Ort '85] B. Ortolani, "Dialogo Uomo-Macchina in Linguaggio Naturale: studio teorico e realizzazione mediante tecniche di Intelligenza Artificiale", Doctor Thesis, Physics Dept., Univ. of Genoa, 1985

[Vic '82] C. Vicenzi, C. Scagliola, "Multiprocessor Architecture for Real-time Speech Recognition Systems", Proc. ICASSP 82, Paris 1982